MANAGING KNOWLEDGE WORK AND INNOVATION

MANAGING KNOWLEDGE WORK AND INNOVATION

2nd Edition

Sue Newell
Maxine Robertson
Harry Scarbrough
Jacky Swan

palgrave
macmillan

First edition 2002
Reprinted seven times
This edition 2009
Published by
PALGRAVE MACMILLAN

Palgrave Macmillan in the UK is an imprint of Macmillan Publishers Limited, registered in England, company number 785998, of Houndmills, Basingstoke, Hampshire RG21 6XS.

Palgrave Macmillan in the US is a division of St Martin's Press LLC, 175 Fifth Avenue, New York, NY 10010.

Palgrave Macmillan is the global academic imprint of the above companies and has companies and representatives throughout the world.

Palgrave® and Macmillan® are registered trademarks in the United States, the United Kingdom, Europe and other countries
ISBN 978-0-230-52201-5   ISBN 978-0-230-36641-1 (eBook)

DOI 10.1007/978-0-230-36641-1

This book is printed on paper suitable for recycling and made from fully managed and sustained forest sources. Logging, pulping and manufacturing processes are expected to conform to the environmental regulations of the country of origin.

A catalogue record for this book is available from the British Library.

A catalog record for this book is available from the Library of Congress.

10   9   8   7   6   5   4   3   2   1
18   17   16   15   14   13   12   11   10   09

CONTENTS

LIST OF TABLES AND FIGURES

Tables

Figures

1

INTRODUCING KNOWLEDGE WORK: PROCESSES, PURPOSES AND CONTEXTS

Chapter Outline

Learning Outcomes

At the end of this chapter you should be able to:

⇒ Define core concepts – knowledge, organizational knowledge, knowledge work, Knowledge Management and innovation – as used in this book.

⇒ Understand different perspectives on knowledge and the importance of these for approaches to managing knowledge work.

⇒ Understand the nature and characteristics of knowledge work and the role of knowledge workers within organizations.

⇒ Understand the history behind managing knowledge in organizations since the turn of the twentieth century.

⇒ Understand the broad issues critical to the management of knowledge and knowledge workers, which will be explored in depth in the remainder of the book.

>> INTRODUCTION

Managing knowledge work and knowledge workers is arguably the single most important challenge being faced by all kinds of organizations. 'Knowledge Management', for example, has been heralded as essential to efforts to improve competitiveness and innovation. Even since writing the first edition of this book (published in 2002), a huge number of new tools and techniques, books, articles and 'how-to' guidelines have been produced in the name of Knowledge Management.

At the same time, many attempts to manage knowledge in organizations have failed to deliver promised improvements (Scarbrough and Swan, 2001). Some have focused too narrowly on generically applicable tools/methods to transfer information, without paying sufficient consideration to the social, organizational and cultural context needed to enable and support knowledge work. Others have forgotten what it is they are actually managing knowledge for – is the purpose to improve the efficiency of current activities, for example, or to do things differently and innovate? Yet others have faltered because they have emphasized particular processes (e.g. sharing knowledge between groups) and forgotten others (e.g. applying knowledge to new tasks). In this new book, then, a major feature is to stress all three of these dimensions of knowledge work: *enabling contexts, purposes and processes.* The need to align contexts, purposes and processes when managing knowledge work is a theme we shall revisit throughout the chapters that follow.

Many of the examples and case studies used throughout this book are drawn from our own research on innovation. This is because innovation is so central to knowledge work – many of the unique skills and experiences of knowledge workers would be largely wasted if they were not provided with the opportunity to put these skills to work in order to do things differently (hopefully better) and to innovate. Innovation also entails the application of knowledge to new tasks and situations in order to develop products, processes and services, and is a prime site for knowledge work.

We start by developing in this introductory chapter a rudimentary understanding of the core concepts we are going to be dealing with – knowledge, organizational knowledge, Knowledge Management and innovation. We are not going to engage deeply in philosophical debates about the precise nature of knowledge – this has been done much better elsewhere (Tsoukas, 2003; Tsoukas and Vladimirou, 2001). Rather, we outline some of the more well-known definitions and frameworks that have been developed in organizational theory and strategy, which help inform our understanding of what it is that firms are trying to do when they claim to be 'managing knowledge'. We also look at how current approaches can be traced back to early ideas about managing work. Such a historically grounded account helps us to see how and why we have arrived at this point, what our possible futures may be and how we can avoid some of the mistakes of years past.

>> WHAT IS KNOWLEDGE?

Philosophers have wrestled over what knowledge is since the classical Greek period. Thus there is a whole branch of philosophy, 'epistemology' – from the Greek words *episteme* (knowledge) and *logos* (word/speech) – that deals with, and debates on, the nature, origin and scope of knowledge. These debates are many and varied but in studies of knowledge work in organizational settings two views stand out. These have been usefully summarized as the 'epistemology of possession' and 'the epistemology of practice' (Cook and Brown, 1999). In short, the epistemology of possession treats knowledge as something people *have* whereas the epistemology of practice treats knowledge as something people *do*.

The epistemology of possession view on knowledge emphasizes its cognitive aspects – knowledge is seen as a possession of the human mind and treated as a mental (or cognitive) capacity, or resource, that can be developed, applied and used to improve effectiveness in the workplace. Those adopting this view often describe knowledge as a kind of pyramid, or hierarchy, comprising data, information and knowledge and even wisdom (Ackoff, 1989) – see Figure 1.1. Data is described as a discrete physical entity, external to the individual, and having no intrinsic value of its own – the dots of ink on this page, for example. Information is data that is organized in some way such that it has a recognizable shape – the words and sentences on this page that are inscribed by data. Like data, information is also 'out there' – an objective property of the world, external to any particular individual, which can be searched, stored, sorted, transmitted, sent and received.

In contrast to data and information, knowledge is a different kind of thing altogether. Knowledge, according to the epistemology of possession, is seen as a personal property of the individual knower who is able to confer meaning on data and information by drawing from his or her own subjective experiences, perceptions and previous understandings. This is the sense in which knowledge

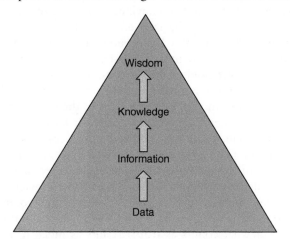

Figure 1.1   A knowledge 'Hierarchy' (e.g. Ackoff, 1989)

is 'possessed' by individuals. Being able to make sense of the words and sentences on this page is about knowledge. What an individual infers from information is related to their cognitive capacity and interpretive schema, or 'frames of reference', which they have acquired through life. It is reasonable, therefore, to suggest that different people, with different past experiences, may infer different things from the same information.

The 'knowledge as possession' view is implicit in much of what is written about managing knowledge work within contemporary organizations. For example, below we outline the very widely quoted work of Nonaka (1994), which talks about how 'tacit knowledge' (the knowledge that individuals have based on their personal experience that is hard to express or articulate) can be converted into explicit knowledge (knowledge that can be 'spelled out' or written down), which can then be communicated to others in the organization who will then also 'know' without having to have had the same experiences. So, according to this view, knowledge is something I possess and, like any of my possessions (say a football), I can then pass on this knowledge (or football) to others.

This 'knowledge as possession' view has, however, been roundly attacked by proponents of the 'epistemology of practice' (Brown and Duguid, 2001; Gherardi, 2001; Lave and Wenger, 1991; Nicolini, Gherardi and Yanow, 2003; Orlikowski, 2002). These writers start from the premise that 'knowledge' is constructed and negotiated through social interaction. Knowledge is, therefore, intrinsic to the localized social situations and practices (practices of saying things as well as doing things) that people actually perform, and not something that can stand outside those practices. Their studies show that social groups as diverse as construction engineers, photocopier technicians, radiologists, tailors, ship builders and alcoholics do not learn to do things by converting tacit knowledge into explicit knowledge which is transferred from one person to another but, rather, by sharing and creating all kinds of norms, stories, representations, tools and symbols which enable the experience of individuals to be related to the knowledge of the wider community. Knowledge is, in effect, 'enacted' through the practices of different groups and inextricably bound up with the way these groups work together and develop shared identities and shared beliefs. For example, chefs have access to recipes that hold explicit written information on what ingredients to use and how to put them together. However, as any good chef will tell you, they do not learn from this, as much as from the actual practice of being an apprentice with a Master Chef within a particular kitchen and social setting that reinforces certain kinds of norms, values and practices. It is this practice that allows them to interpret and apply the recipes effectively and innovatively.

By taking these criticisms on board we can begin to see that the often used saying that knowledge is a person's 'justified true belief' – which dates back to Plato and underpins theories such as Nonaka's – is actually quite problematic (Gourlay, 2006). This is because there are likely to be many possible 'truths' and, so, 'truth' (or what counts as truth) results as much from the negotiations amongst social actors (and the tools at their disposal) as it does from any personally held justifications. What finally comes to be accepted as 'true' is often driven by those who happen to hold positions of power or authority and whose justifications carry more weight (such as the Master Chef). In Western medicine, for example, clinicians' claims about what treatments work, backed by scientific data, usually override competing knowledge claims coming from less powerful groups about alternative therapies. Yet, this was not the case centuries ago and is still not the case in some other societal contexts (Abbott, 1988). Furthermore, if the 'truthfulness' of something can only be judged in relation to personal belief (Nonaka, 1994), then someone could be provided with full justification for something and still choose not to believe it. Hence we can see that knowledge – or claims to knowledge – are social as well as individual and depend heavily on the organizational and cultural context in which such claims are made.

Some proponents of this alternative 'knowledge as practice' view prefer to use the term 'knowing' rather than knowledge, precisely to underline this inter-weaving of what people know with what they do and who and where they are. The term 'knowing' (as a verb rather than a noun) draws our attention to the active, processual and social nature of knowledge (Suchman, 1987). This social and context-dependent nature of knowledge (sometimes described as 'socially situated') needs to be addressed when attempting to manage knowledge within organizations – a theme that will be revisited throughout this book.

Cook and Brown (1999) have attempted, somewhat controversially, to reconcile these different epistemologies of possession and practice, by arguing that it is possible to see processes of knowing and forms of knowledge as equally important and complementary:

> Individuals and groups clearly make use of knowledge, both explicit and tacit, in what they do; but not everything they know how to do, we argue, is explicable solely in terms of the knowledge they possess. We believe that individual and group action requires us to speak about both knowledge used in action and knowing as part of the action.
>
> (p. 382)

Moreover, they are inextricably linked, with knowledge being seen by Cook and Brown as a tool for knowing:

> Organizations are better understood… if knowledge and knowing are seen as mutually enabling (not competing). We hold that knowledge is a tool for knowing, that knowing is an aspect of our interaction with the social and physical world, and the interplay of knowledge and knowing can generate new knowledge and new ways of knowing.
>
> (p. 381)

Working definition of knowledge

The definitional issues will probably never be resolved – indeed, some would argue that if 'knowledge' is naturally contested then why should they be? However, it is useful for us to be clear about our own working definitions (or knowledge claims) when we talk about managing knowledge work. Drawing from the discussion above, then, we define *knowledge* simply as 'the ability to discriminate within and across contexts' (Swan, 2008). Studying 'knowledge' means looking at the varied ways in which actors in particular social situations understand and make sense of where they are and what they are doing. This working definition borrows from Tsoukas and Vladimirou (2001), who theorize knowledge as 'the individual ability to draw distinctions within a collective domain of action, based on an appreciation of context or theory or both' (p. 979). Our working definition is broad enough to encompass the individual cognitive aspects of knowledge as well as its social nature. It also suggests that it is important for us to consider the roles of material artefacts in managing knowledge work – technologies, tools, computers, physical spaces, clocks, schedules and the like – because the ability to discriminate is mediated by them (Barley, 1986; Black, Carlile and Repenning, 2004; Orlikowski, 2007; Orlikowski and Yates, 2002; Schultze and Orlikowski, 2004). For example, knowledge of what is useful, or not, in cooking is mediated by the experiences you have, the tools you are using and the people and cultures that you interact with.

Following along this vein, *organizational knowledge* can be understood as 'a learned set of norms, shared understandings and practices that integrates actors and artefacts to produce valued outcomes within a specific social and organizational context' (Scarbrough, 2008b). Studying 'organizational knowledge' is about understanding the means by which groups of actors develop more or less shared beliefs, behaviours and routines that help shape the organization's capabilities. Organizational knowledge can be reflected in what people say, in what they do, or in the technologies, routines and systems that they use. For example, Hewlett Packard's organizational knowledge is reflected through stated corporate objectives, such as 'everyone has something to contribute: It's not about title, level or tenure' (assuming this is believed!), their relatively flat organizational structure and their employment selection systems and routines that favour diversity in staff.

These debates about the nature of knowledge are not purely academic. The point is that our underlying assumptions about what knowledge is, and whether it is something people have (possess) or do (practice), have a profound influence on the tactics, strategies and analytical tools that we use when attempting to more effectively manage knowledge work. The term *'Knowledge Management'* is one that has come to be used to refer to explicit strategies, tools and practices applied by management that seek to make knowledge a resource for the organization. As a field of study Knowledge Management is concerned with the development of concepts that illuminate or enhance the application of these practices. If your assumptions are that knowledge is possessed, then the major challenge of Knowledge Management is to free knowledge from the individual and make it widely available as an organizational resource, for example, by capturing it in an IT system or by writing it down in guidelines and recipes. If your assumption, on the other hand, is that knowledge is about what people do (and say) then the challenge of Knowledge Management is to provide an enabling context that allows people to do (and say) things differently and, hopefully, better. Therefore, it is important when considering major tools, theories and frameworks for managing knowledge work to be aware also of the assumptions that drive them and the practical issues they lead us to focus on. We turn to this next when we look at three different perspectives on knowledge – structural perspectives, which essentially adopt a knowledge as possession epistemology, and then process and practice perspectives, which adopt a knowledge as practice epistemology.

>> STRUCTURAL PERSPECTIVES AND TYPES OF KNOWLEDGE

Structural perspectives on knowledge draw largely from the epistemology of possession and focus on identifying different types, or forms, of knowledge that people have. Citing Polanyi's (1962) earlier work on 'personal knowledge', two forms or types of knowledge – tacit and explicit – are often distinguished. Tacit knowledge is associated with the skills or know-how that people develop through their own experience in specific contexts (e.g. *knowing how* to ride a bicycle) and has an essentially personal quality that makes it hard to formalize or communicate. In contrast, explicit knowledge is that which has been 'spelled out' or codified, making it more communicable across contexts (e.g. *knowing what* components a bicycle needs to have to make it work and how they should be put together).

An important aspect of tacit knowledge is that we know more than we can articulate or attend to at any point in time. Hence tacit knowledge is often referred to as 'know-how' – it resides in our heads and in practical skills and actions. For example, many of us 'know' how to swim. However, explaining this to someone is extremely difficult. Indeed, if a novice tried to follow our verbal instructions they would probably drown! In fact, the individual's experience of learning to swim for themselves and what the water feels like, coupled with help and instruction, is what leads to the accumulation of tacit knowledge.

However, if everything had to be learned from first-hand experience then learning in organizations would be severely limited. Explicit knowledge, on the other hand, can be readily codified, articulated and communicated to others and is, therefore, seen by some as more useful for organizational learning (Teece, Pisano and Shuen, 1997; Zollo and Winter, 2002). The way to create knowledge in organizations, then, according to the structural perspectives is to identify important tacit knowledge, make it explicit, and convert it back again into the tacit knowledge of others elsewhere in the organization so that it can be applied (Nonaka, 1994).

Frameworks for understanding knowledge types

Structural perspectives are useful in providing frameworks that help us to understand further what kinds of knowledge can be involved in knowledge work. Next we outline three models developed by organization theorists that are particularly helpful in this regard. Of course there are many others we could have looked at but the different principles captured in those selected underpin many of the approaches to managing knowledge work that we see today.

Nonaka's framework (1994)

Nonaka's now well-cited 'SECI' model (see Figure 1.2) sees knowledge creation as a spiraling process of interactions between knowledge types (explicit and tacit). He identified four distinct knowledge conversion processes through which

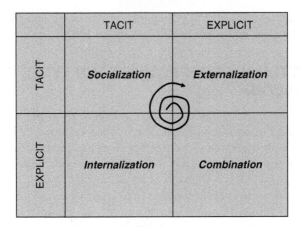

Figure 1.2   The SECI model (after Nonaka, 1994)

knowledge creation could take place: socialization (tacit/tacit); externalization (tacit/explicit); combination (explicit/explicit) and internalization (explicit/tacit). Because Nonaka believes that individual cognition plays an essential part in knowledge creation, he suggests that organizational knowledge creation stems from the individual. If we take the socialization process, for example, this rests on individuals interacting with others and reflecting on their own and others' experiences. This emphasis on knowledge existing only at the individual level is a fundamental difference between Nonaka's framework and the other frameworks discussed later.

This is not to suggest, however, that organizations and their managers do not have a role to play in knowledge creation. Nonaka also stressed that managers need to provide the necessary enabling context for individuals to share and create knowledge. In his more recent elaborations of the SECI model, then, Nonaka developed the notion of 'ba' – a concept originally developed by Japanese philosopher Kitaro Nishida, meaning 'a context which harbours meaning' (Nonaka and Konno, 1998). According to Nonaka and Konno (1998), 'ba' (roughly translated in English as 'place') is 'a shared space for emerging relationships. This space can be physical (e.g. office, dispersed business space), virtual (e.g. e-mail, teleconference), mental (e.g. shared experience, ideas, ideals), or any combination of them' (p. 40). Relating back to the distinction between knowledge and information discussed earlier, knowledge is seen as embedded in 'ba' where it is acquired though individuals' experiences and reflections. Information is knowledge that is separated from ba and so able to be communicated independently – 'Information resides in media and networks. It is tangible. In contrast knowledge resides in "ba". It is intangible' (p. 40). Nonaka and Konno identified, in turn, four kinds of 'ba' that map onto the four kinds of knowledge conversion processes:

- Originating 'ba' – the place where individuals develop empathy, share feelings, emotions, experiences and mental models. This is essential to socialization. It relies on face-to-face contact and is where knowledge creation is seen as starting. An example is an informal exchange around a shared problem or issue.

- Interacting 'ba' – a more consciously constructed place where peers get together to engage in dialogue, challenge ideas and reflect on their own ideas in the light of others' idea. This is essential to externalization. An example is assembling a project team and plan to resolve an issue.

- Cyber 'ba' – the virtual place where new knowledge can be combined with existing information and made available throughout the organization. This is enabled by information communication technology (ICT) and is essential to combination. An example is adding project findings to an Internet database.

- Exercising 'ba' – the place where formal explicit knowledge can be applied through on the job training and active participation. This is essential to internalization. An example is developing training or 'peer assist' schemes to put results into practice.

The SECI model of Nonaka and his colleagues is not without critics. Not least, and despite the notion of 'ba', it presents an overly individualized view of knowledge and is a bit 'slippery' in how it treats knowledge. For example, on the one hand, knowledge separated from 'ba' is not knowledge but information. At the same time, the model continues to classify knowledge as either tacit or explicit, leaving open the question of what explicit knowledge actually is. The SECI model also significantly downplays the differences of interests, power and political dynamics that knowledge creation processes in organizational contexts inevitably encounter. Instead the 'knowledge spiral' – the movement of knowledge from being the possession of an individual to becoming an organizational resource – is depicted as rather smooth, linear, uncontested and unproblematic. These criticisms aside, the model has been very influential and has played an important part in channeling attention, not just to the cognitive, information processing aspects of knowledge creation in organizations, but also to the importance of values and the enabling context in which such values are shared, acquired and played out.

Spender's framework (1996, 1998)

Spender's framework, pictured in Figure 1.3, differs from Nonaka's because it is built on the principle that, in order to understand where organizational knowledge comes from, we need to be concerned with not only types of knowledge (i.e. epistemology), but also where it resides (i.e. ontology). So, as well as incorporating tacit and explicit knowledge, his framework also makes a distinction between individual and social (or collective) knowledge. Combining concerns about what knowledge is (i.e. tacit or explicit) and where it resides (individual or social) means that the four, rather than two, different types of knowledge can be identified: (i) individual/explicit (conscious); (ii) individual/implicit (automatic); (iii) social/explicit (objectified) and (iv) social/implicit (collective).

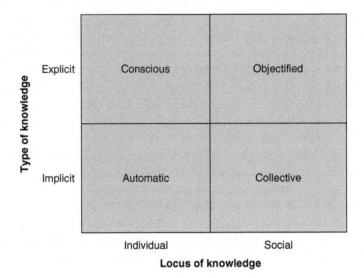

Figure 1.3   Forms of knowledge – Spender's framework

Spender's framework makes a very important additional point, which is that forms of social knowledge can exist beyond the individual. Hence it is possible to make a 'contrast between the explicit knowledge that individuals feel they possess and the collective knowledge on which this explicit knowledge actually stands, and the interaction of the two' (Spender, 1998, p. 238). For example, the culture of an organization is a form of social knowledge that survives beyond the contribution of particular individuals. Spender also saw the creation of organizational knowledge as resulting from interactions between all four types of knowledge. What this framework does not highlight, however, which the SECI model makes explicit, are the processes that allow different types of knowledge to be created in the first place.

Thinking strategically, Spender argues that collective (social/implicit) knowledge is actually the most valuable to organizations because this is a type of knowledge that other firms find difficult to understand and imitate. As we shall see in Chapter 2, if a firm can develop a culture (collective knowledge) that supports knowledge creation then this can be very hard to imitate, even if individuals leave and try to replicate this new culture elsewhere. This idea very much supports the view, still held strongly today, that a firm's 'core competencies' are a crucial strategic resource.

Blackler's framework (1995)

Blackler's framework (depicted in Figure 1.4) was built from a review of existing studies of organizational knowledge at the time. It identifies knowledge types – embrained, embodied, encultured, embedded and encoded:

	Knowledge-Routinized Organisations: *Knowledge embedded in technologies, rules and procedures.*	Communication-Intensive Organisations: *Encultured knowledge and collective understanding.*
Emphasis on collective endeavour	Hierarchical division of labour and control. Low skill requirements.	Communication and collaboration the key processes. Empowerment through integration.
	Example: 'Machine Bureaucracy' such as a McDonalds.	*Example*: 'Adhocracy' such as a large management consultancy
	Expert-Dependent Organisations: *Embodied competencies of key members.*	**Symbolic-Analyst-Dependent Organisations:** *Embrained skills of key members.*
Emphasis on contributions of individuals	Performance of individual specialist experts is crucial. Status and power from professional reputation & qualifications.	Entrepreneurial problem solving. Status and power from creative achievements.
	Example: 'Professional Bureaucracy' such as a hospital.	*Example*: 'Knowledge-intensive-firm' such as a science-based, high tech firm.
	Focus on familiar problems	Focus on novel problems

Figure 1.4 Organizations and types of knowledge (after Blackler, 1995)

Embrained knowledge is knowledge that is dependent on conceptual skills and cognitive abilities. Embodied knowledge is action oriented and is only partly explicit. Encultured knowledge refers to the process of achieving shared understanding, through the development of an organizational culture. Embedded knowledge is knowledge that resides in systemic routines. It can be analyzed by considering the relationships between technologies, roles, procedures and emergent routines. Finally, encoded knowledge is information conveyed by signs and symbols either in manual or electronically transmitted form.

(Blackler, 1995, pp. 1024–1025)

Blackler's framework, like Spender's, suggests that different types of knowledge exist at either the individual (embodied and embrained knowledge) or at the collective level (encultured and embedded). However, each of these knowledge types can be more or less explicit, so giving rise to the fifth kind of knowledge, encoded knowledge. For example, in an organization like McDonalds, culture (encultured knowledge) may be articulated in the form of formal statements and symbols (e.g. the Big 'M' that indicates the McDonalds brand around the world) or may be tacitly known by everyone in the firm and reflected in their behaviours.

What Blackler tried to illustrate, which distinguishes this framework from the others considered above, is that different types of knowledge dominate in different types of organizations. For example, he suggested that a bureaucratic organization making highly standardized products, like McDonalds, will rely predominantly on knowledge embedded in organizational routines and rules. More dynamic and innovative firms, like Hewlett Packard, will rely on either encultured knowledge, if they are communication-intensive, or embrained knowledge, if they are mostly dependent on the knowledge and expertise of the individual's employed. The latter scenario is typical in 'knowledge-intensive firms' which are described in Chapter 2. Blackler's framework is therefore a useful starting point when considering the problems of managing knowledge because it relates the major *purpose* of the firm (e.g. whether they are trying to produce innovative or standardized products and services) to the type of knowledge that dominates and, therefore, to the *processes* and *enabling context* that need to be in place to manage knowledge. The case studies presented in the following chapters in this book will illustrate this important idea.

Critique of structural perspectives

The frameworks outlined above assume, in the main, a 'knowledge as possession' view (Cook and Brown, 1999) and because of this have been challenged for failing to take sufficient account of the more subjective, highly equivocal and dynamic nature of knowledge (Bijker et al., 1987; Weick, 1990). Other critics of structural approaches claim that the separation between tacit and explicit knowledge has been overstated and is not, in fact, a very accurate reflection of Polanyi's original idea (Gourlay, 2006). Indeed Polanyi argued that all knowledge has an indispensable personal component but that, depending on the circumstances, we are only aware of certain aspects at particular points in time. Explicit knowledge, then, is merely that which we are aware of at any given moment, in much the same way as shining a spotlight highlights particular features of a landscape at that point in time. These explicit features are always connected, though, to the things that lie behind in the dark and that can come into view at any moment as the spotlight, and our focus, shifts. Taking this view we can see, in fact, that tacit and explicit knowledge are mutually 'constituted' (Boisot, 1995; Gourlay, 2006; Tsoukas, 1996). In other words they define each other. By attending to something, and making it explicit, we automatically push other things into the background, or into tacitness, so to speak. Gourlay (2006) points out, then, that tacit knowledge may be better considered as a continuum where the degree of 'tacitness' and 'explicitness' is a function of the extent to which knowledge is communicated.

If we consider the example of riding a bicycle, we can see that it may be useful for the novice to be told to hold lightly onto the handlebars. This brings knowledge about how to hold the handlebars into focus, making it explicit. But, at the same time, it pushes other knowledge (e.g. on how to balance weight onto the pedals) further into the background. This is not a trivial point when it comes to managing knowledge because it means that *any* explicit, codified knowledge will *always* be incomplete or partial. It is only by combining this explicit knowledge with tacit 'know-how' developed through experience (e.g. about balance and hand–eye coordination) that tasks can be accomplished.

By focusing on what knowledge is, structural approaches also tend to adopt what has been termed an 'entitative' view of knowledge (Hosking and Morley, 1991). Hence knowledge is seen as 'thing-like' – an object or resource that can be moved around much like other resources such as money. Like other resources the aim is to accumulate it and move it around for the good of the organization. In short, more knowledge equals more profit. However, there is no particular reason, *a priori*, why benefit should automatically follow from having more and more knowledge. As seen with the widespread diffusion of e-mail, it is quite conceivable that information overload might result and/or that existing, embedded knowledge might constrain attempts to do new things. Thus knowledge, unlike money, is not valuable in and of itself, but only where it is applied to specific tasks (McDermott, 1999).

Another criticism of this approach is that it assumes a so-called 'functionalist' view of organizations (Burrell and Morgan, 1979). In other words an organization is depicted as a collection of interdependent parts (e.g. machines and people) that work in harmony towards a common, agreed upon, goal – (e.g. organizational survival and profit). However, this assumes that common goals actually exist in organizations and, therefore, does not address important issues of power and conflict in organizations and in society at large (Foucault, 1980). For example, encouraging individual employees to surrender their knowledge for the benefit of 'the organization' may actually benefit shareholders or senior managers but can, equally, be for the individuals themselves. This is one reason why individuals may choose to 'hoard' rather than share knowledge. Moreover, it is quite conceivable that those in power could use knowledge to further their own interests rather than the interests of the collective organization.

As well as theoretical objections, there are some very practical issues when it comes to using structural approaches to manage knowledge work. For one thing, understanding types of knowledge (e.g. tacit/explicit) and where it resides (e.g. individual/collective) does not actually tell us much about where it comes from or how to *use* it – knowing, in this sense of the word, does not equal doing (Pfeffer and Sutton, 2000). Furthermore, there is now good evidence that Knowledge Management initiatives based solely on this kind of thinking often fail (Walsham, 2002). For example, in an empirical study of an initiative to encourage knowledge transfer in a world-wide bank, Newell et al. (2001) found that the introduction of a Knowledge Management System – a global intranet – designed to capture and share tacit knowledge across the organization had the opposite effect to that intended by senior management. These problems will be discussed further in Chapters 3 and 7.

These points of critique have led people to develop more sophisticated 'contingency' frameworks that show us how strategies for managing knowledge can be linked to specific aspects of the organizational tasks at hand. For example, Hansen (1999) studied innovation in a large electronics company and concluded that strong social relationships with a few people were beneficial for tasks that required the transfer of complex, highly tacit knowledge, whereas weak relationships with many people were more effective where the knowledge involved was less complex and more explicit. This approach is promising as it takes into account *purpose* – that is what knowledge is to be used for. However it still, fundamentally, sees knowledge as a thing or commodity that is valuable for its own sake and tells us relatively little about the processes involved in creating and using knowledge across contexts.

>> PROCESS AND PRACTICE PERSPECTIVES: KNOWLEDGE AND KNOWING

The failure of many initiatives that have attempted to 'capture' and 'transfer' individuals' knowledge have helped fuel shifts towards accounts that take as their focus the development of *processes* and *enabling contexts* capable of supporting knowledge work. This shift can be seen in organization theories which focus on 'knowing' as a social and organizational activity, in contrast to 'knowledge', as a thing or object. Process, and more recently practice, perspectives draw, then, from an epistemology of practice (outlined above – Cook and Brown, 1999).

Our working definition of knowledge – as the ability to discriminate within and across contexts – is based on this processual perspective in that it avoids notions of 'truth' and defines knowledge in dynamic terms as a practice of making distinctions (Tsoukas and Vladimirou, 2001). Process approaches to managing knowledge work draw from theoretical traditions of 'social constructivism', seeing knowledge, or knowing, as a process of 'sensemaking', whereby actors interacting within particular social contexts come to negotiate understandings of the world (Berger and Luckman, 1967; Weick, 2001). Knowledge is, therefore:

- equivocal (subject to different meanings and interpretations);
- dynamic (accepted meanings can change as actors and contexts change) and;
- context-dependent (difficult, if not impossible, to separate from the context in which it is produced).

While structural approaches see a direct relationship between increased knowledge, knowledge transfer and organizational performance (Amidon, 1998), process approaches view this relationship as socially and politically mediated. Whether or not knowledge (or knowing) leads to improvement depends, then, on how tasks, actors and contexts come together (Clark and Staunton, 1989). For example, Clark (2003) describes how the US game of American Football originated from knowledge of the game of rugby in the United Kingdom. However, it was not simply a case of capturing knowledge about rugby and transferring this to the United States. His historical analysis showed how key stakeholders (including players, sports promoters and the media) reinterpreted the British rules of the game and created 'pivotal modifications' that allowed it to be adapted to the particular context in the United States at the time. Hence, in order to generate advertising revenue through media breaks, they introduced shorter 'periods' (instead of halves) and 'time-outs'.

This example shows how the particular interests and interpretations of actors within and across different social and institutional contexts come to bear in reproducing and legitimating particular forms of knowledge and innovation. The process approach also highlights the central role of social networks in translating (not just transferring) knowledge across groups and contexts.

> Knowing is not a static embedded capability or stable disposition of actors, but rather an ongoing social accomplishment, constituted and reconstituted as actors engage the world in practice.
>
> (Orlikowski, 2002, p. 249)

Managing knowledge work, then, is less about converting, capturing and transferring different forms of knowledge and more about building an *enabling context* that connects different social groups and interests, identities and perspectives to accomplish specific tasks or *purposes* (Boland and Tenkasi, 1995). Management initiatives aimed at building so-called 'communities of practice' (Thompson, 2005; Wenger and Snyder, 2000) or social networks (Cross and Sproull, 2004) reflect such a view. These will be explored in Chapter 8.

Practice perspectives

In the last decade there has been a surge of interest in 'practice perspectives' as a way of studying and analysing social and organizational life (Schatzki et al., 2001). In terms of managing knowledge work, however, practice perspectives have had less attention. Even advocates of the so-called 'communities of practice' approach (see Chapter 8) to managing knowledge within firms have emphasized the importance of communities and networks for improving knowledge flows but have left 'practice' relatively untouched (Beth, 2003).

Practice and process perspectives have more in common than not – both see knowing as a social activity and address *process, context and purpose*, for example. However, practice perspectives emphasize in particular the links between knowledge and action, or practice. In short, knowledge is inextricably linked to practice – it flows where practice is shared (e.g. within specialist or functional groups) and sticks where practice is not shared (e.g. across functional departments). It is useful for us to look at practice perspectives more closely because they help us to pay attention to aspects of managing knowledge work that have not been so commonly addressed to date.

Many different kinds of theorists have influenced practice perspectives, including social philosophers (e.g. Dreyfuss, 1991; Wittgenstein, 1958), social theorists (e.g. Bourdieu, 1990), cultural theorists (e.g. Lyotard, 1988) and ethnomethodologists (e.g. Garfinkel, 1967). It is impossible to do them justice here. Definitions of 'practice' include 'action informed by meaning drawn from a particular group context' (Cook and Brown, 1999) and 'socially recognized forms of activity, done on the basis of what members learn from others, and capable of being done well or badly, correctly or incorrectly' (Barnes, 2001, p. 19). However, we can identify some general insights that practice perspectives offer over and above process perspectives to our understanding of knowledge work.

First, practice perspectives remind us that knowledge is 'sticky' – it sticks to practice and is therefore difficult to share where peoples' practices are also not shared. This helps to explain why sharing knowledge across specialist functions or disciplines within an organization, or from one organization to another, is so difficult – even where people appreciate others' ideas, they may not be able to apply them because it would be too difficult to change their current practices. This means that knowledge is not uniformly good but is actually quite paradoxical in relation to organizational performance. On the one hand, division of labour results in different groups performing different practices which means that valuable specialized knowledge can develop. On the other hand, the 'knowledge boundaries' created by specialization pose barriers to knowledge sharing across different groups of practitioners (Brown and Duguid, 2001; Carlile, 2004; Scarbrough et al., 2004). As Carlile (2002) puts it:

> the irony is that these knowledge boundaries are not only a critical challenge, but also a perceptual necessity because much of what organizations produce has a foundation in the specialization of different kinds of knowledge.
>
> (Carlile, 2002, p. 442)

Second, when we perform practice we use many kinds of material and physical objects, not just words and thoughts. Material objects are not just tools that people use to achieve ends, however, they also set limits around what practices are actually possible. For example, Orlikowski (2007) describes an online business meeting where laptop computers, Internet connections, phone lines, cables, connectors, pens, mute buttons on telephones – in her terms, the 'stuff' of everyday life – serve to 'scaffold' the social activity of the people involved. She uses the metaphor of 'scaffolds' to highlight the ways in which temporary material arrangements help constitute particular kinds of social activity *in real time*. Practice perspectives on knowledge work draw attention, then, to the 'materiality' of social activity (Orlikowski, 2007; Schatzki, 2001). In other words they focus on the ways that all human activities, including knowledge work, are interwoven with non-human, material artefacts, objects and physical arrangements. While there is considerable debate around exactly *how* this interweaving takes place (the importance of human versus non-human agency, being a particular bone of contention – Latour, 1988), practice perspectives agree that the social world is 'a field of embodied, materially interwoven practices centrally organized around shared practical understandings' (Schatzki, 2001, p. 3).

This has important implications for managing knowledge work. On the one hand, it means that the ability (or lack thereof) to transform knowledge and innovate depends, at least to some extent, on what Schatzki (2001) describes as the 'solidifying inertia' of material layouts (p. 3). Bicycles rely fundamentally on the wheel and are still very much the same today as they were centuries ago, for example. On the other hand, material objects (mobile technologies, drawings, prototypes and so on) can also act as critical tools for Knowledge Management.

An important point, however, is that this is not a one-way relationship – the design of material objects (e.g. the layout of the meeting room) influence human activity but also result from it. This is an issue we will return to in Chapter 3.

Third, practice perspectives remind us that knowledge work actually takes place in a broader 'field of practices' (Schatzki, 2001). For example, the practices of medical professionals are part of the broader field of scientific practice. This includes 'epistemic practices' (or 'knowledge cultures') that govern how knowledge is created and legitimated – in science via the rules of scientific method, for example (Knorr-Cetina, 1999). Therefore, to manage knowledge work, we also need to be sensitive to the broader institutional contexts and interconnected sets of practices in which that knowledge work is located. The notion of 'the field of interconnected practices' reminds us that change in one area of practice potentially disrupts a wide range of other practices. It is for this reason that creating and using knowledge in interdisciplinary settings can be so challenging. As Drexler noted at the first conference on nanotechnology (in 1989), 'unfortunately, interdisciplinary subjects have a way of escaping from any discipline whatever' (Drexler, 1989).

Fourth, practice perspectives emphasize not just the socially situated nature of knowledge, but also the *investment* of knowledge in peoples' practice (Carlile, 2002). In other words, practices often take considerable time and effort to establish and, once established, can be reinforced by a whole range of other, interconnected practices. For this reason they are difficult to change, even where there is good evidence to do so. For example, new integrated IT systems are notoriously difficult to introduce into organizations because people find it very difficult to change from their current 'legacy' systems. Moreover, even if one group is willing to change, they may face challenges in introducing the system because other groups can not (or will not). As we shall see in Chapter 7, this applies equally when introducing Knowledge Management systems.

>> PERSPECTIVES COMPARED

Table 1.1 provides a summary of the distinctions between structural, process and practice perspectives on knowledge and managing knowledge work. In the chapters that follow we want to understand knowledge *work* – that is, where people work with knowledge in order to accomplish things – not knowledge for its own sake. Because of this, we draw more heavily from the process and practice perspectives as these: (a) take closer account of the core aspects of knowledge work – *knowledge processes, purposes and enabling contexts*; and (b) balance attention to the social *and* the material/technological aspects of knowledge work.

Having identified core concepts and approaches to knowledge work, in the next section we look at historical approaches to managing knowledge in organizations. This historical overview, albeit brief, is important in understanding why knowledge work is so important today and why formal Knowledge Management programmes sometimes repeat the mistakes of the past.

Table 1.1   Perspectives on knowledge work compared

	Epistemology of Possession	Epistemology of Practice	
	Structural	Process	Practice
View of social life	Individuals navigate in an objective external world through cognitive processes	Individual & collective interpretations embedded in social interactions, roles & structures	Materially interwoven (human & non-human) practices centrally organized around shared practical understandings
View of Knowledge	Knowledge as a cognitive entity – a resource to be accumulated, captured, transferred	Knowing as a social & organizational activity – socially constructed through interactions in particular contexts	Knowing as practice – constituted by and constituting fields of interconnected practices
Major locus of knowledge	Embrained and embodied in the skills and heads of individuals or organizations	Embedded & encultured in social context	Embedded, embodied and invested in practice
Link between knowledge and organizational performance	Knowledge directly related to, and functional (good) for performance	Relationship between knowledge and performance socially & politically mediated: reflecting interests of powerful groups	Relationship between knowledge and performance mediated through practice: Knowledge paradoxical for performance – sticks at practice boundaries
Major focus for managing knowledge work	Transfer/convert knowledge from one type (e.g. tacit to explicit) or location (individual, organizational) to another	Share, translate & legitimate knowledge amongst interacting groups	Transform knowledge through overlapping practices
Major tasks of Knowledge Management	Capturing/transferring knowledge, e.g. using IT	Translating knowledge across social groups, e.g. by building social networks & trust	Transforming practice and transversing boundaries of practice, e.g. using objects and creating communities of practice

>> SCIENTIFIC MANAGEMENT AS KNOWLEDGE MANAGEMENT

The importance of managing knowledge to improve the production process is not new. As long ago as 1890 Alfred Marshall suggested that knowledge was the most powerful engine of production. However, it was not really until the advent of Scientific Management at the beginning of the twentieth century that firms began to actively explore how to manage knowledge in work settings. Frederick Winslow Taylor developed the principles of Scientific Management in 1911. This new (at the time) approach to the organization of work – in particular, manual work – had a very profound effect on management, many features of which have endured to the present day.

Scientific Management emerged in the United States during the industrial revolution at a time where there were major advances in technology and mass production was on the increase. Managers of ever larger organizations were grappling, then, with the problems of controlling ever increasing volumes of work. Moreover, this was being carried out by a largely untrained workforce made up of immigrants from Europe or native American workers who had come from the agricultural regions of the United States. These workers were generally unskilled in factory work, many had little understanding of the English language and the majority had little or no experience of working in a factory environment.

Frederick Taylor began to develop the principles of Scientific Management based on his experiences at the Midvale Steel Company, where his career took him from machine shop labourer, through foreman to chief engineer. Having been involved with several wrangles with shop floor workers during his time as a foreman, Taylor believed that the prevalent system of production at that time – craft production – was highly inefficient. This was because it was largely left to the groups of 'craft workers' themselves to plan and carry out work tasks as they saw fit using loosely defined 'rules of thumb' acquired through years of experience. Hence, the knowledge concerning the way work was to be carried out resided, in effect, within 'the head and the hands' of the workers. This, Taylor believed, left organizations vulnerable to a lack of discipline and 'systematic soldiering' – the deliberate slow pacing of work and restriction of output – because it was not in workers' interests to produce any more than they absolutely had to.

To overcome these problems, Taylor believed that work processes should be organized differently, being divided up into a series of simple sub-tasks which could be standardized and tightly prescribed. Workers could then be selected 'scientifically' (Taylor, 1911) according to the task(s) they were to perform. Workers would no longer be responsible for planning the organization of work; instead they would only be required to carry out these simple, standardized sub-tasks in an efficient manner.

Taylor also argued that it should be the task of managers to observe work processes and determine the most efficient way to organize and schedule them – effectively acting as engineers. The Business Process Reengineering efforts of today are to some extent reminiscent of this approach. Hence, whilst with the craft system the knowledge required to carry out work had resided in the 'head and the hands' of the workers, with the new system of Scientific Management engineer-managers would extract and capture this knowledge by systematic observation. They would then use these observations to redesign the work process that workers would then follow. In short, managers would be the heads, and workers the hands, of the organization. To use today's terms, we can see, then, that these managers were in fact attempting to manage knowledge.

After leaving Midvale, and carving out a career as an independent consultant, Taylor carried out some of his first systematic studies around 1898 at the Bethlehem Steel Corporation in the United States, with impressive increases in productivity. His most famous study (a story that he rewrote several times, each time with more impressive results) was of a Dutch pig iron handler called Schmidt. At the start of his studies, 75 men were loading an average of 12.5 tons per man per day. Schmidt followed Taylor's simple but detailed instructions regarding when to load the pig iron and walk and when to sit and rest, with no interaction with other workers. By following these instructions specifically, Schmidt increased his output to 47.5 tons per day. He was able to maintain this output for three years of studies and received a 60 per cent increase in wages compared to his peers (Taylor, 1911).

Following the impressive results at the Bethlehem Corporation, other firms were keen to apply Scientific Management principles. However, the improvements in productivity were accompanied by widespread hostile reactions from workers because the work was inherently boring and left workers little or no latitude to apply their knowledge and skills. In addition, in many firms management chose to introduce the principles rather selectively to reduce the number of workers required and, because the skills required were now simpler, cut rather than increase wages. This often led to strikes such that the Federation of Labor came to vehemently oppose Scientific Management. In 1911 a House of Representatives Committee was set up to investigate Taylor's methods, concluding that Scientific Management did provide useful techniques for the management and organization of work. However, because of continued hostility and significant concerns about the potential for industrial unrest in arms factories in wartime, congress banned the adoption of the approach in the defense industry.

Despite this knock–back, Henry Ford applied and further developed Scientific Management principles for the production of cars. At the turn of the century, highly skilled craftsmen had been employed to build cars using handcrafted parts manufactured on general-purpose machines. However, with the introduction of Scientific Management and rationalization at the Ford automotive plant, single-purpose machines were introduced on which anyone could be easily trained to produce standardized parts. The knowledge and many of the skills required to build a car had in effect been *embodied* in the machine. However, workers still controlled the *speed* of production. It was not until Ford developed the concept of the assembly line, still used today – where the car moved past the men, instead of men moving past the car – that Ford was able to achieve what he considered to be total control of the production process.

Importantly, Taylor and Ford both had very instrumental views of human nature, believing that workers were purely rational, economic beings motivated solely by monetary incentives. They therefore believed that management–labour relations could actually be improved because workers would have the opportunity to earn more (but not too much more) money in return for gains in efficiency. However, these beliefs were fundamentally mistaken and as worker fatigue and boredom set in, absenteeism rose significantly and the quality of the work decreased. Later, the 'Human Relations' school, led by the pioneering work of Elton Mayo at the Hawthorne plant of the Western Electric Company, led to the development of different approaches to the organization of work based on group work and group responsibility for work tasks. This demonstrated that workers have social, not just monetary, needs and are also motivated by intangible rewards such as job satisfaction and recognition of a job well-done.

It would be a mistake to think that we have witnessed the end of Scientific Management. The underlying principles are still applied across sectors today, especially, where efficiency, standardization and cost minimization are the main drivers of competition. Take, for example, the rise of fast food chains like McDonalds or the ever increasing number of call centres outsourced to low-wage countries. Many of the problems around quality of products or, increasingly, services are now addressed technologically, with mechanisms for surveillance and quality control being built into the core technologies used by workers (Sewell and Wilkinson, 1992). For example, call centres across a range of sectors now use sophisticated information technology to monitor the number of calls taken by workers and the quality of the interaction between client and worker. Essentially the idea with these systems is still to take knowledge, and all the uncertainty that this creates, out of the work (and workers) and place this in the hands of management and the technologies that they choose to use.

>> MANAGING KNOWLEDGE IN THE 'INFORMATION AGE'

Whilst this earlier work alerts us to the fact that managing knowledge has long been seen as important in organizations, the so-called 'Knowledge Era' or 'Information Age' has seen major advances in this idea. This can be traced to wider debates about the organization of work and the sources of wealth creation in contemporary society. A whole 'new' language has arisen around concerns that it is knowledge, and not other resources such as labour or capital, that is the main source of competitive advantage across sectors. This language is now used widely in management and in politics and includes such terms as: the learning organization, Knowledge Management, strategic management of core competencies, the knowledge-based view of the firm, knowledge-based systems, knowledge-intensive firms, intellectual and social capital, knowledge capital, talent management and so forth.

The fashionable labels come and go and, as predicted in the previous edition of this book, 'Knowledge Management' has largely lost its ground as 'flavour of the month' (Scarbrough and Swan, 2001). The emergence and demise of these management fads, however, is itself continued testimony to the phenomena which they address – that is, the growing knowledge-intensity of business, the impact of discourse on patterns and styles of management, the seemingly endless importance of information and communication technology (ICT) on work and work relationships, and the importance of change and innovation for organizations facing increasingly turbulent environments. These factors are not the product of fashion but of history – a convergent set of forces which have unleashed fundamental patterns of change on advanced industrial economies.

These forces have been examined in a number of different studies of industrial, occupational and organizational change in more recent decades. In 1969, Drucker emphasized that knowledge had become the crucial resource of the economy. Daniel Bell, in 1973, also described the potential for the development of a post-industrial society dominated by knowledge workers operating in knowledge-intensive firms. This would be a society organized around knowledge for the purpose of economic development, social control and institutional innovation and change. Other work in the 80s and 90s (e.g. Castells, 1996; Drucker, 1988; Gibbons et al., 1994) indicated the extent of such changes in advanced economies since the days when Scientific Management principles were first introduced. Such studies have outlined important characteristic features of the current era. These include the following:

(i)   The extent to which knowledge has been 'globalized', or freed up from material, physical and geographic constraints.

(ii)   The economic value of intangibles, such as new ideas, software, services and network relationships.

(iii) The convergence of computing power and communications technology, with a new generation of web-based technologies having major impacts on the structuring of work and occupations.

(iv)   The importance of knowledge as a primary means of production, acting upon itself in 'an accelerating spiral of innovation and change' (Castells, 1996).

(v)   An emphasis on normative, or cultural, rather than hierarchical forms of control so that knowledge workers effectively manage and discipline themselves (and each other).

(vi)   Fundamental changes in the ways knowledge itself is produced – no longer just in 'ivory tower' academic organizations or R&D departments (Mode 1) but *as it is applied* in new contexts (Mode 2) (Gibbons et al., 1994; Nowotny et al., 2003). The different dimensions of these modes of knowledge production are summarized in Table 1.2.

Table 1.2   Mode 1 and Mode 2 knowledge production

Mode 1 knowledge production	Mode 2 knowledge production
Problems defined by academic and professional communities	Knowledge produced in context of application
Disciplinary knowledge	Transdisciplinary knowledge
Homogeneity	Heterogeneity
Hierarchical and stable organizations	Heterarchical and transient organizations
Quality control by the 'invisible college'	Socially accountable and reflexive

Source: Adapted from Nowotny et al. (2001).

Taking a more critical approach, it is important that we continue to ask questions about the extent to which these changes have been as widespread, or as inherently positive, as predicted by the likes of Drucker or Gibbons et al. As we have seen, in some types of work – call centres being an example – there is little evidence of workers being freed from hierarchy or being actively engaged in using their own knowledge as a means of production. New web-based and increasingly mobile technologies also, clearly, create their own problems. On the one hand, they can decentralize work and free people and activities from the constraints of physical location or even identity. At the same time, however, they can depersonalize the experience of work, generating problems of social isolation, or can intensify it by shifting home–work life balance. They can also increase opportunities for more subtle forms of surveillance and control.

Positive or negative, however, the changes heralded by the 'Information Age' are undoubtedly having a visible impact on the way organizations are being structured. Many have indeed shifted away from the traditional command and control structures of Taylor's time (the classic bureaucracy) towards flatter, decentralized structures and more flexible, open-ended, fluid and networked arrangements (see Chapter 3). If we look at high-technology sectors such as the biopharmaceutical industry, for example, we see this characterized by loose constellations of firms, alliances and mergers, outsourcing and partnering arrangements, licensing deals and so forth. The rise of networked organizations (sometimes referred to as polycentric organizations), virtual modes of organizing, and more open-ended, collaborative forms of innovation and product development (Chesbrough, 2004) illustrate further the extent to which organizational structures have evolved in pace with changes in technology that break down traditional boundaries of time and space.

These changes in structure have, however, generated new problems for managing knowledge in the current era that are equally, if not more, significant than those experienced in Taylor's time. For example, when outsourcing is introduced, or mergers take place, the implications in terms of 'losing' valuable knowledge are often not recognized until it is too late. More open-ended, collaborative arrangements for organizing work and product development also generate significant challenges in terms of who owns intellectual property (Chesbrough, 2003a, b). And, when businesses are restructured around virtual teams and networks, and stretched across time and space, they also inevitably lose opportunities for casual sharing of knowledge and learning invited by physical proximity. As Prusak put it (1997):

> If the water cooler was a font of useful knowledge in the traditional firm, what constitutes a virtual one.

> (p. xiii)

Indeed, it has been suggested that in fact one of the reasons that Knowledge Management initiatives became so popular in the late 1990s was because they offered an antidote to some of the profound organizational problems posed by these changes of organization in the 'Information Age'. The emphasis in

Knowledge Management was, at least initially, on identifying, extracting and capturing the, often tacit, 'knowledge assets' of the firm so that they could be both fully exploited and fully protected as a source of competitive advantage. For example, Dow Chemical, which earns a high income through technology licensing, replaced a data archive described as 'a disorganized mess of intellectual capital' with a widely accessible database to keep track of their many patents.

The use and limitations of Knowledge Management systems, introduced to exploit the company's intellectual or knowledge assets, are explored in detail in Chapter 7. From this historical overview we can see that in some respects 'Knowledge Management' is actually pretty similar to Scientific Management, in so far as both aim to capture the knowledge that resided in 'the heads and the hands' of the workers. However, the task of extracting and capturing the knowledge of work processes 'held' in the heads of workers has become far more complex as traditional forms of work have gradually been replaced by what we now refer to as knowledge work.

>> WHAT IS KNOWLEDGE WORK?

If we look back at the definition of knowledge above we can see that all work, even Schmidt's pig iron handling, requires the application and use of some knowledge. You could argue, then, that all work is knowledge work. However, as we shall see in Chapter 2, using the term in such a broad-brush way is not very helpful when thinking about managing knowledge work.

The term 'knowledge work', as used here, refers more particularly to organizational activities and occupations that are 'characterized by an emphasis on theoretical knowledge, creativity and use of analytical and social skills' (Frenkel et al., 1995, p. 773). 'Knowledge work' in these terms encompasses both what is traditionally referred to as professional work (e.g. accountancy, scientific and legal work) and more contemporary types of work (e.g. consultancy, software development, advertising and public relations). In these kinds of work, knowledge acts as the main input into the work, the major way of achieving the work and the major output. This kind of work, and the organizations that focus on it, are explored in more depth in Chapter 2. Suffice to say here, it is with this kind of work that we are most concerned in our book.

The term 'knowledge worker' encompasses, then, both professionals and those with other discipline-based knowledge or more esoteric expertise and skills – for example advertising, media, consultancy – whose major work tasks involve the creation of new knowledge or the application of existing knowledge in new ways. Knowledge workers typically have high levels of education and specialist skills combined with the ability to apply these skills in practice to identify and solve problems. What is significant about these types of knowledge workers is that, unlike the kinds of shop floor workers Taylor was dealing with, or the call centre workers discussed above, knowledge workers are the organization's primary means of production. If we take the view, also, that specialist knowledge is deeply embedded in practice (the epistemology of practice view), this means that knowledge work does not lend itself particularly well to knowledge capture or standardization. Therefore those engaged in these types of work need to be left to make their own decisions about what and how to do their work.

>> CONCLUSIONS

In this chapter we have focused on introducing and providing terms and providing a historical overview of how and why knowledge work has become so important for organizations in the twenty-first century. In this we have seen how process and practice perspectives have become more prominent over recent years, in part due to the limitations and critique of purely structural approaches and knowledge typologies. Table 1.3 summarizes some of the major concepts introduced in this chapter:

We can conclude from this that managing knowledge work in the twenty-first century is less about direct control and capture of knowledge in machines or systems – as in the days of Taylor and Ford – and more about providing an enabling context that supports the processes and practices of applying knowledge for specific tasks and purposes. Knowledge workers resist the command

Table 1.3 Core concepts

Concept	Working Definition	Field of study
Knowledge	The ability to discriminate within and across contexts	Concerned with the ways in which actors in particular social situations understand and make sense of where they are and what they are doing
Organizational knowledge	A learned set of norms, shared understandings and practices that integrates actors and artefacts to produce valued outcomes within a specific social and organizational context	Concerned with the means by which actors develop beliefs, behaviours and routines that shape the organization's capabilities
Knowledge Management	Explicit strategies, tools and practices applied by management that seek to make knowledge a resource for the organization	Concerned with the development of concepts that illuminate or enhance the application of these practices
Knowledge Work	Organizational activities and occupations that are 'characterized by an emphasis on theoretical knowledge, creativity and use of analytical and social skills'	Concerned with the analysis of organizational conditions, or enabling contexts, that allow such work
Knowledge Worker	Professionals and others with disciplined-based knowledge or more esoteric expertise and skills whose major work tasks involve creating new knowledge or applying existing knowledge in new ways	Concerned with the ways in which knowledge workers are organized, motivated and managed
Innovation	The application of knowledge to new tasks and situations	Concerned with the ways in which new products, processes and services are developed and delivered

and control structure of Taylorist times and demand a new form of management and organization more reminiscent of the orchestra than the traditional manufacturing firm. Like musicians, knowledge workers seek outlets for their creative abilities and become absorbed in interesting challenges and the stimulation of working with other specialists. This poses new challenges for management in knowledge-based organizations that we shall consider through the course of this book, which are to:

- Develop *enabling contexts* – including organizational cultures, structures, opportunities for collaborative forms of work and coordination, reward and recognition systems and career opportunities – that support knowledge work.
- Understand *knowledge processes* – that is the processes and practices through which knowledge is shared, integrated, translated and transformed (but also hoarded, constrained and protected).
- Deploy knowledge for specific *purposes* – that is to accomplish specific tasks as set by particular interest groups (and not assuming that knowledge is necessarily good, or good for its own sake)
- Align *context, knowledge processes and purpose* in the management of knowledge work.

Throughout the following chapters our emphasis is on combining theories with practical examples and case studies – many of which are drawn from our own research – that enable us to better understand knowledge work and its management through aligning processes, purposes and enabling contexts. In the next chapter, however, we focus on the management of knowledge-based or 'knowledge-intensive firms', as they tend to be referred to in the literature as these pose distinctive challenges for managing knowledge work. Using the case of 'ScienceCo', we explore in particular the structural and cultural contexts that support and enable knowledge work.

Summary of key learning points

>> Knowledge is highly contextual thus distinguishing it from information or data.

>> Two major ways of understanding knowledge underpin approaches to managing knowledge work: the epistemology of possession and the epistemology of practice.

>> The epistemology of possession treats knowledge as something people have and tries to identify types and forms of knowledge – knowledge creation is seen as involving the conversion of one type of knowledge to another.

>> The epistemology of practice treats knowledge (or knowing) as something that people do and tries to understand processes by which people and organizations come to know and apply this knowing in practice – knowledge creation is seen as an ability, rooted in action and social practice.

>> Structural approaches to managing knowledge assume an epistemology of possession, while process and practice approaches assume an epistemology of practice.

>> The principles of Scientific Management can be seen as an early attempt to manage knowledge. They are still applied today in many sectors.

>> An industrial shift to the 'Information Age' or 'Knowledge Era' has witnessed new forms of knowledge production and a growing awareness of knowledge work as a major source of wealth creation across organizations and nations.

>> 'Knowledge Management' became popular on the back of this shift as a means of coping with growing uncertainties of knowledge work in the twenty-first century. Approaches that aim to extract and harness the knowledge of the individual worker are actually quite reminiscent of Scientific Management.

>> The management of knowledge workers is of strategic importance, in particular, to firms that compete on the basis of innovation.

2

KNOWLEDGE-INTENSIVE FIRMS

Chapter Outline

Learning Outcomes

At the end of this chapter you should be able to:

⇒ Understand the concept of knowledge-intensive firms and differentiate between different types of knowledge-intensive firm.

⇒ Understand the structural and cultural conditions relevant to the management of knowledge-intensive firms.

⇒ Understand the different ways in which these structural and cultural conditions interact to provide an enabling context for knowledge work in knowledge-intensive settings.

⇒ Appreciate the importance of achieving a 'fit' between structure and cultural conditions for the successful management of knowledge workers.

>> INTRODUCTION

The first chapter introduced and explained the notion of 'knowledge work' and 'knowledge worker'. Here we focus our attention on firms where the majority or even the entire workforce consists of knowledge workers – hence the term 'knowledge-intensive firm' – and consider the distinctive management challenges posed by this particular type of 'expert' workforce. Even today in what many refer to as the 'knowledge based economies' of the developed world, knowledge workers are still a relatively scarce resource within the labour market as their particular knowledge, skills and expertise are not generally widely available (Horwitz et al., 2003). Knowledge workers therefore tend to have considerable choice and latitude regarding their place of work – particularly within knowledge-intensive firms – and management are required to find ways of attracting and perhaps more importantly, retaining an expert workforce as the costs of replacement in terms of time and money are significant.

Knowledge-intensive firms tend to be service-based organizations often competing in their respective sectors based on their ability to solve complex problems and provide solutions for clients. Law firms, accountancy practices, management consultancies, investment banks, architectural practices, advertising and public relations agencies are all good examples of knowledge-intensive firms. Many of these types of firms tend to organize in distinctive ways in order to (a) attract and retain knowledge workers and (b) promote innovation and in some instances creativity. Sustaining an expert workforce who are willing to create and share knowledge is crucial if knowledge-intensive firms are to achieve competitive advantage in the long term. Yet it is the workforce in these firms that to a large extent owns the means of production, not management. Developing and, more importantly, *sustaining* an expert workforce is therefore possibly the most important strategic issue that confronts management within these firms over time.

In this chapter we are going to consider the structural and cultural conditions which, in combination, support the management of knowledge work and promote the recruitment and retention of knowledge workers in knowledge-intensive settings. In so doing we focus on the *process* and *practice* of knowledge work. We illustrate the importance of the interaction and integration of these organizational elements through the case of ScienceCo. The distinctive organizational arrangements that developed in this firm, characterized by an atypical culture, serve as a useful example of the importance of creating an *enabling context* for the conduct of knowledge work – particularly the design of core work processes which involve creativity and innovation.

>> TYPES OF KNOWLEDGE-INTENSIVE FIRM

Alvesson defines knowledge workers as 'qualified labour' (Alvesson, 2004, p. 8). However, this is a somewhat broad definition. Here we use the term 'knowledge worker' to encompass both professionals and groups with other

Table 2.1 Types of knowledge-intensive firm

	Strategic focus	Resources	Examples
Client-based	Client relations	Individually controlled	Law and accountancy practices
Problem-solving	Creative problem-solving – innovation	Team-based	Advertising agencies, software development, web design firms
Output-based	Adaptation of ready solutions	Controlled by the organization	Some large management consultancy firms

Source: Adapted from Lowendahl (1997).

forms of disciplined-based knowledge or more esoteric expertise and skills, for example advertising, media, whose major work tasks involve the creation of new knowledge or the application of existing knowledge in new ways. It follows then that different types of firm employ different types of knowledge workers. Lowendahl (1997), for example, suggests that the crucial strategic difference between knowledge-intensive firms is the role of the professionals employed, that is, the characteristics of the resource base and the types of project targeted. She identifies three generic types of knowledge-intensive firm premised on the firm's strategic focus (see Table 2.1).

Alvesson (2004) distinguishes between two major types of knowledge-intensive firm; R&D companies and professional service firms. Professional service firms deal largely with intangibles and those employed often deal directly with clients while R&D companies typically produce tangible products and contact between employees and the customer are less direct. This largely concurs with Lowendahl's typology which only differentiates further on the basis of what is produced for the client in terms of either bespoke or readily adapted solutions/products (be they tangible or intangible). The term 'knowledge-intensive firm' is therefore used as a generic term to encompass many different types of firm operating across sectors. Traditional professional service firms such as law and accountancy firms, for example, are seen as a subset of knowledge-intensive firms and have existed as long as the organized professions. These types of firm generally organize along partnership lines with recognized codes of practice and clearly defined 'up-or-out' career paths. Despite the changing nature of some of the established professions (Muzio and Ackroyd, 2005), the majority of professional service firms still tend to be structured and organized along similar lines – often referred to as the professional bureaucracy (Mintzberg, 1979). Professional bureaucracies are organized along traditional hierarchical lines. Legal professionals will occupy the senior positions within the firm and a range of non-legal professionals will manage discrete functions within the firm such as human resources, finance and so on. Small professional service firms tend to be organized along traditional partnership lines otherwise known as the P2 form whereby the senior partners of the firm also manage the firm (Greenwood, Hinings and Brown, 1990). Larger ones are often referred to as Managed Professional Bureaucracies (MPBs) (Cooper et al., 1996) and employ a variety of professionals as well as legal professionals and administrators to deal with the management and operation of the firm. Notably within the larger MPBs, professionals often work as part of large teams (i.e they do not necessarily individually control resources) addressing the needs of similar large, corporate clients. Professional service firms are characterized by a clear hierarchical, partnership structure and well-defined career paths, and the management of this type of firm is already well-documented in the management literature (Lowendahl, 2000).

Some knowledge-intensive firms, in particular large consultancy firms, are also often loosely referred to as professional service firms. The way in which the very large, global consultancies such as Accenture, McKinsey and Price Waterhouse Coopers organize does tend to resemble that of the traditional professional service firm (although they tend to be output-based rather than client-based). However, whilst these categories overlap, the features of knowledge-intensive firms are broader and, importantly, some of the features ascribed to the traditional professions are not necessarily apparent in all knowledge-intensive firms. For example, distinctive features of PSFs such as codes of ethics, strong professional affiliations and specific educational entry requirements leading to restricted access need not, and do not, exist in many knowledge-intensive firms.

More contemporary forms of knowledge-intensive firms emerged in the latter part of the twentieth century including media, advertising and public-relations agencies, software development companies, and many other high-tech and specialist consultancy firms. Around the start of the new millennium we also witnessed the emergence of virtual, Internet-based knowledge-intensive firms offering specialist services to both individual clients and the general public (e.g. Napster, Friends reunited). It is the issues around organizing and managing within these typically smaller, knowledge-intensive firms operating in knowledge-based sectors that are going to be specifically addressed here in this chapter.

Not surprisingly, a precise definition of a knowledge-intensive firm is elusive and it is clear from the term itself that it is a socially constructed, broad-ranging and yet quite ambiguous concept. Alvesson (2004, p. 17) loosely defines knowledge-intensive firms as 'organizations that offer to the market the use of knowledge or knowledge-based products...'. The core of activities in these companies is based on the intellectual skills of a very large proportion of the labour force deployed in development, and often also in the sale of products and in service work and he goes on to define a knowledge-intensive firm as 'an organization broadly recognized as creating value through the use of advanced knowledge' (p. 29). However, the term 'advanced knowledge' here is somewhat ambiguous. Unfortunately, because there is no precise definition there has been a proliferation of articles on the subject of knowledge workers and knowledge work in what might be considered fairly traditional work settings, which has led some commentators to suggest that all work is in fact knowledge work (Knights et al., 1993). However, in this chapter we are not using this broad definition but instead focus on those sectors in today's knowledge-based post-industrial economy which compete on the basis of their ability to create, apply and share professional and discipline-based knowledge. This includes sectors where the skills and expertise required are not necessarily acquired through formal education and qualifications but where knowledge is still the basis for competition. For example, many skills that are applied within the field of ICT, such as software development, web page design and so on, are skills that are often largely self-taught and almost develops intuitively by those individuals with a particular interest in IT. In many instances it is not necessary to have a degree in computer science in order to become a software expert or web developer. It is therefore quite difficult to give a precise definition of a knowledge-intensive firm in terms of the particular skills and expertise required.

From a critical perspective, Alvesson (1993, 2001) suggests that knowledge-intensive firms might be more usefully seen purely as 'systems of persuasion' – relying primarily on their persuasive strategies (esoteric skills) rather than expert knowledge or skills *per se* to convince clients of their superior ability and expertise to satisfy client expectations. This might be the case in some service-based knowledge-intensive firms, for example, some advertising agencies, but certainly not all knowledge-intensive firms. Whilst there is therefore a lack of clarity and a degree of ambiguity around the term 'knowledge-intensive firm', it is a useful one with which to encapsulate a broad range of firms operating across sectors in knowledge-based, post-industrial economies. What is indisputable is that many types of knowledge-intensive firm emerged in the late twentieth and early twenty-first centuries and now such firms constitute important industry sectors within a post-industrial economy. In this chapter we address the ways in which they organize and the drivers for particular modes of organizing. We next turn to describing the distinctive characteristics of knowledge work and knowledge workers.

>> THE DISTINCTIVE CHARACTERISTICS OF KNOWLEDGE WORK AND KNOWLEDGE WORKERS

Autonomy

Generally knowledge workers expect to have considerable autonomy in their work. The nature of the work, which is often characterized by creativity and problem-solving, demands autonomy. It is the knowledge workers themselves who tend to be the most appropriate people to decide how to initiate, plan, organize and coordinate their major work tasks. Unlike other kinds of workers, knowledge workers possess or 'own' the organization's primary means of production – that is, knowledge. They therefore expect and demand autonomy and management is not really in a position to deny them. This is not to say that knowledge workers work alone, typically they work in teams of varying sizes with varying degrees of inter-dependency. In addition, it is not always the case that management in knowledge-intensive firms shares the same levels of skills and expertise as the expert workforce they are trying to manage. Therefore, knowledge workers' demand for autonomy, in combination with an insufficient understanding of the work being conducted in some instances, means that management is typically not in a position to directly control or even manage knowledge work processes. Therefore, it is perhaps more appropriate within a knowledge-work setting to suggest that management's role is to provide the necessary *enabling context* that will *facilitate* knowledge work. Further evidence for this is provided in more recent research conducted by Amabile et al. (2004, 2005). Amabile and colleagues conducted research focused on the cognitive aspects of creativity and adopted a social psychology methodology. In total 222 knowledge workers, working in 26 teams across 7 companies and 3 industries completed a daily questionnaire which sought information to establish the relationship between positive affect (mood) and creativity. A positive mood was found to be positively associated with creativity and this lingered through to the following day (Amabile et al., 2005). Moreover leadership behaviour was found to have a significant influence on subordinates in that leader behaviours was found to precipitate subordinate perceptual and affective reactions, which in turn influenced subordinate creative performance (Amabile et al., 2004).

Knowledge base and working methods

Different types of knowledge worker rely, create, share and apply different types of knowledge in their work. Thus in different knowledge work settings distinctive 'epistemic cultures' can be found (Knorr-Cetina, 1999), epistemic cultures being 'those amalgams of arrangements and mechanisms.... – which, in a given field, *make up how we know what we know'* (Knorr-Cetina, 1999, p. 1; italics authors own). Such cultures are characterized by different social, discursive and material practices, including different levels of interaction with natural objects, sign systems and so on. When we consider the different epistemic cultures associated with different forms of knowledge work we start to appreciate the 'the complex texture of knowledge as practiced' (Knorr-Cetina, 1999, p. 2) and how this might differ across different knowledge work contexts. Robertson et al. (2003) found significant differences in knowledge creating practices across a scientific consultancy and a legal consultancy which was explained in terms of institutionally embedded means of legitimating knowledge across scientific and legal contexts. These included different emphases on experimentation versus interpretation, different forms of personal networking, and significant differences in the relative importance of codifying knowledge. In scientific professions for example, claims to knowledge are legitimized by the application of the scientific method (principally experimental) to natural and biological phenomena. Once established and replicated through the scientific method and validated by the scientific community, such knowledge claims transcend particular contexts (Collins, 1985). In contrast, 'lawyers point to the law finding of judges and the law making of legislatures' (Halliday, 1985, p. 426). Thus the knowledge claims of the legal profession extend only to particular jurisdictions and particular points in time. It is also important to recognize that, as well as the broad epistemological differences that exist between professions, such differences are also found amongst different specialisms within a broad professional grouping (Drazin, 1990). This has implications for management inasmuch as attempts to introduce standard work practices and procedures (e.g. Knowledge Management systems and tools), may be perceived as contrary to the ongoing epistemic practices and an unnecessary distraction from core work processes.

Co-location

Another distinguishing feature of the type of work conducted by knowledge workers in knowledge-intensive firms is that there is often the need to work remotely from the employing firm, typically physically located at the client firm. This physical co-location of knowledge workers can be an important management issue to be addressed. For example, client firms may well be inclined to offer permanent employment to knowledge workers who produce good results and who might prove to be a lot less expensive if employed directly by the client rather than on a consultancy basis. The client firm might therefore be in direct competition with the employing firm for the services of knowledge workers. Not only is management therefore required to focus on strategies to aid retention in relation to direct competitors to the firm, they must also consider the development of retention strategies in relation to their client firms.

In addition, knowledge workers are typically organized in teams with more or less interdependence depending on the nature of the task. Physical co-location can therefore also be problematic for team-working even when sophisticated ICT is made available. The complexity of knowledge working often makes face-to-face modes of interaction the only viable communication medium for sharing and creating knowledge at critical points in the process. Here then, management again is required to develop strategies and mechanisms that will enable the coordination and integration of knowledge work processes across the team without necessarily directly intervening in those processes.

'Gold collar' workers

The distinctive characteristics of knowledge workers and knowledge work processes led to the term 'gold collar' worker being applied to knowledge workers (Kelley, 1990). This term implies that these workers need to be managed skilfully, provided with excellent working conditions and generally afforded exceptional, or at least very good, terms and conditions of employment. There are exceptions to this naturally, particularly in large knowledge-intensive firms, such as large management consultancies (cf. Alvesson and Karreman, 2007). However, in small- and medium-sized knowledge-intensive firms, leaders and managers of the firm typically offer superior employment conditions which can be viewed as providing an enabling context for knowledge work (Baron et al., 2001).

In addition to terms and conditions of employment, modes of organizing need to be developed which will be conducive to knowledge work and viewed favourable by knowledge workers. Management must therefore pay careful attention to both the structural and the cultural conditions that exist within the firm. Knowledge-intensive firms thus typically need to organize differently compared to more traditional firms where workers are not necessarily the direct productive force of the organization and, in many respects, are easy to replace. There are still relatively few in-depth empirical studies of the management of knowledge-intensive firms (though see Alvesson, 1995, 2004). Articles on the topic however continue to proliferate and many focus on what is perceived to be the major problem of motivating knowledge workers (O'Neill and Adya, 2007; Thompson and Heron, 2006). These articles are somewhat limited in their focus and do not directly address aspects of the wider organizational context. Here however we are concerned primarily with developing a more holistic account and focus on what constitutes an enabling context for knowledge work within knowledge-intensive settings. The generic structural and cultural conditions which are considered to facilitate the management of knowledge-intensive firms are considered in conjunction with some of the structural or cultural barriers that might mitigate against successful outcomes from knowledge work processes.

>> FACILITATING KNOWLEDGE WORK – ORGANIZING AS AN ADHOCRACY

The way in which knowledge-intensive firms structure and organize internally will be crucial where innovation and creativity are the basis on which the firm competes. Whilst it will be particularly important for management to offer good terms and conditions of employment to knowledge workers, the way in which the major work processes are managed and coordinated will be equally significant. An approach to organizing needs to be developed that is synergistic with knowledge work and provides an enabling context for the practice of knowledge work.

The way in which many knowledge-intensive firms organize tends to reflect the more general trend towards flatter, less bureaucratized ways of organizing that are becoming more common across all sectors in the twenty-first century (see Chapter 3). In general terms, knowledge-intensive firms try to organize highly organically and flexibly, generally around teams. Henry Mintzberg (1979) identified five archetypal structural forms that characterize the way firms organize. He suggests that where creativity and innovation – typically in the form of developing novel solutions to client problems – are a conscious strategy, as often tends to be the case within knowledge-intensive firms, then an 'adhocracy' is the most appropriate organizational configuration. The adhocracy is almost the complete opposite of the traditional bureaucracy. An adhocracy genuinely de-emphasizes a hierarchical structure in preference to a dynamic organizational structure based on self-formed and self-managed project teams, decentralized decision-making and minimal formalization in terms of policies, rules and procedures. Within an adhocracy, Mintzberg suggests, control tends to be based on professionalism and shared, organizational values – referred to as cultural or normative control – rather than on more typical forms of direct control such as direct supervision and adherence to rules and procedures. To summarize this analysis, Table 2.2 highlights the distinctive characteristics of the adhocracy in comparison to the traditional bureaucracy.

The adhocracy can also be contrasted with traditional professional service firms where conflict can often arise between competing professional and organizational values (Raelin, 1991). For example, professionals will naturally want to complete client work to the best of their professional abilities, applying discipline-based knowledge (legal, financial, scientific) to client problems. However, time is always considered to be a precious resource in these firms and directly related to the fee structure. There can therefore, on occasion, be conflict between the professional values of the lawyer or accountant, for example, to do a 'good job' and the needs of the firm to manage the firm's resources across the client base as efficiently as possible. According to Raelin, managing partners within these types of professional service firm are required to find ways of mediating these conflicting tensions.

This conflict of values, however, is not necessarily so apparent in some more contemporary types of knowledge-intensive firm where the notion of 'professionalism' is broader and tends to refer to general beliefs and expectations around high standards of performance and a dominant work ethic. This is explored further later in this chapter. Thus, in general, the informal,

Table 2.2 The bureaucracy and the adhocracy compared

Bureaucracy	Adhocracy
Multiple level hierarchy	Minimal hierarchy
Work processes organized around functional groups	Work processes self-organized around teams
Many formal rules, policies and procedures	Few or no formal rules, policies and procedures
Direct control characterized by supervision	Normative control characterized by self-management
Centralized decision-making	Decentralized decision-making
Coordination achieved through explicit rules and procedures	Coordination achieved though mutual adjustment
Highly mechanistic form	Highly organic form

loosely coupled organizational context of the adhocracy is considered to provide the necessary autonomous working conditions in which individuals can spend time experimenting with ideas and more generally engaging in creative and innovative work. Whilst it may seem somewhat atypical for management to choose to organize in this way, this approach tends to be adopted in many contemporary knowledge-intensive sectors such as software development, new media, specialist consultancies and so on. It has been shown that any significant shift from this mode of organizing can be highly detrimental to both organizational performance and employee turnover. Baron et al. (2001), for example, conducted a large-scale, longitudinal survey of software firms in Silicon Valley over a ten-year period which focused on modes of organizing, performance, CEO and employee turnover. Baron's team discovered that across a population of 173 software firms over time there were four dominant organizing templates. These templates were characterized by what was considered to be the primary motivation to work for the firm (attachment), the primary selection criteria and the primary means of co-ordination and control. Across the five templates the nature of the work conducted within the firm across the star, engineering and bureaucracy was considered to be the major means of attachment, attracting knowledge workers to these firms and promoting retention. The commitment template was characterized by knowledge workers' strong emotional attachment to the firm (love) and money was the major means of attachment in firms characterized as autocracies. Typically skills were the major selection criteria applied although firms adopting the star template selected on the basis of future potential. The star template firms also relied largely on self-control and professionalism as the basis for co-ordination and control, whilst the engineering and commitment templates relied on cultural control. These are summarized in Table 2.3.

The majority of firms in the sample were identified as either Engineering (34 per cent) or Commitment (13 per cent) types and 11 per cent of the sample were also identified as Star types. Only 6 per cent organized as bureaucracies and 7 per cent organized as autocracies where the CEO adopted a command and control mode of organizing. The remainder of the sample were classified as hybrids. The majority of firms therefore relied primarily on professional or

Table 2.3 Organizing templates that characterize high-tech knowledge-intensive firms

Type	Attachment	Selection	Co-ord/control
Star	Work	Potential	Professional
Engineering	Work	Skills	Cultural
Commitment	Love	Fit	Cultural
Bureaucracy	Work	Skills	Formal
Autocracy	Money	Skills	Direct

Source: Adapted from Baron et al., 2001, p. 968.

cultural (normative) control (see below) rather than formal co-ordination and control mechanisms as a means to co-ordinate work. This supports the idea that an organic, informal and flexible mode of organizing is preferred in these types of knowledge-intensive firm (the notion of cultural or normative control is explored in depth later in the chapter). Notably, firms which adopted a bureaucratic or autocratic model had significantly higher employee turnover than those adopting a commitment or star model. Often over time, with a change in CEO came a change in organizing and the most de-stabilizing in terms of employee turnover, and firm performance was the shift from star or commitment types to the bureaucracy. This tended to occur when firms went public and shareholders demanded more traditional modes of management. The very few firms that shifted from a star model (arguably the template that most closely resembles the adhocracy) to bureaucracy experienced the highest employee turnover. Baron et al.'s research therefore clearly demonstrates that the majority of knowledge-intensive firms do tend to organize largely informally and traditional bureaucratic modes of organizing are not suitable if innovation is required.

More recent research by Robertson and Swan (2004) also highlighted that subtle shifts in organizing template from an adhocracy to a 'soft bureaucracy' (again largely legitimated by the public flotation of the firm onto the stock market) can also have a significant detrimental effect. Soft bureaucracy is considered to be a new, subtle form of bureaucratic control and domination characterized by 'ambivalent structures of governance, within which domination is not essentially exerted by means of, for example, violence, direct punishment or local hierarchical supervision, but through sophisticated managerial strategies' (Courpasson, 2000, p. 142). Control in 'soft bureaucracies' is thus characterized by four distinctive components: (1) a specific combination of impersonal and personal obedience; (2) centralization as a means of legitimating political decisions; (3) control based on soft coercion and protection; (4) control which fuses external and internal legitimacy. In short, the aim is to manage knowledge-intensive firms to be 'both simultaneously innovative (retaining the appearance of worker autonomy) and yet able to control innovation' (Robertson and Swan, 2004, p. 130). Ultimately however Robertson and Swan (2004) demonstrate that whilst soft bureaucracy may be one way of subtly controlling knowledge workers, the negative effect in terms of morale and subsequent performance may be significant. Their research also supports Baron et al.'s earlier research which highlighted that going public, and the demands of the market (shareholders) for greater formalization can start to erode the enabling context for knowledge work.

>> STRUCTURAL CONSTRAINTS ON KNOWLEDGE WORK

Development of organizational 'best practice'

Research has demonstrated that even when the structural conditions are generally supportive of knowledge work tasks, it is still very easy for creativity and innovation to be stifled (Starbuck, 1992). Firms are therefore cautioned to try and avoid the development of particular norms and practices that might constrain innovative behaviour. For example, informal routines that have developed over time can quickly start to become standardized ways of working embedded in physical capital, routines and even organizational culture. These informal routines can develop into knowledge that becomes codified into firm-specific 'best practice' templates, such as systematic auditing procedures and tools for project planning and development. As the usage of these tools spreads and comes to be seen as almost mandatory within the firm, then innovation can be constrained as consideration of new tools, concepts and ways of working tends to be precluded. This, however, is perhaps less likely to happen in scientific contexts where experimentation is a dominant epistemic practice and notions of 'best practice' are somewhat redundant.

Monitoring of time

Starbuck also highlights that in many knowledge-intensive firms, such as consultancies and advertising agencies, time spent working on client projects is often monitored and rigorously accounted for, as it is billable time and needs to be carefully documented to the satisfaction of management and the client. This monitoring, however, can often inhibit innovative behaviour even when timescales have been mutually agreed between the project team and the client – as should be the case in a genuine operating adhocracy. Where this is common practice knowledge workers often reduce or ultimately fail to spend time searching for, creating or acquiring new knowledge and actively learning. This 'redundant' time (Nonaka, 1994) is considered to be particularly crucial for innovation and yet is simply not available within those knowledge-intensive firms that are intent upon monitoring and controlling billable time.

Growth

Starbuck also emphasizes that, over time, knowledge-intensive firms often have a tendency to attempt to diversify and grow and this is not always a sensible strategic decision. Increasing growth and diversification often lead to increasing formalization, layers of hierarchy and increasing numbers of support staff which can all ultimately lead to the firm experiencing problems. As Starbuck states, 'when support staff come to outnumber experts greatly, or when knowledge-intensive firms (KIFs) claim expertise in too many domains, KIFs lose their halos of expertise and their credibility' (1992, p. 737). Mintzberg in fact suggests that the adhocracy is a typical organizational form only in young, start-up, entrepreneurial firms. He argues that over time adhocracies evolve into other archetypes – in the case of knowledge-intensive firms they often evolve into professional bureaucracies. The firm necessarily becomes more formalized, introducing, for example, levels of professional management in an attempt to manage basic requirements such as efficiency improvements.

As discussed earlier in the chapter, this shift in structure and organizing may however be counterproductive where innovation is the basis on which the firm competes. Research conducted by Lowendahl (1997) demonstrated that a strategy of growth can be counterproductive, particularly for those firms that compete on the basis of their ability to solve complex problems for clients. A compromise, however, might be achieved by creating new, autonomous business units as soon as the firm reaches a particular size or introducing internal markets around a project based form of organizing. These new business units should ideally be led by those who recognize the need for an enabling context and the importance and significance of low levels of formalization and decentralized decision-making for knowledge work processes. A number of high-tech firms operating in Cambridgeshire in the United Kingdom (often referred to as 'Silicon Fen') have adopted this strategy. 'Spinning out' new firms as opposed to organizational growth is the approach these firms have adopted in order to manage the exploitation of new innovations developed in-house. These firms are therefore consciously attempting to continue to operate as adhocracies-stimulating innovation but avoiding organizational growth.

>> CULTURAL CONDITIONS IN SUPPORT OF KNOWLEDGE WORK

Many knowledge-intensive firms do attempt to structure and organize along the lines of an adhocracy, recognizing that this approach provides an enabling context for knowledge work. However, as discussed in the previous section, this highly informal approach to organizing can often be problematic to sustain in the long run. In order for an organization to survive in the long term, it must be able to achieve and sustain a competitive level of profitability. When firms organize predominantly around self-formed and self-managed knowledge-based teams, it can be very difficult for the leaders of such firms to both develop and manage efficiency criteria even when the firm remains small.

The nature of much of the work that is carried out can be both ambiguous and intangible and is therefore difficult to measure, control or even quantify. For example, advertising agencies develop 'ideas' for clients and specialist consultancy firms develop bespoke solutions to client problems. In these cases, it is extremely difficult for managers or even knowledge workers themselves to estimate the resources required in terms of time, expertise and skills to successfully complete client projects. In addition successful outcomes cannot always be guaranteed as innovation is an inherently uncertain process. In many instances successful outcomes can only be measured by the degree to which the client is satisfied with the outcome. Rational, qualified judgements that highlight means–ends relationships are difficult or impossible to make.

Furthermore, it has already been emphasized that knowledge workers will, to a greater or lesser extent, resent any attempt to directly monitor and control their work, demanding and requiring as they do high levels of autonomy in order to carry out their major work tasks. The leaders of knowledge-intensive firms are therefore always seeking ways to manage the fundamental underlying tension that exists between efficiency and autonomy. Whilst structural conditions which emphasize flexibility and self-managed team-working are important preconditions facilitating knowledge work tasks, the cultural conditions within the firm will be at least as important in ultimately creating an enabling context for knowledge work processes that are largely conducted autonomously. It is the cultural conditions within a knowledge-intensive firm that primarily promote 'responsible autonomy' (Friedman, 1977), where employees use their work autonomy to advance the interests of the organization and not just their own personal interests.

Cultural (normative) control

Whilst leaders of knowledge-intensive firms will be keen to employ individuals with particular skills and expertise, their general requirements will be rather broad, recognizing that diversity across the workforce is considered to be a significant factor promoting innovation (see, e.g. Grant, 1996; Lowendahl, 1997; Nonaka, 1994). In Chapter 1, it was highlighted that the nature of knowledge production is changing and increasingly knowledge production relies on the combination of knowledge from a variety of fields and disciplines. Not only does this create a challenging environment in which to work from the perspective of the individual knowledge worker (see Chapter 4 for a detailed examination of the challenges faced by multi-disciplinary, inter-dependent teams), diversity also generates significant management challenges in a very loosely organized environment. A form of management grounded in cultural or normative control has been suggested to be an appropriate approach to adopt within these organizational environments. The suggestion is that leaders of these types of firm are in a position to create and develop a corporate culture which workers will want and choose to identify with. By identifying with the organization it is assumed that workers internalize the dominant organizational ideology – values, beliefs and norms – and consequently behave in the interests of the firm.

The arguments around the role of corporate culture have been developing at least since the 1980s and the 'business excellence' ideas of that period (Peters and Waterman, 1982). Deal and Kennedy (1982), Kanter (1984), Schein (1983, 1992), also promoted the idea that it is the primary task of leaders of organizations to develop and actively reinforce *strong* organizational cultures. 'Improvements in productivity and quality, it is argued, flow from corporate cultures that *systematically* recognize and reward individuals, symbolically and materially, for identifying their sense of purpose with the values that are designed into the organization' (Willmott, 1993, pp. 515–516; italics author's own). Naturally this 'leader-led' organizational culture will be characterized by an organizational (core) value system that represents the long-term interests of the firm. This represents the basis of cultural (normative) control in organizations.

Importantly, in this literature strong organizational cultures are those that are shared across the firm, strengthening the firm through integration and enhanced productivity. This integration perspective on organizational culture (Martin, 1992) and much of the literature that advocates the promotion of a strong organizational culture posit culture as an organizational variable that can be directly shaped by the behaviour and core values of the leaders and management of the firm. These core beliefs permeate the whole organization over time and serve to influence the values and norms of behaviour of the rest of the workforce. There is an emphasis on homogeneity, consensus and, importantly, within the context of a knowledge-intensive firm, predictable behaviour which, in this context, is characterized by an impressive work ethic and communitarian loyalty (Alvesson, 2004). This view has persisted over time and more recent literature in this area reinforces the idea that normative control is an important aspect of the enabling context for knowledge work (Pyoria, 2007). What tends to be overlooked here, however, is that whilst predictable behaviour is sought with regard to knowledge workers displaying responsible autonomy, in other respects predictable behaviour is not advocated as this may not necessarily lead to innovation and creativity.

The way in which leaders of firms can actively create and shape organizational culture is explained in detail in Schein's work (1982, 1993). He suggests that leaders are in a position to implement primary embedding mechanisms and secondary reinforcement or articulation mechanisms, which will symbolically reflect and are consistent with the dominant, core values held by the leaders. Specific employment policies and practices such as the criteria used for recruitment and selection, performance management and reward are examples of what Schein refers to as primary embedding mechanisms. Organizational design and structure together with formal statements of organizational philosophy typically found in firms' mission statements are examples of secondary reinforcement mechanisms. Schein suggests that if leaders of firms implement all 12 mechanisms in a consistent and coherent manner then, over time, core organizational values will become shared values across the workforce leading to performance and productivity improvements. Alvesson (2004) also emphasizes the importance of symbolism and symbolic leadership, as an important aspect of creating and sustaining a strong organizational culture within knowledge-intensive settings.

From this perspective, if the leader of a knowledge-intensive firm wished to emphasize the importance of knowledge sharing – as might be expected in knowledge-intensive firms – then mechanisms that directly or indirectly rewarded knowledge sharing would need to be introduced. For example, knowledge workers might be financially or symbolically rewarded for contributing to projects they were not directly employed to work on. In this way, by implementing this embedding mechanism in conjunction with other mutually reinforcing mechanisms, Schein suggests that knowledge sharing behaviour in the firm can be encouraged and promoted as knowledge workers begin to recognize that knowledge sharing is a core value within the firm.

Multiple perspectives on organizational culture

There is an overriding assumption in Schein's work and all of the business excellence literature that it is feasible and practicable for leaders of firms to actively create and shape an organizational culture which promotes integration and consensus around dominant organizational values. An expert, highly skilled and often highly educated and diverse workforce might, however, quite naturally hold a wide range of beliefs and values, particularly when diversity extends to national culture. Therefore it cannot simply be assumed or taken for granted that knowledge workers in knowledge-intensive firms will necessarily be willing to subsume their identity and personal value systems to those of the firm. The integration perspective on culture (Martin, 1992), which this literature reflects, assumes certain structural preconditions such as a well-defined hierarchy and highly centralized decision-making. These, as we have seen, are often not in place within knowledge-intensive firms – particularly those that organize as adhocracies. It may therefore be highly problematic to operationalize this approach to 'culture management' in a knowledge-intensive setting. The extent to which the leaders of such firms are in a position to shape beliefs, particularly in such an informal organizational context, is in fact highly questionable.

Leaders of knowledge-intensive firms may therefore have to acknowledge that knowledge workers will naturally hold a variety of beliefs, which cannot necessarily be altered or subsumed within a single organizational value system. This is referred to in Martin's (1992) work as the fragmentation perspective on culture. The fragmentation perspective suggests that culture is better viewed as a metaphor rather than a variable – something an organization *is* rather than something an organization *has*. From this perspective culture is only loosely structured and partially shared, emerging dynamically as organizational members experience each other, events and the organizational context over time.

The fragmentation perspective provides support competing and contradictory value systems held by individuals across the firm, which is often the case in knowledge-intensive firms populated by a highly skilled, diverse workforce. This perspective acknowledges ambiguity, recognizing that within organizations individuals might experience a lack of clarity or simultaneously hold multiple meanings and beliefs. Lack of clarity can result from unclear structures, fuzzy boundaries or imprecise goals. These are likely to be apparent within a knowledge-intensive firm organized broadly as an adhocracy. It may well be the case, then, that knowledge-intensive firms display cultural characteristics more reminiscent of the fragmentation perspective rather than the integration perspective.

Leaders of such firms therefore need to acknowledge and accept that differentiation and fragmentation rather than integration might predominate, and recognize that they are only in a position to loosely manage organizational culture, for example, by promoting perhaps just one specific value or belief that knowledge workers will naturally wish to identify with. Research by Alvesson and Robertson (2006) demonstrated that in several different types of consultancy settings, leaders and management employed a variety of strategic and symbolic mechanisms to construct an elite organizational identity with which consultants readily identified; this served as an overarching way of integrating knowledge workers within these firms. Consultancy firms appear to be particularly appropriate settings for the construction of elite social identities because of the type of people employed (often of high academic ability) and the nature of much of the work that is conducted (ambiguous and intellectually demanding). Consultants in these firms provide their expertise to other professionals – the majority of their clients are highly skilled themselves – therefore a high level of self-confidence is required. A construction of self and the organization as elite and therefore clearly superior in vital respects can be important resources on which to draw to promote and reinforce the required self-confidence. Moreover an elite identity was found to be a significant mediator of consultancy work for a variety of reasons. First, an elite identity was found to promote self-discipline which sustained a desire to accomplish high standards of performance. Secondly, perceiving these firms to only recruit 'the very best' served to attract applicants and generate high retention rates. Finally, a shared belief that consultants themselves and the firm as a whole were 'elite' generated a strong image that generated high calibre clients.

Typically, organizational elites have been considered the privileged few who control organizational resources and have considerable power and influence both organizationally and to some extent at a societal level (Hill, 1995; Kabanoff and Holt, 1996). Thus in much of the extant literature the elite is located at the apex of an organization. Alvesson and Robertson, however, demonstrated that the notion of belonging to the elite can exist across whole firms. By promoting an organizational ethos that is more or less generally accepted and shared, rather than attempting to instil and reinforce a dominant core value system, there is a greater likelihood that knowledge workers will start to see the firm as a 'good' place to work. As far as is possible in such a diverse, loosely structured environment, this approach is more likely to aid retention and promote responsible autonomy within the firm. One example of this is provided by Timothy Koogle, the founder of Yahoo!, a leading web portal, who argues that his organization became successful largely because he promoted the idea that employees should communicate freely with one another and as far as possible engage in genuine consensual decisions making (Greenberg and Baron, 2000). This ethos was considered to be essential in the fast-paced world of the Internet and at the same time intuitively appealing to the knowledge workers employed.

>> CONCLUSIONS

This chapter has highlighted the structural and cultural conditions that provide an enabling context for knowledge work processes characterized by creativity and innovation in knowledge-intensive settings. Some of the conditions that can act as barriers to knowledge work were also discussed. It needs to be emphasized, however, that the limited research that has been conducted in such firms highlights that there is no single 'best management practice' here. Many knowledge-intensive firms operate in niche markets – offering very specialized services – and the way in which many of these firms choose to organize is often quite unique and highly context-sensitive. Generally, the structuring and organizing of these firms will be loose, informal and flexible characteristic features of the adhocracy. Whilst the adhocracy might appear to be a somewhat chaotic, relatively unmanaged context, it is perhaps useful to consider the way in which this configuration has been operationalized in a scientific consultancy firm based in the United Kingdom. The way in which structural and cultural conditions interact to promote knowledge work processes is explained in the following case study and illustrates the complex conditions actively promoted over time which have ultimately mediated the tensions around efficiency and autonomy within a knowledge-intensive setting. First the case is described and then two questions are posed.

In Chapter 4 we focus on the actual process of knowledge creation or knowledge generation and adopt a micro-level of analysis. We move from a firm-level analysis of the way in which modes of organizing and organizational conditions can develop in support of knowledge work processes to an analysis of the dynamics of knowledge creation processes within a project team setting. Before this, however, Chapter 3 looks more broadly at new organizational forms and the role of ICT in supporting these new forms.

CASE STUDY 2.1
SCIENCECO MANAGING AN EXPERT WORKFORCE

ScienceCo was founded in 1980. It is a medium-sized, technology-based consultancy company, located on the outskirts of London. It operates today on a global basis. At the time of its inception, the founder wished to create a consultancy environment that would not only develop solutions in response to client problems, but also stimulate invention and innovation more generally. Eighty-five per cent of the workforce are highly educated scientists and technologists, who rely primarily on their expertise and knowledge rather than equipment or systems to provide inventions and innovative solutions for manufacturing, engineering and pharmaceutical companies around the world.

Since 1980, the firm has grown from a small entrepreneurial business employing a handful of scientific consultants specializing in engineering and communications to a medium-sized company employing about 200 people and incorporating other scientific disciplines such as biotechnology, applied sciences and information systems. The workforce is truly international, incorporating 19 different nationalities. In defining the type of projects that ScienceCo conducted for their clients, it is important to understand the difference between invention and innovation. Consultants working in interdisciplinary project teams develop completely new concepts and products that are marketed as intellectual property rights (IPR) to clients and project teams. They also develop innovative solutions to client problems using existing concepts, ideas and technologies in new ways. The firm has been responsible for the invention of major scientific and technological developments that are recognized and used throughout the world. One such item is the electronic security tag, which since its invention has been manufactured and marketed by the Swedish firm Esselte. ScienceCo is primarily in the business of creating new knowledge and applying existing knowledge in new ways.

A crucial issue for management at ScienceCo has always been attracting and retaining a highly skilled, expert workforce of international standing in order for the firm to grow and successfully compete on a global basis. Thus developing an appropriate organizational environment in which expert consultants are keen to work has been of paramount importance. The following sections outline the organizational structure, human resource practices, patterns of IT usage and organizational culture that have developed within the firm over time.

>> ORGANIZATIONAL STRUCTURE

Attempts have been made to maintain a fairly flat organizational structure throughout the firm's development. Even today, there is fundamentally only one level of management, consisting of the founder (now Executive Chairman), Chairman and Managing Director. Decision-making within the firm has typically involved significant numbers of consultants as well as management. A worker committee, the Board of Management, which consists primarily of consultants and one or two support staff, make recommendations to management regarding day-to-day operations and organization. Management communicates constantly with the whole of the firm (generally using e-mail) regarding new projects and potential future projects. Turnover and profitability are also communicated to everyone on a monthly basis. Consultants are encouraged to innovate outside of client project work, and they can request financial resources for this through the Innovation Exploitation Board. This forum includes consultants from across the firm, as well as the management team, who meet regularly to discuss the feasibility of new ideas proposed by consultants. All members of the management team are also active consultants, contributing to project team-working within the firm.

Consultants are organized across three divisions within the firm according to their particular scientific expertise. These are Business Innovation (BI), Technology, Internet, Media and Entertainment (TIME), and Engineering (ENG). While divisional managers head up divisions, there are actually no hierarchical levels either within or across divisions. Divisional managers tend to be those individuals who are prepared to take on some minimal administrative responsibilities such as recording revenue generation and monitoring the projects that are being managed by consultants within their own division. In many cases, divisional managers are actually remunerated less than other consultants within their division (see section on 'Performance management') and they also actively contribute to project working across the firm.

Divisions have emerged, merged and disbanded in a reactive manner over time, based on the client project work in hand. In 1980, there were only two skill groups, Engineering and Communications. However, in 1990, a divisional structure was introduced in order to provide improved financial accountability. By 1996, seven divisions existed including two business consulting divisions, Information Systems and Applied Sciences. The Life Sciences division emerged at this time from the Applied Sciences division when enough biotechnology projects had been secured to ensure the divisions' sustainability in the medium term. By 2000, however, Life Sciences had again merged with the Engineering division together with Applied Sciences. Business Innovation by this time incorporated both business divisions and the Information Systems division. Despite the existence of divisions, consultants tend to work in an interdisciplinary manner across divisions within small project teams. This occurs because the nature of client requirements generally requires cross-disciplinary skills and expertise. These project teams are self-forming and self-managed. Project team-working is discussed in more detail within the section on 'Performance management'.

>> RECRUITMENT AND SELECTION

For many years, the firm did not employ a Human Resources (HR) manager. However, in 1995, based on predicted and expected project work, the firm was faced with a requirement to increase the expert workforce by 15 per cent (and this was projected to continue annually, compounded). The firm recruited a Human Resources manager to develop a more formal recruitment and selection process, and to develop ways of maintaining high retention rates across the firm.

In the past, consultants had typically been recruited informally by word of mouth, drawing upon consultants' global personal networks of colleagues and contacts. In order to make the recruitment process more effective, the HR manager developed good relationships with two international recruitment agencies that had offices throughout the world. Once provided with a person specification and a brief that described very broadly the type of work carried out by the firm, they provided shortlists of candidates on an ongoing basis. In terms of the selection process, the founder had always insisted that candidates take an AH6 intelligence test and Cattell's 16PF personality test. Given that the majority of candidates shortlisted by the agencies generally had a PhD in a scientific discipline, it was virtually impossible for any candidate to fail the AH6 test. It was also difficult to 'fail' the 16PF because the firm did not look for an 'ideal' profile other than 'openness' and a 'willingness to experiment'. Consultants were simply keen to see what sort of personality profile candidates had. Thus, almost all candidates who had been shortlisted proceeded to an initial short interview with the HR manager and the relevant divisional manager.

During this preliminary interview, the HR manager stated that candidates were expected to demonstrate a strong understanding of their own and, more importantly, other disciplines, because of the need to work in interdisciplinary teams sharing knowledge. They were also expected to be 'almost naturally innovative' and have a strong commercial awareness. The HR manager stated,

> It's quite a unique mix we are looking for. All the way through the selection process, we give out big indicators to say the sort of organization we are. It's quite aggressive maybe, and I'm sure interviewees will pick up quite a lot of arrogance on the part of the company. But the messages we are giving out are more about confidence in what we do and how we do it rather than us thinking we are better than anyone else.

And approximately 25 per cent, which typically equates to four candidates, progress to a second interview. The firm was not overly concerned about the high numbers of candidates rejected. Management is only interested in individuals with either a PhD or particular expertise within a scientific discipline, who are fluent in English, have some commercial/industrial experience, and who are prepared to adopt the role of a consultant. This role involves marketing their own and, more generally, the firm's abilities and expertise. It is therefore a relatively unique set of characteristics which is sought in candidates.

The second interview focuses on assessing the candidate's ability to market to clients, their overall level of expertise, and their ability to work within interdisciplinary project teams. This second interview is a panel interview involving a number of consultants from several divisions, who 'quiz' the applicant in some depth on their knowledge of their own and other science- or technology-based fields. Panel members are randomly drawn from across the firm, based on availability at the time of the interview. If the panel agrees on a candidate, then the candidate will be recommended for appointment to the MD.

In 1996, typically, 16 candidates were interviewed for each post, and for each of those interviewed, approximately ten CVs would have been received from the recruitment agencies. The selection process is described as 'rigorous' by the HR manager. He emphasized that the interviews focus primarily on the candidates' ability to 'fit in' to the ScienceCo way of working. This involves willingness and ability to collaboratively share knowledge across different science- and technology-based fields, both within project teams and more generally. The HR manager commented,

> You get a CV, and the person has a PhD, and they've worked for a pretty high-powered research agency, and that's brilliant. You've got to see them, but you know that there is a pretty strong chance that the moment you meet them you're going to know what they're not – they're not one of us.

>> PERFORMANCE MANAGEMENT

Only one formal system exists at ScienceCo, and this is the performance management system that was introduced in 1990. This system was introduced at the same time as consultants were allocated to divisions. Before this, individual consultants' performance had not been managed. The system focuses on divisional revenue targets (DRTs) and personal revenue targets (PRTs). Management establishes these targets at the beginning of each financial year, and they are monitored monthly. The same monthly PRT applies to all consultants, regardless of age, experience and so on. Hence, DRTs are the accumulation of PRTs, premised on the number of consultants within the divisions. By default, then, the larger divisions had to generate more revenue.

Revenue is generated through project work that is generally priced at a flat rate rather than a fee rate. A lead consultant emerges on client projects. Typically, this is the consultant who has the most contact with a particular client. The 'lead' consultant is responsible for negotiating the value of the project with the client, after careful consideration of the resources that will be required in terms of breadth of expertise and time. Lead consultants will use e-mail to inform consultants throughout the firm about potential new projects and the skills and expertise that will be required. Once the value of a project has been determined with the client, it is the responsibility of individual consultants who want to work on the project to negotiate with the lead consultant regarding the amount of project revenue they will be allocated. As there are no formal systems to record these negotiations, e-mail messages serve as a record of any negotiations that take place. The allocation of project revenue contributes to the individual consultants' PRT and the DRT to which they are assigned.

Management described PRTs as a scheme for making people sell their skills to other people in an effective manner:

> It is a micro economy. It is a free market for expertise. Over the years it has been the subject of much controversy as it puts a lot of pressure on people, and it is in this way that we try to maintain a competitive (some would say combative) environment. It does create tension, but at the same time, it enhances innovation given by the rate at which new ideas come out of the organization.

In order to achieve PRTs, consultants generally work on a small number of projects at any one time, commanding a percentage of the overall revenue from each one. Achievement of PRTs consistently over time is expected of everyone, other than the most inexperienced consultants and recent recruits. The majority of consultants usually achieve their PRT. However, consistency across whole divisions is problematic and occasionally divisional managers find it difficult to achieve their DRT. At the end of each financial year, divisional managers performance-rank those within their division, based on achievement of PRTs and contribution to overall sales. This is a transparent process and individual consultants are free to discuss, and in some instances dispute, their overall ranking position. When divisional managers have agreed on their rankings within their division, they meet with the management team to agree on overall ranking across the firm. Individual consultants are then awarded percentage increments according to their ranking. Underperformers are tolerated in the medium term. Consultants who do not achieve PRTs over time will not receive a salary increment, but they are actively encouraged and helped by management to improve performance the following year. Management has never introduced salary scales within the firm, and no formal career structure exists because there is a no formal hierarchy. Individual consultants are therefore awarded a percentage increase based on the salary they have personally negotiated with the MD on their appointment to the firm.

It is also important to recognize that consultants manage their own time both within and outside of project working. Consultants are free to choose their hours of work and length of vacations. This means that some consultants work continuously, occasionally for months at a time and then take extended vacations, up to 2–3 months at any one time. Other consultants choose to work regular hours and take shorter breaks. Divisional managers only expect to be made aware of vacations (time and length) and consultants are trusted to manage their time effectively.

>> TRAINING AND DEVELOPMENT

Professional development is particularly important to all consultants at ScienceCo. In order to stay at the top of their professional fields, consultants must be aware of any developments in their field, and they need to participate in activities that offer the opportunity for further professional development. Again, consultants are responsible for identifying their own requirements in terms of courses, conferences and workshops. Management simply provides the necessary financial resources, which in some cases are considerable. It is assumed that consultants will organize their workloads accordingly, in order to participate in professional development without any significant disruption of project work occurring.

Training for consultants has never been considered an issue within the firm. Management has always believed that the quality of the people employed negates any need for systematic training. It is assumed that if dedicated training is required, for example, in the use of particular software application for project work, then consultants are sufficiently skilled to train themselves at times that suit them.

>> IT USAGE

Significant resources have always been made available for investment in any technology that might facilitate project working. An e-mail system was introduced in 1990 to facilitate communication between consultants. By this time, the firm had grown to around 100 consultants, and the opportunities for regular face-to-face contact with everyone were rapidly diminishing. The e-mail system began to be used extensively almost immediately, as there were very few formal systems or procedures in use for communication, and on any 1 day, significant numbers of consultants would be working remotely at client firms. By 1996, consultants were receiving between 100 and 150 e-mails each day, and despite attempts to curtail the use of e-mail for trivial matters, consultants today still receive about this number. This is because no protocols are used to classify mail sent, other than to attach a prefix of SOC for 'social' communication and INNOV for an e-mail where the sender is searching for information.

It is the e-mail system that is generally used to broadcast requests for information when putting together proposals for clients. Anyone who wants to be involved in a potential project initially communicates in outline their potential contribution, in terms of skills and expertise, via e-mail. The system works well in this respect as the medium is good for communicating low-level information, quickly and across the whole firm. However, the level of e-mail communication consultants are exposed to on a daily basis is recognized generally as a significant burden. Norms have developed, such as sending replies to everyone in the firm and failing to edit the title of e-mails to ensure that it relates to the content of the e-mail. These norms, while making the use of e-mail relatively thoughtless, informal and simple, have generated a somewhat chaotic and haphazard system of communication. For example, some consultants, when faced with ever-increasing numbers of e-mail, choose not to bother reading the majority, and only use the system when absolutely necessary.

Other technologies such as groupware technologies are occasionally used and intranets have been set up in and across divisions. Consultants are aware that packages such as Lotus Notes can provide useful project documentation. However, the majority of projects continue to be documented in a highly idiosyncratic manner because project leaders are free to provide documentation in whatever way they deem appropriate. Client requirements need to be fulfilled in this respect. However, if the client is satisfied with the documentation produced, no further effort is directed at producing, recording and classifying project documentation in a consistent manner across the firm. Again, consultants are trusted to produce high-quality project documentation, without recourse to formal standards, systems or procedures.

The use of both groupware and intranets tends therefore to be spasmodic and piecemeal. For example, groupware, such as Lotus Notes, only tends to be used when geographical constraints impose a need to work in this fashion. Consultants prefer project team-working to be face to face, rather than via Lotus Notes discussion threads. Groupware technology is not generally considered rich enough to adequately convey some types of information and knowledge required during project work. In many instances, when significant decisions or results need to be shared across a project team, the technology is simply used to schedule a telephone conference call.

>> CULTURE

As stated in the introduction, from the outset the founder wanted to promote an innovative environment and one that would stimulate creativity. With this in mind, he attempted to develop and perpetuate an environment characterized by an absence of hierarchy, rules and formal procedures. An emphasis was placed on maintaining an egalitarian environment, one in which everyone was in principle free to contribute to decision-making, and one that allowed individuals' relative freedom to be creative. While the founder was keen to promote a corporate culture around a small set of core values specifically regarding the importance and value of creativity and innovation, to both the firm and society more generally, he respected individuals as individuals. He did not, therefore, attempt to develop a strong culture that encompassed particular norms of behaviour. The ScienceCo way of working is therefore characterized by a lack of prescription, informality and idiosyncrasy.

The heterogeneity and diversity of the workforce exemplify the importance placed on individuality within the firm. Not only are 19 different nationalities represented, there are also significant differences across the firm with regard to age, experience and general attitudes and behaviour. Individuality often tends to be manifest symbolically in dress, ranging from the bizarre (e.g. running shorts and vest in the depths of winter!) to the more traditional conformist dark suit and tie. During project working, however, diverse groups of individuals with differing expertise are expected to work together jointly, developing solutions to client requirements or problems. While conflict inevitably arises across such a range of diverse individuals, the environment is one in which individuals feel free to speak out without recrimination. Consultants are trusted to resolve any differences that might arise without recourse to the management team, so that ultimately client requirements are satisfied.

While everyone agrees that the environment is highly informal and this is considered to be one of the major attractions of working in the firm, consultants do have different perceptions of what constitutes organizational reality. For example, while everyone agrees that the organization is almost flat, it is widely recognized and acknowledged that a dynamic, informal hierarchy exists based on expertise. However, consultants do differ (in some cases quite considerably) in their opinions as to the hierarchical ordering based on their own personal experience of working with others in the firm. As one consultant stated,

> Nobody in theory has a job title. Single status applies but obviously some people are seen as more powerful, more influential, higher status than others – based purely on what they are seen to contribute to the organization in terms of big projects or particularly innovative ideas.

Individuals across the firm can therefore command powerful positions within the informal hierarchy. Their position will be based on their ability to both acquire new business and command large proportions of project revenue that contribute to their PRT. Positions within this informal hierarchy, however, are transient and relatively ephemeral, as new clients and new projects requiring different skills and expertise are acquired over time.

>> QUESTIONS

1. Define and explain six critical organizational factors that have contributed to ScienceCo's growth and ability to retain an expert workforce.
2. What are the potential problems that might arise over time in this organizational context?

Summary of key learning points

>> Knowledge-intensive firms rely on their workforce for their competitive advantage. Therefore employee retention is a crucial strategic issue within these types of firm.

>> 'Knowledge-intensive firm' is a generic term that encapsulates a broad range of firms operating across sectors in a post-industrial economy.

>> Knowledge-intensive firms can be classified as client-based, problem-solving or output-based.

>> Knowledge workers are often referred to as 'gold collar' workers, acknowledging the autonomy and exceptional working conditions they are generally afforded.

>> The adhocracy, characterized by a dynamic organizational structure based on self-formed and self-managed teams, is considered to be an appropriate configuration where innovation is the basis on which a firm competes.

>> Structural constraints on knowledge work include the development of organizational 'best practice' templates, monitoring of knowledge workers' time and organizational growth.

>> Responsible autonomy is more likely to be achieved if management acknowledges that organizational culture is likely to be characterized by differentiation and fragmentation rather than consensus and integration. Hence management should only attempt to loosely manage culture, aiming to promote an organizational ethos that knowledge workers find accessible and can readily identify with, rather than a dominant core value system.

3

NEW ORGANIZATIONAL FORMS THAT SUPPORT KNOWLEDGE WORK: THE ROLE OF ICT

Chapter Outline

Learning Outcomes

At the end of this chapter you should be able to:

- Understand the complex relationships between technology and organization
- Recognize that technology, including ICT, cannot determine work practices
- Understand how the material properties of technology, the institutional context and human agency all interact in influencing how technology is used in practice
- Appreciate how new forms of organization can support knowledge work
- Understand the role of ICT in these new forms of organization
- Recognize that implementing some form of ICT will have emergent and sometimes unintended consequences
- Understand that changing work practices and organizational structures using ICT involves a process of negotiation and often compromise, that will occur over time
- Understand how new organizational forms also, in some ways, create problems for knowledge-intensive work

>> INTRODUCTION

In Chapter 2 we identified some of the defining characteristics of knowledge-intensive firms (KIFs). We also noted that not all knowledge work takes places in KIFs. Rather, organizations of all kinds – even those that continue to apply Scientific Management principles to the organization of work (such as call centres) – have workers who deal extensively with information and knowledge and/or workers whose main output is information and knowledge. However, it is also the case that some organizational forms appear to be more conducive to knowledge work than others. Hence, in this chapter we look more broadly at new organizational forms that are often associated with knowledge work. We look, in particular, at how these can be supported by ICT. In doing this it is important to explore, in general terms, the relationship between technology and organization and, perhaps more importantly, reflect on the processes of change since, as we will see, adopting some form of new technology does not, in any straight-forward sense, automatically lead to conditions conducive to knowledge work.

Early accounts of the relationship between technology and organization were somewhat simplistic, suggesting that technology *per se* would 'revolutionize' the nature and, perhaps more importantly, the location of work. Thus, the advent of the Internet, the World Wide Web, the mobile phone, teleconferencing, groupware and so on was presumed to mean that people would naturally start to work virtually (many from home), and that geographical distance would no longer be a barrier to communication and work. This has led many to assume that knowledge work will automatically be enabled by ICT. Others argue, however, that technology *per se* cannot affect change. Rather, new technologies provide constraints on, and opportunities for, human action. Moreover, this human action is embedded in a particular social and institutional context. This institutional context simultaneously empowers and controls behaviour because it legitimizes some forms of behaviour while simultaneously 'prohibiting' other forms.

Once we have understood this, it becomes clear that organizations should not simply expect that the adoption of technology *per se* will successfully promote knowledge work, especially where knowledge workers (such as professionals) have significant power to resist technology. Rather, change needs to be negotiated through time as users come to learn, though participation, how they might use the technology (or not) to support (or not) their daily work practices. This is illustrated in the case at the end of the chapter, where we find a university struggling to get knowledge workers to adopt an enterprise system when the needs of users had largely been ignored during the design phase. The system is eventually accepted, but only after significant change is made in the post-implementation environment, that is, once the system is actually being used in practice. All this said, it is clear that technology does have an important role to play in managing knowledge work, especially as organizations and markets become more widely distributed, often on a global basis.

In this chapter, then, we explore the relationship between technology and new organizational forms that can potentially support knowledge work and knowledge workers and recognize the importance of taking a process perspective (see Chapter 1) on managing the introduction of any kind of technology – seeing this as a complex, and typically highly political, organizational change process. The chapter begins by looking at the general relationship between technology and organization and then provides the example of teleworking to illustrate the human, structural and institutional influences on this relationship. The chapter then goes on to explore new organizational forms that are potentially more conducive to knowledge work and how these have been influenced by new forms of ICT. We illustrate the problems of introducing ICT to effect organizational change with a case study of a university that was seeking to 'professionalize' practices through introducing an enterprise resource planning (ERP) system. In this case, ignoring the needs and wishes of powerful faculty was not effective but this was only recognized in the post-implementation phase when changes had to be made to the system design to accommodate this group and their administrators.

>> THE RELATIONSHIP BETWEEN TECHNOLOGY AND ORGANIZATION

In thinking about the role of technology (and in particular ICT) in facilitating knowledge work within an organization, it is important to first look in more general terms at the relationship between technology and organization. This will help us to understand that introducing an ICT to support some aspect of knowledge work will not, in-and-of-itself, lead to the desired effect.

Early researchers exploring the relation between technology and organization developed accounts which were 'deterministic' – that is, they assumed either that the organization somehow determines which technology can be adopted or that the adoption of technology determines what kind of work can be carried out. For example, in one of the earliest studies, Woodward (1965) argued that different types of technology were associated with different forms of organization. Others followed suit, considering different attributes of technologies and their relationship to organizing and organizational structures (for example, Perrow, 1967). These are referred to as 'contingency theories' – where an organization's structure and/or processes are seen as contingent on, or dependent on, the type of technology that is used. In this sense, these authors also implied that the technology determines or causes a particular form of organization. For example, it was suggested that the more complex and unpredictable the production system technology, the more likely were organizations to adopt organic rather than mechanistic structures (Burns and Stalker, 1961).

In studies of ICT this was taken one step further, with authors assuming that ICT could 'drive' or 'force' organizational change – so, if an organization adopts a Knowledge Management System (KMS – a type of technology discussed more fully in Chapter 7), this would lead to improvements in the extent to which individuals would share knowledge. Such a deterministic view of technology is very simplistic and is not supported by empirical evidence. As

Robey and Boudreau (1999) point out, even the idea that ICT 'enables' change is problematic (sometimes it might even disable change). Rather, we need to recognize that there is a complex, dynamic and reciprocal causal relationship between ICT (or indeed any kind of technology) and organization, with outcomes that are emergent and difficult to predict in advance. For example, a hospital may implement a patient record system with a view to improving the sharing of information across different medical specializations. However, the actual effect of this may be that people from different departments stop talking to each other – because now records are available from a central repository and a specialist does not therefore need to talk to his/her colleague to ask for the record. This may actually reduce coordination and so ultimately decrease, rather than increase, knowledge sharing.

Indeed, some authors have gone a step further by suggesting that the concepts of technology and organization cannot be separated from each other because they are actually 'mutually constituted', or as Orlikowski (2007) calls it – constitutively entangled. She provides an example of the use of blackberry in a small office environment. In this office, people came to expect to answer and send e-mails 24 hours a day, 7 days a week. But, Orlikowski, argues, it is not that the Blackberry technology has particular social impacts. Rather, technology and its use are each constituted by the other – each shape and are shaped in turn by the other.

The assumption that technology drives organizational change in a deterministic manner (or indeed that organizational designs drive technology adoption) is also problematic because it ignores the agency of human actors in influencing choices about both the technology and the organization (Child, 1972). Moreover, it also ignores institutional pressures and the material properties of the technology itself. We turn to consider these issues next.

>> HUMAN AGENCY AND THE SOCIAL CONSTRUCTION OF TECHNOLOGY

In Chapter 1 we saw how process perspectives treat knowledge as an ongoing social accomplishment, being constructed through and from social interaction. Technologies are, in effect, bodies of knowledge (Weick, 1990) – indeed the 'ology' in technology refers to a branch of knowledge or learning. A significant tradition has developed, then, in understanding technology also as a social construction. These social constructionist accounts view technologies as fundamentally social objects (Bijker et al., 1987; Weick, 1990). Individuals and groups shape both the design and the adoption of technologies depending on their interests and perspectives (Bijker et al., 1987). Thus, all technologies represent the particular set of choices that designers have made – designers make assumptions about users and how they will use the technology, and this influences the way they design the technology. Furthermore, users shape the way technologies are actually used in everyday practice because most technologies can be used in multiple ways – they are 'open-ended' in other words (Orlikowski, 2000). Weick

(1995) refers to this as the 'interpretative flexibility' of technologies, arguing that technologies are fundamentally equivocal because they can be interpreted, and made sense of, in different ways by different people. This explains why individuals and groups can 'enact' (or act out) the same technology in different ways. Technologies, according to this view, are a bit like the props on a stage – they can be picked up and used by different actors for different purposes (an umbrella might be used as a weapon, for example!). Orlikowski (2000) argues, then, that the use of any kind of ICT is best seen as a process of enactment. Implementing a new ICT system in an organization will not deterministically change knowledge workers' practices. Rather, enactment emphasizes how knowledge workers appropriate a given technology in different ways as part of their ongoing everyday practices, as described next.

In some cases, people may enact the technology so that they do not have to change their work practices, even where the technology was introduced precisely in order to facilitate practice change. Thus, people may simply ignore the technology or use it only very minimally, so that it does not interfere with their established practices. For example, when Powerpoint was first introduced as a technology into an academic environment, many professors continued to use the old overhead transparency technology – handwriting on a sheet of clear plastic and using a projector to project this on to a screen. It took many years for some to 'convert' to the Powerpoint technology; and indeed many never have.

In other cases, a new technology may be used, but not in the way intended. For example, users may create 'add-ons' to a new ICT system that enable them to continue to do work in the way that they always have done it. Thus, there are many examples of people who download data from a new corporate IT system and reformat this into an Excel spreadsheet that allows them to work in the way they always had prior to the implementation of the corporate system.

In other cases, users may draw upon the new technology to substantially change their work practices, even in ways that were not anticipated by the designers. For example, using a customer relationship management (CRM) system, those in a sales department, may change their former habit of cold-calling potential customers randomly and instead use the CRM system to identify those most likely to be receptive to their calls and then target promotional offers at this group without any cold-calling. This may, or may not, be a more productive use of their time, but the point of the example is that it is not the CRM system *per se* that changes the work practice, but rather the users, as knowledgeable and inventive practitioners, find ways to use the system to support them in doing their job (or conversely find ways to avoid using the system or find ways to adapt the system to suit their needs). Knowledge workers, in particular, often have ability, and the power, to enact technologies in ways that suit their interests, as we see in the case at the end of this chapter, where university professors were able to resist a technology that was designed to try to get them to change practice against their will. This important role of human agency in enacting technologies and innovation processes is a recurrent theme throughout this book and will be revisited, in particular, in Chapter 9.

>> INSTITUTIONAL PRESSURES AND THE MATERIAL PROPERTIES OF TECHNOLOGY

It is important to realize that the social construction of technology does not occur in a vacuum (Bijker et al., 1987). Rather, this process will be influenced by the institutional context. Institutional research considers the ways in which social and historical forces shape the actions of organizations (DiMaggio and Powell, 1983). Organizations are embedded in 'a web of values, norms, rules, beliefs, and taken-for-granted assumptions' (Barley and Tolbert, 1997, p. 93). These institutional influences both enable and constrain action. Institutional perspectives, then, alert us to the ways in which technologies are embedded in complex social, economic and political networks. Thus, political, economic, cultural and societal institutions exist in any given context and influence behaviour by 'constituting rules, defining key players, and framing situations' (Scott, 1995, p. 137).

This approach directs attention to the ways in which institutional influences shape the design and adoption of technologies. Institutional theorists alert us to the fact that the adoption, or uptake, of technologies is driven by social pressures for legitimacy and not simply by their efficiency in solving problems. Once a particular technology becomes very popular, for example, it is hard for an organization (or an individual) to resist using it without appearing to be 'out-of-touch'. An example here is enterprise resource planning (ERP) systems, which are IT systems that support business processes across an enterprise, working from a single database so that data theoretically flows across work processes without unnecessary duplication. So, customer information collected by a sales person will be available for those in marketing or service, without each function having to input their own customer data (ERP systems are discussed more fully in Chapter 7). ERP systems are very common today in all kinds of business environments to the extent that it can be hard for an organization to maintain legitimacy as an efficient organization if it fails to adopt such a system – just as turning up to a job interview for a high-profile city-bank job in jeans and a sweat-shirt would undermine the legitimacy of a job applicant; or not having a mobile phone or not being on facebook when all one's friends are makes someone 'not cool!'.

Some institutional accounts can be rather deterministic, ignoring how individual actors have flexibility in responding to and indeed shaping their environment. So, while there may be strong pressures about what you wear to your city job interview, you still could turn up in jeans and a sweat-shirt and there is even a tiny chance that you get a job (please note, however, that we are not advocating this!). Thus, while institutional accounts alert us to very real constraints of wider societal pressures on the action of individuals, groups and organizations, they may overstate how deterministic these pressures actually are. In contrast, other theories, notably structuration theory (Giddens, 1984), in addition to recognizing the constraining influences of the existing environment (i.e. existing social, political, cultural, economic structures), also recognize the ability of actors to shape these structures over time. Indeed, proponents of structuration theory argue that structures exist as constraints only to the extent that actors enact these structures in their ongoing everyday activity, thereby privileging human agency over structural constraint. There are ongoing debates about the relative influence of institutional and structural constraints versus human agency – debates that we are not going to be able to resolve here. However, outlining these debates does highlight the importance of recognizing the ways in which the design, diffusion and use of all kinds of technologies that can potentially support knowledge work are influenced by both the institutional environment and also the actions and interactions of human actors.

More recently, it has also been pointed out that accounts of how technology is designed, adopted and used have tended to ignore its material and physical properties. What is becoming increasingly clear is that technologies are simultaneously social and *physical* (Orlikowski and Barley, 2001) artefacts – the physical properties of technologies influence the ways they can be used. In other words, the material properties of a technology both constrain and afford its use. For example, the traditional design of the telephone system constrained use to particular physical locations because of the need for land-line connections. Today, mobile phone technology frees up the use of the phone so that people's communication becomes much less geographically restricted. Such a difference reflects the material properties of the technology, which therefore constrain (and enable) the options available to designers and users (Barley, 1990; Orlikowski, 2006, 2007). So, returning to the Blackberry example, Orlikowski (2007, p. 1444) writes,

> The performativity of the BlackBerrys is sociomaterial, shaped by the particular contingent way in which the BlackBerry service is designed, configured, and engaged in practice. For example, the 'push email' capability inscribed into the software running on the servers has become entangled with people's choices and activities to keep devices turned on, to carry them at all times, to glance at them repeatedly, and to respond to email regularly. Such activities are only relevant in the circumstance of messages being continually pushed to handheld devices, and of shifting interpretations and interests that become bound up with the constantly available electronic messages. It is not a matter of the technology interacting with the social, but of constitutive entanglement.

This suggests that in order to understand the impact of technology on knowledge work we need to integrate the influences of human agency and the *purpose* to which technology is being put, the *processes* entailed in its construction, its material properties, and the institutional *context* that enables (or disables) its design and use. Addressing these characteristics – purpose, process and context, in this case in relation to technology as a particular form of knowledge – is a recurring theme within this book. We can illustrate this by considering the phenomenon of teleworking.

>> TELEWORKING

ICTs potentially allow many knowledge workers to work remotely from 'the office' and as such, theoretically, to be freer – freer to decide when to work, how to work, where to work and so on. It is no longer necessary to be physically present to have access to most organizational information and indeed to be in contact with others. E-mails can be sent to anyone from almost anywhere in the world and files and other information can be downloaded to be worked on, again almost anywhere. So, a software engineer, working on a project to design a new software package, can be working with a team that is geographically distributed across continents, communicating with them using e-mail, videoconferencing and other groupware technology. Indeed, each member of the team could possibly be working from their own home, or even from the beach if they found this a conducive place at which to write software! While not all jobs can be done virtually, and most jobs demand some physical presence some of the time, it is the case now that many workers could work, at least part of the time, from their home or some other remote location of their choice. This is particularly the case with knowledge workers (Perez et al., 2007). We will refer to this as teleworking (others call it virtual homeworking, e-work or telecommuting) to distinguish it from virtual working, which implies a person is working with others when they are not physically co-located but this may still be in an on-site work environment. This is an important distinction because teleworking, not virtual working, contravenes the separation of work and home that has characterized paid employment for many since the Industrial Revolution.

ICTs are an enabler of such altered work arrangements – the material properties of mobile technologies make teleworking a realistic option. True, some people have continued to work from home throughout the industrial era, for example, women working from home in cottage industries where work, such as garment-making, is taken to individuals' homes for completion. However, developments in ICTs open up this option to a much greater range of workers, including knowledge workers. Nevertheless, the development of ICTs *per se* does not drive such change. Indeed, research has tended to show that, despite the fact that developments in ICTs make it potentially possible for many people to work at home at least some of the time, the numbers who actually do this are very small (Bailey and Kurland, 2002). For example, Korte and Gareis (2002) reported that only 6.1 per cent of workers in Europe regularly work from home and this figure appears to be fairly consistent across countries (e.g. Schweitzer and Duxbury (2002) report a figure of 6 per cent in Canada). More recent data from Australia suggests that the numbers might be increasing, with 30 per cent of respondents indicating that they at least occasionally worked away from their normal place of work during business hours (Australian Government, 2008). Nevertheless, even given that they were including anybody who ever worked away from their normal place of work, they still found that 70 per cent of workers never do this.

So, while ICTs provide the opportunity for knowledge workers to work from home at least some of the time, the evidence suggests that in fact very few make use of this opportunity. Moreover, this is the case despite the fact that the balance of evidence shows that teleworking has benefits for the individual, for the organization and for society. From the perspective of the individual, research shows that most people like teleworking, finding that it allows them to better balance the demands of a family and a job. For example, Gajendran and Harrison (2007) found that teleworking had positive effects on perceptions of autonomy and actually reduced family-work conflicts. From the perspective of the organization, there are also benefits associated with teleworking. For example, it has been suggested that teleworking allows firms to tap the expertise and skills of workers in high demand who do not wish to be tied to permanent employment and of workers who cannot be physically present during the normal working day because of other demands on their time, especially childcare. Teleworking is also advocated as a way of reducing capital costs and overheads (because fewer offices and buildings will be needed if people are working from home). Finally, from the perspective of society, teleworking is seen to be beneficial because it reduces commuting and all the associated costs, especially costs in relation to the pollution of the environment – a topic that is high on the list of priorities in many countries right now because of climate change concerns.

So we are left with a question – why has the proportion of knowledge workers engaged in teleworking remained small, despite the opportunities afforded by advancements in ICTs and despite the obvious benefits for individuals, organizations and societies? To address this question we can take an institutional-level perspective – teleworking has not become more widespread because it challenges existing norms and practices. In particular, teleworking challenges existing norms about control that are central within the context of employment relations. These mechanisms of control vary by the type of work. For clerical and factory workers, their output is tangible and so easily measurable. This measurable output means that workers can be readily monitored and controlled. However, managerial, professional and knowledge work is primarily mental and interpersonal/social, and so is difficult to monitor. In this situation, physical presence has been used as a proxy for productivity. You are assumed to be working hard if you work long hours. This helps to account for the long-hours culture that has become ubiquitous in many countries. Moreover, knowledge workers have come to believe that they will only be promoted if they are visibly present in order to be noticed. Staying late and arriving early can be particularly important in this respect, even to the extent that in some cases workers use their agency to 'fiddle the system' by going home but leaving their work station open and their jacket on their chair, to suggest that they are still around and working! Given this 'game', what would be the point of working long hours from home where no one could see the effort that was put in?

Many managers, then, do not appear to trust their employees to work at home fearing that if they are not visible they will exert less effort. At the same time, workers are reluctant to work from home, because they fear that this will reduce their visibility and therefore their potential for promotion. From the institutional perspective, then, teleworking, at least as a substitute for working 'at the office', will only become more widespread when these deep-seated attitudes and cultural norms change, regardless of any advances in ICTs which can support teleworking, and the obvious benefits of such an arrangement. From an agency perspective, knowledge workers may not take advantage of teleworking if they perceive that this gives them less opportunity to make a good impression with their boss.

Having said this, another trend that is today 'visible' for knowledge workers can mean working from home, *after* having spent a long day at the office! Thus, we have seen already how the advent of blackberry and other handheld mobile devices can encourage a 24/7 mentality in some contexts, which means individuals are actually expected to be and expect to be available for work, anytime and anyplace, even when on holiday. In doing this, some workers may well be conforming to the 'presentism' culture even whilst not physically at the office – sending e-mails to the boss at 3 a.m. in the morning, for example, can be a tactical ploy to illustrate commitment rather than a response to flexible work opportunities from home. Nevertheless, being available 24/7 arguably makes knowledge workers less, rather than more, free. This led Donnelly (2006, p. 95) to conclude,

> Many knowledge workers are likely to remain 'enslaved', like traditional employees, as their temporal/ locational flexibility is restricted by the needs of their employer(s), client demands and expectations, 'professionalism', network relations and career ambitions. As a result, claims that knowledge workers remain 'free workers', may involve greater rhetoric than reality.

>> NEW ORGANIZATIONAL FORMS AND ICTS

As seen above, developments in ICTs provide opportunities for new forms of knowledge work. They also open up new possibilities for organizational designs more generally. In particular, ICTs may enable the creation of organizational designs that provide more supportive environments for work that is knowledge-intensive. As has already been suggested in Chapter 2, knowledge work is best conducted in 'organic' and informal settings, with egalitarian cultures and where horizontal, as opposed to vertical, communication dominates. Such work settings are very different to the traditional bureaucratic 'top-down' forms of organization advocated by Scientific Management (and outlined in Chapter 1). Bureaucratic organizational forms certainly continue to exist, but it is evident that new forms of organizing are emerging which are much more fluid and dynamic than these traditional structures.

These new forms of organizing have looser structures which allow them to be more flexible (Volberda, 1998). This is achieved by breaking down the large bureaucratic structure into subsystems or modules. These smaller units can adapt more quickly to changing circumstances. In other words, even in a complex system, there is the potential for rapid evolution, if that system is broken down into a set of stable subsystems. These subsystems can then each operate nearly independently of the processes going on within other subsystems, so that rapid change can be accomplished. Decomposability or modularity is thus seen as the solution to managing increasing complexity, with social networks supported by ICTs linking together the different parts, whether internally or externally (Castells, 2000).

Of course, we must remember that ICTs do not themselves lead to the creation of these new organizational forms. Indeed, ICT is able to facilitate both decentralized and centralized modes of organizing, as is illustrated by the case at the end of this chapter. Harris (2006) also reminds us that many organizations remain largely bureaucratic and controlling and argues that the idea that we are in a 'post-bureaucratic' era has been overstated by some. In reality, organizations, especially if they are large, have some very bureaucratic structures as well as some more flexible/modular structures; indeed, this is deemed to be important to help an organization to be both flexible and innovative in order to respond to change as well as be efficient. There is a literature now, for example, on the so-called 'ambidexterity' of organizations – organizations that have structures that allow them to simultaneously explore and exploit knowledge (Raisch and Birkinshaw, 2008) in order to be both efficient and flexible/innovative at the same time.

Despite these caveats, we can nevertheless identify a number of characteristics associated with more flexible forms of organizing, including:

1. *Decentralization through the creation of semi-autonomous business units (BU)*: This allows each BU to focus on a particular market niche and so respond more flexibly and adaptively to the needs of the particular market niche.

2. *Flatter, less-hierarchical structures*: This has been achieved through removing layers of middle managers. With fewer managers, close supervision and control are less possible, so that power is devolved down the hierarchy, giving individuals more autonomy (or empowerment) in their work.

3. *Cross-functional project teams*: Rather than have each function work relatively independently and pass things 'over the wall' to the next function in the process, people are brought together to work in cross-functional teams, as discussed in Chapter 5. The objective is to encourage a faster response rate so that lead times, for example on new product developments, are considerably reduced.

4. *Interorganizational networking*: Rather than attempt to integrate new required skills and competencies into the organizational hierarchy, orga-

nizations are increasingly working in collaborative alliances and partnerships with other organizations or using outsourcing arrangements to service particular internal requirements. This enables organizations to innovate much more quickly since they can access knowledge and expertise that are not held internally. These linkages between networking and innovation will be explored further in Chapters 8 and 9.

5. *Globalization of business*: Organizations are increasingly geographically distributed, working on a global rather than a national basis. This has been achieved either through the acquisition of businesses in other countries (as in the BankCo case in Chapter 7), through partnership arrangements, or through internal international growth. This allows them to capitalize on global market opportunities and so potentially grow in size and profitability.

While developments in ICTs have not determined the changes outlined above (and explored further in the chapters that follow), they have made these options more feasible and have opened up global markets for all kinds of organization as well as opportunities for organizations to work together in the development of innovations. For example, Ozcelik (2008) describes how not-for-profit organizations are using the Internet to increase access to information to widely distributed stakeholders, to facilitate interaction with their stakeholders and to improve their fund-raising efforts. The Internet, in turn, allows potential donors to get far more information about the various organizations they might give to than was previously available (see, e.g. www.globalgiving.com – a website where organizations anywhere in the world can post their social projects for which they are looking for funding). Moreover, these new forms of organizing, supported by ICT, can be more conducive to knowledge work and to the support of knowledge workers, albeit as already seen they do not automatically 'free' employees from organizational constraints.

In understanding the role of ICT in relation to these new organizational forms, Earl and Fenny (1996) describe three imperatives for successful global business – global efficiency, local responsiveness and transfer of learning – and analyse how ICT can potentially have a role in relation to all three imperatives. Global efficiency implies that an organization coordinates and consolidates its various activities so that it achieves economies of scale. This requires, for example, the collection of comparative performance information from its operations around the globe. Global ICTs such as ERP systems – discussed further in Chapter 7 – allow this information to be collected in a common form so that these global efficiency decisions can be made.

Local responsiveness implies that organizations must respond to the requirements and idiosyncrasies of local markets – the 'global car' needs to be modified to suit the particular local conditions where it is sold, for example. Production system ICTs which support high variety are helpful here. This philosophy is obviously very different from the earlier mass production era outlined in Chapter 1, where single products were produced with few options and variants: Henry Ford was reported to have once said, 'My customers can have any colour car, as long as it is black'!

Finally, in relation to knowledge processes, a global business needs to ensure that it focuses on sharing knowledge and learning so that expensive reinvention is prevented. ICTs such as e-mail and teleconferencing can help to facilitate dialogue among professionals so that learning is shared. This is the aim of the Knowledge Management initiative at BankCo, described later in Chapter 7. Of course, this is not to say that globalization, and especially attempts at globalization, did not occur before developments in the Internet and the World Wide Web. History is replete with examples of nations, if not corporations, attempting to expand their global empire. Nevertheless, it is clear that advances in ICTs have played a role in advances in the globalization of work, as well as in the other features of the new organizational forms discussed above.

>> FACILITATING ORGANIZATIONAL CHANGE USING ICT

ICTs may potentially support organizational change in relation to all three of the imperatives defined by Earl and Fenny (1996), but we have already considered how ICT will not directly determine or even indirectly influence change independent of the human actors involved. We look briefly in this section at some ways in which desired organizational change might be promoted.

In understanding how ICT is used in knowledge-intensive organizations we should begin by recognizing that a key feature of today's ICT, including KMS, is that most are packages that support knowledge processes – for example, knowledge sharing across the whole organization. This is rather different to traditional ICT that was developed to support specific work tasks (the pace of assembly line production, for example). Packages are adopted by organizations 'off-the-shelf' so to speak, and can be configured, within specific constraints, just as an off-the-shelf suit can be slightly modified by a tailor. The advice, however, is to not customize such packages or attempt to completely modify the software to suit the particular organization (just as it may not be sensible to buy an off-the-shelf suit and then try and completely redesign it). This implementation without modification is referred to as the 'vanilla' system. We discuss this more fully in Chapter 7. A good example of a currently popular package that is aimed at facilitating knowledge processes and that many organizations are trying to adopt is sharepoint. Sharepoint is a Microsoft product which claims, according to the Microsoft website, to 'provide a single, integrated location where employees can efficiently collaborate with team members, find organizational resources, search for experts and corporate information, manage content and workflow, and leverage business insight to make better-informed decisions'.

The integrated nature of a package, like sharepoint or any other enterprise-wide system, means that ideally user representatives from different parts of the organization should be involved in the implementation project. However, given the complexity of such systems, it is perhaps not surprising that so many organizations struggle with their ICT projects – the Standish Group (2007) estimated that 70 per cent of software projects fail. Successfully implementing a so-called 'knowledge processing' system like sharepoint, therefore, requires managing organizational change. Understanding how to effect change using ICT is therefore extremely important. There are two important points to remember in relation to this (Wagner and Newell, 2007):

1. Achieving a workable solution does not mean that within an organization there needs to be consensus over all issues related to the ICT. Rather, the important issue appears to be coordinating action that will allow broad goals to be achieved, even if this involves compromise along the way. This is because consensus about how to configure an ICT is likely to be very difficult, given the diversity of users who will be affected. Different groups will want different things included/excluded and if consensus is sought this is likely to lead to a stalemate. We will see this illustrated in the Uni case at the end of the chapter.

2. Achieving a workable solution is more likely if treated as multiple cycles of design (by which, in relation to packaged software, we mean configuration and perhaps some customization), implementation and use rather than a single phase of design followed by implementation and use. There are a number of reasons for this:

   a. Legacy thinking: Evidence suggests that users find it difficult during the early stages of requirements definition to see beyond their current practices and anticipate how things could be done differently if they had new tools, for example, to enable more knowledge sharing within and across functions. This is because much work practice is rooted in everyday interactions (Suchman, 1987) so that trying to appreciate a new way of working by just looking at the technical system is difficult. Add this to the users' limited technical knowledge (Beath and Orlikowski, 1994) and it becomes understandable why, when users are involved in the initial configuration/customization phase, their main concern is that the new system will enable them to do what they did before – with 'as little change as possible'.

   b. Vanilla implementations: Packaged software does allow configuration options, but only within fixed parameters and the general advice is to avoid, as far as possible, customizations to the package. Given this context, it begs the question of the point of user involvement if users are not listened to because of the desire for a 'vanilla' implementation?

   c. Motivation: A final problem during the pre-implementation phase is actually getting users to be interested in participation. This lack of engagement is a reflection of human nature, where we only become interested in something when it is salient to us and when we can actually begin to learn about the technology through practice and participation (Wenger, 1998). Moreover, even where users genuinely want to be involved, they are often distracted by more urgent things that they are faced with, especially for knowledge workers who are typically very busy.

Given these issues, it is often only when project completion is imminent and the reality of new work practices becomes apparent, that users begin to evaluate the new system more closely and raise concerns about how the system has been configured and/or customized. This often leads to resistance and the need for post-implementation modifications. Effective resistance may be even more likely where technologies are aimed at knowledge workers because these kinds of workers usually have more power than other kinds of workers. Therefore, instead of emphasizing user participation during the pre-implementation phase it can be very helpful to view technological innovation as an iterative process involving interactive episodes of design, implementation and use. These episodes, and the nature of the innovation process as a whole, are explored further in Chapter 9.

Today, methodologies like rapid prototyping can be used as part of this iterative process, where rather than trying to design the finished system, engineers get out a 'quick-and-dirty' version and then let users play and react to it. During these cycles the reality of the new system will certainly become salient and knowledge workers will inevitably become more interested as they begin to learn from their situated practice. Most importantly, it is during these iterations that knowledge workers will really look at what the new system offers and be concerned about whether it makes their job easier or more difficult. Where the new system is seen to make their job difficult, as in the case presented at the end of the chapter, there will be significant user resistance. In other words, trying to achieve consensus before implementation about how the technology will be used appears to be an unrealistic target. Rather, a more realistic goal may be to provide people with a system that makes their jobs not significantly more difficult and at the same time provides them with the prospect that they will be able to do even more in the future – knowledge workers, as knowledgeable actors, will then themselves learn to exploit the system as they enact the technology in their daily work.

Once a system is in use, one way of helping knowledge workers understand its potential is to provide an off-line version where they can 'play around' to identify what happens when they do certain things on the system. This type of access may be restricted in the live environment because of the repercussions if they complete transactions in different ways, but in the off-line 'sandbox', this experimentation can help users, including knowledge workers, understand the potential (and weaknesses) of the system as currently designed.

>> NEW ORGANIZATIONAL FORMS AND KNOWLEDGE LOSS

One final point to make in this chapter relates to the downsides of the new organizational forms which can support knowledge work and knowledge workers, an issue touched upon briefly in Chapter 1. More specifically, while more modular organizational forms are more conducive to knowledge-intensive work, paradoxically they also make it more difficult to exploit knowledge across the stretched organization. In bureaucratic organizations, job descriptions, rules, procedures and so on were clearly defined and the hierarchy of command provided a clear pathway for communication. In the newer, flatter, organizational forms, there are potentially more opportunities for knowledge to be lost or reinvented in new contexts. So, knowledge is lost between BU, between organizations involved in inter-organizational alliances, across projects and across geographical locations. Moreover, since hierarchies have been flattened, there are fewer middle managers left who can act as intermediaries and try to coordinate and provide a communication link across these boundaries.

In traditional bureaucratic structures, control and information exchange were achieved by having each manager in the hierarchy only responsible for a small number of subordinates. Managers thus had a relatively narrow 'span of control' and were able to closely supervise and control their subordinates. They would then pass on information about their section to the manager above, who also had a narrow span of control. With the flattening of organizational structures, the span of control of each manager in the organizational hierarchy is much greater. So, while in the past a manager may have supervised only seven to ten subordinates, today they may be supervising 50–60 or even more. In this situation it is not possible to know what each subordinate is actually doing and to closely control and monitor their activities. The subordinates must therefore control their own activities to a much larger extent. They are empowered to make their own decisions.

As seen in the previous chapter, this is entirely appropriate for knowledge work and knowledge workers, which cannot be tightly controlled and organized. However, it does mean that middle managers may struggle to act as the communication conduits within an organization (the knowledge intermediaries) – they do not know in much detail what is happening within their particular sphere of responsibility nor do they necessarily have time to engage in such information gathering activities. It is not surprising, then, that often other intermediaries (consultants, for example) will be brought in to conduct this intermediary work. Thus we can see how new organizational forms create challenges for knowledge work (especially with regards coordination) – challenges that can themselves generate new opportunities for knowledge work and knowledge workers. Indeed, it has been suggested that the rise of Business Process Reengineering in the late 1980s/early 1990s – where organizations were flattened and streamlined around business processes – acted as an important precursor for the following fad in Knowledge Management in the mid-1990s (Scarbrough and Swan, 2001).

Organizations have, in essence, become so stretched and virtual that important opportunities for face-to-face social interaction have been lost. So, in a situation where knowledge is seen as perhaps *the* most valuable resource of a company, organizational forms have been developed to nurture knowledge creation. However, these very same organizational forms that help to nurture knowledge creation also provide more opportunity for knowledge loss. 'Knowledge Management' initiatives can be seen as an attempt to resolve this paradox (although it should also be noted that the spread or diffusion of Knowledge Management initiatives has also been promoted by a 'bandwagon' effect). We discuss these topics in Chapter 7, when we look specifically at Knowledge Management systems as well as Enterprise Systems, both of which are described as systems that can help organizations 'manage their knowledge'. In the next chapter we focus down on the micro-processes that are involved in knowledge creation.

>> CONCLUSIONS

In this chapter we have considered the ways in which advancements in ICTs are opening up new possibilities for the design of organizations which are more supportive for knowledge-intensive work. However, we have also seen that these advancements in ICTs will not automatically or deterministically lead to the adoption of new organizational forms or new arrangements for organizing, as is sometimes naively assumed. Rather, the way the new ICTs are used, and their effectiveness, will depend on complex interactions between technology, organization, context and users. In relation to knowledge work, we have shown how ICTs play an important role in shaping, and being shaped by, *purposes* (e.g. applications of knowledge to new tasks), *knowledge processes* (e.g. knowledge sharing across geographical locations) and *enabling contexts* (organizational and institutional). We used the example of teleworking to illustrate this and discussed how the implementation and use of any kind of ICT involved a process of negotiation over time. We examine this more closely through a case study presented next. This case is about a university implementing an ERP system. We discuss ERP systems in Chapter 7, for now it is sufficient to understand that ERP is an IT system that stores data in a central database so that all departments are working from the same data. In order to make this work, all departments need to define and use data in the same way and follow the same process in carrying out their work.

CASE STUDY 3.1
UNI UNIVERSITY AND ITS NEW ERP SYSTEM*

In the summer of 1996 Uni, an elite US university, began modernizing its administrative information systems through a two-year ERP implementation that was officially announced as a project to benefit all constituencies. Uni was one of the first universities to select ERP and chose to work with ConsultCo Corporation in order to develop two software modules – grants and contracts activities. That October the project structure was formed and functional teams were created with co-business and technical leaders. The composition of teams was mostly Uni middle-level managers from Central Administration whose permanent positions had been back-filled for the duration of the project. Although an experienced ERP project manager had been hired, the real authority lay with the teams who communicated directly with Uni's newly appointed Vice President for Finance and Administration.

Once underway, the project team found that ConsultCo's technical experts were not on-site as often as expected, leaving team members working with an incomplete software suite and having to imagine how the grants and contracts module would be integrated. Worried about the project's progress after a year of high-level theorizing, Uni hired consultants to audit the readiness of the software for its scheduled 'big bang' implementation in October 1998. Their findings caused Uni to modify expectations and switch to a phased implementation strategy adopting a revised deadline of July 1999 for the fully integrated suite. This date marked the beginning of Uni's year 2000 fiscal calendar and as such it represented the deadline for retiring legacy systems at risk of the millennium bug. Uni met its 'drop dead date' in that the skeleton ERP was operational on the first day of the new fiscal year but the user interface and reporting environment still required significant development. The suboptimal roll-out of the ERP was complicated by user resistance to the grants and contracts design. The academic constituencies who had expectations of an improved working environment were unable to complete crucial administrative tasks. Faculty demanded changes in the ERP's design as well as interim support for their administrators whose workload increased dramatically in the ERP-enabled environment. For more than two years the project team was involved in post-implementation design changes before finally receiving buy-in from the academic community. The chronology of events is graphically illustrated in the below timeline.

---

* This case is co-authored by Erica Wagner and Sue Newell. Adapted from Wagner and Newell (2004).

In the next sections two contentious episodes that nearly caused the derailment of Uni's ERP project are described. These episodes have been selected because they illustrate the kinds of factions that one might typically come in contact with during large software projects where multiple stakeholder groups and knowledge workers are involved in the implementation. The first episode adopts an internal-external perspective which is important to consider in light of the growing trend for contractual relationships between client organizations and external experts such as software vendors. Whereas the second episode concentrates on the goals of knowledge workers who share broadly in the university mission but also have unique aims, goals and ways of working.

>> UNI-CONSULTCO CONFLICT

The Uni-ConsultCo strategic partnership was created to benefit both parties through the development of a higher education ERP suite. This product would form the basis of Uni's administrative infrastructure and would help ConsultCo enter an untapped vertical market. ConsultCo sought the industry expertise of Uni in order to help the software vendor modify their government/public sector ERP product to meet university needs. The result would be the creation of a new product which both Uni and ConsultCo would continue to fine-tune over time through migrations to new releases of the ERP product. Through coordinated action Uni and ConsultCo were expecting to achieve this common aim because alone neither had all the necessary skills to create a higher education enterprise solution.

However, during the first two years of the project ConsultCo failed to become enrolled in the project to the extent that Uni expected – being largely absent from the project site:

> I had a sense that [ConsultCo] didn't even staff this thing for a year... when I asked questions at a cocktail party like... 'how big is your staff now?' [I'd learn]... it's up to two people. They would catch themselves and say 'No, no, no... We've got seven now'. Then they'd reveal things like 'we assigned our first person in April '98'.

Uni felt the level of resources provided by ConsultCo were inadequate and a misrepresentation of their partnership agreement and struggled to move forward because of this:

> ... Without the [ConsultCo] guys here with us we were still talking philosophies and strategies... and had not even set up the system and figured out the decisions that needed to be made.

The lack of resources provided by ConsultCo was understandable, given that Uni represented one client within a small vertical market which had limited growth opportunities; and they staffed the project to reflect this. ConsultCo approached development as a modification to their government package which they wanted to do in the most efficient manner possible so that they could see the highest return on investment given the market potential. Over time, those on the Uni team came to realize this:

The thing about [ConsultCo] is, they have made a commitment to higher ed but it's much harder than... they thought it was going to be because they thought we were much more like governmental than we really are... They have made an investment and they continue to invest in this market but you have to wonder how long they're going to do that. There are only about 50 institutions that comprise the [US] market...

In contrast, the project represented a major commitment for Uni in terms of time and resources and was a substantial capital investment that was expected to have long-term implications for their operation and governance. A project leader reflects on this situation:

The strategic development partnership [is] a risky implementation because you don't know what you're going to get – it's dependent on a future release – you're not quite sure at the last minute whether your partner's going to say 'sorry, I can only do five of these features'... It's almost like trying to fly a plane and you're not quite sure whether you're going to land in LA or Chicago. So you're constantly re-charting your flight path.

When the original October 1998 deadline arrived, ConsultCo was still developing one of the modules and decided to completely redesign the other. Their absence, coupled with the failure to produce tangible products, lead Uni team members to organize themselves more closely to one another and simultaneously reinterpret their relationship with ConsultCo. Uni began considering alternative ways to achieve its goal given its reliance on ConsultCo – what did ConsultCo want and how best should Uni negotiate with them? It was clear that ConsultCo needed from Uni discipline expertise with regards to university grants management and Uni team members began to realize that their modernization initiative was more complex because of the partnership with ConsultCo due to the vendor's need to create a marketable product:

We're going to have to find good ways to work together because [ConsultCo] is committed to doing a pre-award [grant] system... because they want to market this product to higher education institutions and pre-award is an important part of the business. This is where we find we have the most duplication because we don't need a pre-award system. [Functional team member]

Uni had a well-respected grants management office that administered the external funding process for faculty. Uni was happy with the current operations of this office and their accompanying IS, however they lacked the ability to centrally manage the way in which academic faculty budgeted and spent their award dollars. So while Uni would have preferred to leave pre-awards out of the scope of the ERP project, they realized that they were in an interdependent relationship with ConsultCo who saw pre- and post-award activities as parts of the same process, both of which were necessary to develop as part of a higher education solution that would be sold to research institutions. Uni saw the potential to leverage their grants management expertise in order to obligate ConsultCo for repayment to Uni sometime in the future.

As Uni began to reinterpret their partnership with ConsultCo by seeking compromise, the VP decided to mediate divergent goals and beliefs by using his power and influence to get things done. The VP began by exerting his power over the project and hired an enterprise computing expert as Technical Director of Administrative Systems whose charge was to stop waiting for ConsultCo and 'ramp up' the technical development in time for the Y2K deadline. In addition to refocusing the project team through strong leadership, the VP and newly hired Director felt that it was necessary to give ConsultCo an ultimatum. The Technical Director explains,

> We were in crisis in late spring of '98. The grants management piece was simply not working and [the other module] had not even been delivered. And so it was clear to me [and others] that there was no way we were going to meet the July '99 date [given] the state we were [at in] May of '98. That's the first time...that we were going to tell [ConsultCo] that we were going to chuck 'em on grants – that we were going to come up with an alternative strategy. That would have been bad news for them because that's how they want[ed] to sell this market...So we went through the discipline of [asking] 'what would we do instead'? And it was ugly, messy, not ideal – but we were prepared to do it. We really meant business – if they couldn't execute we were not going to install.

The VP was influential in achieving concessions from ConsultCo because of his ability to mobilize Uni resources towards alternative development activities during a crucial time when the project was experiencing paralysis. In-house technical expertise was mobilized:

> ...I had the geniuses working for me...I asked them to do the detailed homework and gave them full empowerment...so that we could create the development that had to be done...and that required taking the geniuses from other groups like the Warehouse [team] and making it happen [Technical Director of Administrative Systems]

The VP also made a personal visit to ConsultCo headquarters where he indicated that there was indeed 'no free lunch' available for the vendor but rather they had an obligation to repay Uni for its commitment to developing the higher education product. While the project team 'geniuses' continued to develop an alternative solution for grant and labor functionality, ConsultCo produced what they called 'essential' functionality in time for Uni's fiscal year 2000 and Uni chose not to drop ConsultCo as a development partner. Their continued involvement with the vendor is directly related to their own interests for a robust product which they understand will only be achieved if they are able to influence ConsultCo's behaviour and development trajectory by visiting the vendor and being involved in product functionality decisions, despite the costs involved:

> We sent a team of people out to California for two weeks in June to do Beta testing on the [new] versions of those applications...It costs a lot of money to do that and it costs a lot of resource time but we think that it's worth it in the long run [Team leader].

>> CONFLICT BETWEEN ACADEMIC CONSTITUENCIES AND CENTRAL ADMINISTRATION

During implementation team members focused on professionalizing the university's administrative practices in order to ensure institutional governance and mediate financial and regulatory risk. This goal was spearheaded by the Financial Management (FM) team leader who persuaded project members of this agenda and through coordinated action they purposely excluded legacy grants management practices (based on a commitment accounting approach) from the Enterprise System design in preference for a corporate accounting approach based on time-phased budgeting interpreted as more rigorous. This is in the FM team leader's story:

> I would say that the mentality that we've had...for managing is primitive...and it's old-fashioned...the corporate world left it many years ago...Many faculty think of things fundamentally wrong. We want to move people towards a management model where we're going to ask [them] to put together a time-phased budget and management plan.

The FM team leader went on to liken the legacy accounting approach to Quicken – a simplistic software program for the management of personal finances:

> If they don't like it, we ought to fire 'em – and get new users!...It's a...retreat...I taught Karate for many years – you know what? If you're afraid to fight, you'll never fight! Got to decide to get up there and get hit...[we're] spending millions and millions of dollars to go forward, not to duplicate what we had...[Uni] needs more than a copy of Quicken for each grant – we have 4,000 grants...we don't do that here any more. I mean – we just don't!

The rhetoric of this story excludes the possibility of other views in favour of squashing the old ways of working. In the interviewee's mind, everyone should be on the same page – sharing common aims – or they have no place at the university. The content and tone of his message illustrates little respect for the different views across the university.

When the ERP was rolled out to the Uni community it was met with resistance from academic administrators who were unable to inform their faculty members about the financial details of their grant and contract awards using the time-phased approach embedded in the ERP. Academic faculty, in turn, became deeply unhappy about the ERP because they were unable to receive the answers they needed in order to do their jobs effectively. At this time the project entered paralysis because the project team was unable to gain political support from the academic departments. It is in this moment of controversy that all parties involved realize the lack of common aims and begin to consider how they might advance their particular interests. A dissenting central leadership voice shares his interpretation of this controversy:

> We took an environment that wasn't complex and added a level of complexity that was a 100 fold...in the old world people invented shadow systems around the accounting system in order to do their jobs...They understood how to take faculty

information here, and central university information there and make them both accurate... But with the ERP central administrators win!

Frustrated by this situation and cognizant of the increased stress levels of their staff, powerful faculty members reminded the VP of his official promise that the ERP would improve University administrative practices for the entire community. Faculty and their administrators joined forces and used their power to secure a meeting with the Provost, VP and project leadership where they gave an ultimatum threatening to build local systems and use the ERP only as a data repository unless the legacy functionality replaced the time-phased approach. Their influence is illustrated in the narrative of a faculty administrator:

> I took the message over to the [project team], and said... 'we have looked at e creative way of using the ERP for [grants] and it's become clear to us that we need commitments... we're poised... to create our own system but I would like to present this as a University issue and I want to know whether or not you would like to join us in this effort'. Boom, boom, boom. All of a sudden it... happened... overnight. They had a working group that quickly went into designing a customized system.

As a result of these meetings the project began to move out of paralysis. The legacy commitment accounting system remained live and new, 'bolt-on' tools were developed that customized the ERP system, so that faculty needs were met. The expectation was that by appeasing faculty with regards to grants management, the ERP as a whole would be more likely succeed.

Compromising on system functionality was not something that the project team had envisioned having to do. However, the project team came to realize that if they were going to successfully move users out of shadow systems and into the integrated ERP environment they were going to have to temper their hard-line approach. The team thus reprioritized their post-installation development activities and created a customized piece of software that was bolted onto the ERP software.

>> QUESTIONS

1. What does the case illustrate about the relationship between technology and organization in the context of knowledge work?
2. Given that at the start there was a common goal between Uni and ConsultCo, why did the cooperation break down? What does this tell you about cooperation between different groups of knowledge workers?
3. Why did different stakeholders within the University have different understanding and perceptions of the ERP? What does this tell you about knowledge?
4. Do you think the results would have been different in this case if the users of the ERP had not been knowledge workers (i.e. university professors)?
5. What are some principles/lessons that you might take from reading this case about organizational change efforts that are based on IT and their impact on knowledge work?

Summary of key learning points

>> Organizations often use ICTs to accommodate knowledge work. However, the impact of ICTs on knowledge work is influenced by human agency, the physical properties of particular ICTs, and the institutional context in which the work is undertaken.

>> Knowledge work is often undertaken by workers who are geographically distributed, using ICTs. ICTs have a role in, but do not determine, the kinds of distributed forms of work, including teleworking, that are used by knowledge workers.

>> Teleworking can be beneficial for the knowledge worker, the knowledge-intensive firm and the knowledge society. However, it is not as widely used as it might be because it challenges existing norms about the control of workers (workers cannot be trusted) and about what constitutes measurable performance (visible presence), even in the context of knowledge workers.

>> More generally ICTs afford opportunities for, but do not deterministically create, new organizational forms that are supportive of work that is knowledge-intensive. This includes organizational forms, which are more decentralized, less hierarchical, based on teamworking, use interorganizational networks and are globalized.

>> There are three imperatives for successful global business – global efficiency, local responsiveness and transfer of knowledge and learning. ICTs can play a role in these activities, although they can also be facilitated by other means.

>> Achieving organizational change to support knowledge work through ICT is difficult – compromise will often be necessary and modifications in the post-implementation environment should be anticipated and welcomed.

>> Paradoxically, while new organizational forms are conducive to the support of knowledge-intensive work, they also make it more difficult to manage knowledge since they open up more opportunities for knowledge loss. 'Knowledge Management' initiatives can be seen as an attempt to resolve this paradox.

4

MANAGING KNOWLEDGE CREATION IN TEAMS

Chapter Outline

Learning Outcomes

At the end of this chapter you should be able to:

⇒ Understand the dynamics of knowledge creation as it takes place through collaboration.
⇒ Recognize the problems of collaborative work as well as its potential.
⇒ Appreciate the critical role of trust in processes of knowledge creation.
⇒ Identify the role of integration mechanisms in facilitating the development of trust.

>> INTRODUCTION

Chapter 2 focused on managing knowledge workers and explored a consultancy firm as an example of a knowledge-intensive organization which deals with managing this type of work all the time. This highlighted the growing importance of knowledge as an organizational asset and considered some of the issues associated with the effective management of knowledge work and knowledge workers. In this chapter we look more at the micro-processes and practices involved in knowledge work, focusing on team and project dynamics. We do this because knowledge creation is typically an activity that is accomplished through collective processes rather than by individuals working alone. We look at why knowledge creation typically involves some sort of collaborative effort and also consider the problems surrounding such collaboration. Moreover, concentrating on collaborative knowledge creation is important because, as Grant (2000) observes, most management principles and most 'Knowledge Management' (KM) efforts within organizations have focused on improving the use of existing knowledge (i.e. knowledge exploitation) in order to enhance efficiency and ignored the processes and practices necessary for the generation or creation of new knowledge. Some of the more recent Communities of Practice literature (see Chapter 8) does address knowledge creation, but nevertheless, there remains more literature on knowledge exploitation than knowledge exploration, at least in the KM literature.

>> THE IMPORTANCE OF COLLABORATION IN THE KNOWLEDGE CREATION PROCESS

Whether the objective is to develop a new product or service or to design and implement a new organizational technology, such as a new ICT system, the availability of knowledge will be key – knowledge of the markets and customers, knowledge of the available technologies, knowledge of the standards and regulations that will apply, knowledge of materials, knowledge of distribution processes and so on. These different knowledge bases must be brought together so that new knowledge is created which leads to the development of the new product, service or organizational process. Typically, this diversity of knowledge will not be known by a single individual, but rather will be dispersed both within the organization (e.g. across functional groups or disciplinary departments) and across organizations (e.g. knowledge relevant to the development of a new drug will be distributed across doctors working in hospitals, scientists working in universities, employees in pharmaceutical companies and regulators working in the Federal Drug Administration (FDA) or its equivalent). Thus, knowledge creation is typically not something that is done by a single person. Rather, knowledge creation is typically the outcome of bringing different types of knowledge together by involving a number of individuals from different professional and disciplinary backgrounds and often from different organizations in collaborative efforts of some kind. Multi-disciplinary project teams would be a good example of such a collaborative effort.

Sometimes, the knowledge of these different individuals can be brought together in a fairly mechanistic way, so that little interaction is needed across the group – this is referred to as multi-disciplinary work. For example, in a university setting, individuals from different departments (disciplines) in a business school might come together to design an MBA, but in doing this, each discipline maintains its core identity so that the programme is taught as a series of courses, each with a single disciplinary focus. At other times, however, individuals and groups from the different disciplines may interact and work closely together so that knowledge is generated which is new and different to what could have been produced by any discipline working alone – this is referred to as trans-disciplinary work. It is this trans-disciplinary knowledge generation which is more challenging but which also holds the promise of more innovative solutions. For example, again in a university setting, individuals from different departments (disciplines) might get together to design an MBA, but this time the courses that are developed are not based on the traditional disciplines, but instead are thematically based and rely on the integration of knowledge from across the different disciplines that produces new concepts and frameworks that can provide a more holistic understanding of phenomenon. For example, one theme may relate to the social responsibility of business and include a focus on how to promote economic activity in developing countries to reduce poverty. This requires thinking and the generation of ideas that spans disciplines, for example, across the arts and sciences as well as business disciplines.

>> TEAM-WORK AND SOCIAL AND INTELLECTUAL CAPITAL

In organizational contexts, bringing together individuals from diverse backgrounds will often be done through the use of projects, since projects stand outside traditional hierarchical controls, allowing those involved to have more decision discretion and autonomy and so more opportunity to 'do things differently' – a pre-requisite for creating something new as in trans-disciplinary knowledge generation. We look at project-based forms of organizing fully in the next chapter; here we focus specifically on knowledge creation within teams, a goal of many projects that are set up by organizations. A project team will have a specific objective, for example, to design and implement an ICT system to support information sharing across geographically dispersed business units, or to develop a new type of breakfast cereal that will be attractive to teenagers, or to reduce the negative environmental impact of an organization's activities or to find a way to rebrand a company's products or services. These examples demonstrate that knowledge creation can lead to intangible outputs as well as tangible outputs. The successful completion of these tasks will depend on selecting project team members with appropriate knowledge, skills and expertise, so teams ideally will be chosen so that their members have a mix of knowledge and capabilities. We can refer to this as the intellectual capital of the group – the 'knowledge and knowing capability of a social collectivity' (Nahapiet and Ghoshal, 1998, p. 245). Intellectual capital, and its mix across the team, is important. Moreover, it is also important that those involved in the team are aware of, and understand and respect, the knowledge and skills of the others who are involved, since it is pointless having a team member involved who has expertise which is important but never used. This has been referred to as team cognition (He et al., 2007): 'the mental models collectively held by a group of individuals that enable them to accomplish tasks by acting as a coordinated unit'.

It is unlikely, however, that those involved in a team will have all the relevant knowledge and expertise necessary, whether to design a new system, or develop a new product or service *per se* or to ensure that it is accepted and implemented by all those for whom it is intended. Rather, team members will need to network with a range of other individuals in order to appropriate the necessary knowledge as well as communicate convincingly to all those who will be impacted. This wider group of people who will be involved in the innovation process can call the stakeholders. For example, if a project team has been brought together to find ways to reduce an organization's carbon footprint, they will need to find out how energy resources are currently being used, think creatively about ways to reduce this energy use, and then convince people to actually implement the suggested solutions – even if some of the solutions are actually very simple, say switching off laptops and PCs rather than leaving them on all night. If the project team tries to work on the project in isolation they are likely to not only ignore relevant and important information but also to have any solutions identified not implemented because those that need to change their practices have not been involved in the thought processes that lead to the new solutions and so are unlikely to understand or buy-into the suggested changes. Thus the project team needs to engage with a range of stakeholders. In doing this they will be drawing upon their collective social capital. Nahapiet and Ghoshal define social capital as 'the sum of actual and potential resources within, available through, and derived from the network of relationships possessed by an individual or social unit' (1998, p. 243).

Nahapiet and Ghoshal identify three types of social capital – structural, cognitive and relational. Structural social capital refers to the actual network ties between individuals, through which knowledge is potentially shared. We look at this aspect of social capital more fully in Chapter 8 when we examine communities of practice. Cognitive social capital refers to the overlap in frames of reference and understanding that allows connected individuals to share knowledge – just because there is a network connection does not necessarily mean that people will be able to share knowledge effectively since without some shared understanding communication will be difficult. We explore this below in relation to different types of knowledge boundaries that can exist between individuals, especially when they come from different backgrounds. Finally, relational social capital refers to whether or not those with a connection trust each other – so, again, there may be a connection but if there is a lack of trust between the parties, then sharing knowledge will be very problematic. We explore this issue of trust later in this chapter.

>> CREATING SYNERGY WITHIN TEAMS

Cross-functional team-working within organizations is often portrayed as the key to creativity and success for firms today and there is a long tradition in psychological research on team-working demonstrating how 'the whole *may be* more than the sum of the parts'; in other words, how a diverse range of individuals can create, through synergy, ideas which go beyond what any single individual could have produced individually. Similarly in the 'Knowledge Management' literature, where there is an emphasis on knowledge creation, collaboration, interaction and team-working are seen to be crucial. For example, the knowledge creation model developed by Nonaka and Takeuchi (1995) puts heavy emphasis on social processes of dialogue and interaction. Thus, three of the four key processes in their SECI model (socialization, externalization, combination and internalization) that depicts how knowledge is created in organizations through the conversion between tacit and explicit knowledge involve social processes: socialization, externalization and combination (see Chapter 1 for fuller description of the SECI model). In other words, most of the processes that are described in the model depend on dialogue and interaction over a prolonged period. Occasional contact between members of different departments, customers or clients is not enough, they argue, because this does not allow for the sharing of tacit knowledge that is essential for knowledge creation. Instead, interactions must occur over a prolonged period within what they describe as an enabling context. As we saw in Chapter 1, Nonaka and Konno (1998) call this enabling context 'ba'. Ba may well involve a physical space where face-to-face interaction can occur, but can also involve virtual space (e.g. using e-mails, intranets, video conferencing, blogs, social networking) and most importantly it involves developing a shared mental space (shared experiences, emotions, ideas).

The classic example provided by Nonaka of this need for social interaction was of developing an automatic bread-making machine. The project team who were trying to develop this new technology came up with numerous prototypes but none of them was actually very successful in creating bread to the quality produced by bakers. One member of the project team then decided to go and actually work with a master bread baker to try and understand what he did to make quality bread. From this, we are told, the project member came to understand how the baker was 'twisting' the dough in a particular way and his communication of this insight back to the other project members allowed them to subsequently develop an effective automatic bread-maker. Through observation and practice (socialization) the project member was able to acquire the tacit knowledge of the bread-maker that the bread-maker was not able to himself make explicit.

The central idea here, then, is that creativity develops from the interaction of people with different knowledge sets or as Dougherty (1992) calls this – different 'thought worlds'. Differences in knowledge will often tend to generate a conflict of ideas, but this conflict – that Leonard-Barton (1995) has termed 'creative abrasion' – can positively influence creative thinking. This positive influence will occur if the individuals involved can sustain a meaningful and synergistic conversation with the others. This depends on more than simply social skills, which enable team members to 'get along' with each other. It also depends on those involved having cognitive skills which allow them to appreciate and understand the technical knowledge of others – the team cognition referred to earlier. Iansiti (1993) refers to this as having T-shaped skills – depth in a particular discipline but combined with a breadth of understanding of other disciplines. This cognitive skill allows those involved to go beyond merely tolerating the ideas of others to interacting meaningfully at a cognitive level to facilitate 'creative abrasion'.

In addition, shared mental models among team members allow the team to construct a shared understanding of their situation. This is dependent on the team members working closely together over a prolonged period, since with prolonged interaction individuals can share information over and above that required for each individual to do their particular job. This has also been referred to as knowledge redundancy. Knowledge redundancy affects a team's absorptive capacity (Cohen and Levinthal, 1990). Absorptive capacity refers to the capability to recognize the value of new and external information, absorb it and apply it productively. Absorptive capacity in relation to the capability of synthesizing the knowledge of other team members is unlikely unless some knowledge redundancy or a T-shaped skill profile exists.

Team-working is, then, a key mechanism that can provide the enabling context for knowledge creation where mutual understanding of deep tacit knowledge can be achieved based on shared experiences over a prolonged period. Rich personal interaction is necessary in order for those involved to get sufficient opportunity for the sharing of tacit knowledge. Given this need for rich personal interaction a key issue has become how to encourage this when those interacting never meet each other because they are geographically dispersed. We will discuss this further in Chapter 7 when we look at codification strategies that can be used to facilitate knowledge sharing and knowledge creation but to pre-empt, it is clear that ICTs can facilitate this as long as those involved understand how the different ICT can be used effectively (Banker et al., 2006; Fuller et al., 2006). In this chapter we next turn to some of the problems of team-working that make knowledge sharing and collective knowledge creation problematic.

>> PROBLEMS OF TEAM AND PROJECT WORK

Teams are often presented as *the* organizational panacea that will tackle all the problems of organizational life, including, as here, knowledge creation. Teams, it is claimed, can satisfy both individual needs (e.g. for sociability and self-actualization) and organizational needs (e.g. for productivity and innovation). However, the literature on team-working, while advocating its potential synergistic effects, also emphasizes some of the problems of developing and sustaining collaborative working – problems which are frequently overlooked in prescriptive accounts of the benefits of team-working for knowledge creation. There is now an extensive literature on the problems that can occur when people work together in teams. This dates back to very early work by Ringlemann (1913), who found that for some tasks (e.g. tug-of-war games) there was a reduction in individual effort as the number of people engaged in a collaborative task increased. So in a tug-of-war situation, the more people there are on each side the less effort does each individual actually exert. This is sometimes referred to as the social-loafing phenomenon and has been found to be more common where individual contribution to the team effort cannot be easily identified (Latene et al., 1979). At the present time there is a whole list of team-working problems or phenomena that can be cited from the literature. We now consider several that are pertinent to knowledge sharing and knowledge creation in teams.

Knowledge boundaries

Perhaps the most prominent obstacle inhibiting the sharing of knowledge across a multi-disciplinary team is created by knowledge itself! The seminal work, that helps us to understand how knowledge can itself be a barrier to knowledge sharing, is by Paul Carlile (2002, 2004). Carlile develops a framework which depicts three kinds of knowledge boundary – syntactic, semantic and pragmatic – and which also indicates that for these different boundaries to be overcome, knowledge must be transferred, translated and transformed, respectively, as described below (see Figure 4.1). Given these knowledge boundaries, Carlile identifies boundary objects as an important means for facilitating the sharing of knowledge across specialist knowledge domains (Star and Griesemer, 1989). Boundary objects can be either concrete objects (e.g. a blue-print, a drawing, a prototype) or abstract concepts (e.g. a vision, a symbol), but their common and defining characteristic is that they contain some 'interpretative flexibility' (Bijker et al.,

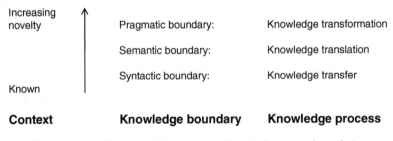

Figure 4.1 Framework for managing knowledge across boundaries

1987) that allows them to be used to provide a common frame of reference for communication across different knowledge and practice domains. For example, Nicholas Negroponte's vision to provide 'one laptop per child' helped to bring together the many different stakeholders who are needed to actually achieve the goal of producing a cheap and durable laptop for children from poor countries. Even though this vision is unlikely to be fully achieved in the foreseeable future the progress that has been made would undoubtedly not have occurred without his mobilizing vision that acted as a boundary object for the many different people involved.

Unpacking the three different types of knowledge boundary, the first and easiest knowledge boundary is a syntactic boundary, created by differences across groups from different backgrounds in terms of the grammar, symbols, labels and languages that are used. So, for example, someone from England may use the term 'boot' where someone from the United States may use the term 'trunk' to describe the space, usually at the back of the car where luggage can be stored. If two people from these different countries are communicating and do not know that a different word is used to describe this space, they may misunderstand each other – as when an English person says to an American, 'put your things in my boot' and then is surprised to see the American trying to put his papers into his shoe! Or, as another example of something a US friend said to her UK mother-in-law, when describing over the phone what her husband was wearing as they were about to go out to dinner – 'he looks very nice in his vest (i.e. jacket) and pants (i.e. trousers)!' One of the failed NASA projects was the result of different groups of scientists, who were working on different parts of the space craft, using different measurement systems so that the parts did not fit together effectively once deployed on Mars. This type of problem is common because of the way different communities create their own unique language (and typically associated acronyms!) in order to facilitate their own interactions. Once the differences are recognized they can be fairly readily overcome through creating a common language so that a 'sender' can represent their knowledge in a way that a 'receiver' will understand.

Semantic boundaries refer to differences in accepted interpretations and meanings amongst actors. At semantic boundaries, the critical issue for sharing knowledge is one of 'perspective taking' – the process whereby one group comes to recognize and accommodate differences in interpretations such that 'the unique thought worlds of different communities of knowing are made visible and accessible to others' (Boland and Tenkasi, 1995, p. 359). Carlile relates the shift from syntactic to semantic boundaries to task characteristics. As task novelty increases, he argues, differences in the amount or specialization of knowledge that actors possess, and the dependencies of actors on one another's knowledge to complete the task, become increasingly unknown. In such circumstances, common syntax may no longer be adequate to transfer knowledge and, consequently, new, shared meanings need to be created that allow the sharing of knowledge. At the semantic boundary, knowledge cannot simply be transferred but needs to be translated, so that actors are able to appreciate the differences in knowledge they have by taking on the perspective of the other. For example, one person from an engineering background trying to communicate to another from a legal background may need to take the perspective of the lawyer in terms of trying to explain the risks associated with a particular technological solution, because risks are going to mean different things to these two parties – for the engineer maybe the risk of one component of the technology failing and having a knock-on-effect on some other component and for the lawyer the risk of a lawsuit that may arise if something goes wrong.

Finally, there are pragmatic knowledge boundaries created by differences in interests between those involved in the collaborative effort. So, even if people have come to appreciate the others' perspective, they may still not agree about a solution because they do not want to change their own practice. This is because of different interests that impede people's ability to share, assess and apply knowledge. In this sense, Carlile reminds us that we are 'invested' in our own particular practices so that there are things 'at stake' if changes in practice are proposed, especially since it is usual that change will not have an equal impact on all those affected, some likely to be more negatively affected than others and so more likely to resist the change. According to Carlile, the transition from a semantic to a pragmatic boundary occurs when task novelty and dependency increase (so creating uncertainties), and where actors have different vested interests and incentives (so creating potential conflict). Under these circumstances, the interests of one actor may create negative practice consequences, for the other and the shared interpretations developed for dealing with differences at the semantic boundary are insufficient to generate the level of collaboration required. At this type of boundary, therefore, knowledge (and practice) must be *transformed* to encourage specialists to translate each other's knowledge and practice, and to transform their own practices as a result. For example, doctors may resist a change which allows nurses to prescribe certain drugs because they may perceive that this undermines their own knowledge base and legitimacy. The doctors' knowledge will need to be transformed if they are to come to accept that nurses can do this. Sometimes offering incentives may be important to encourage this transformation, since the incentive can help people to adjust their practices without undermining their sense of legitimacy.

These knowledge boundaries are particularly important in relation to understanding the problems of collaboration and collective knowledge creation. Nevertheless, there are other aspects of group dynamics that also impede collective knowledge creation in teams and projects that we consider next.

Conformity

The famous experiments on conformity by Stanley Milgram (1964) demonstrated the extent to which individuals obey the instructions of an authority figure even when they are asked to behave in a callous way towards an innocent other. In these experiments a naive subject was asked to give progressively higher levels of electric shock to a supposed 'learner' (actually a confederate of the experimenter who therefore never actually received any shocks) every time this learner made a mistake in remembering a list of paired words. The subjects in this experiment certainly did not enjoy doing this, and indeed the majority of those who conformed (about 65 per cent of those participating) protested strongly and urged Milgram to stop the experiment and check that the learner was not suffering unduly (the learner was located in another room so that there was only an audio connection between the teacher and the learner). Despite these protestations, however, Milgram's command – 'you must continue' – was enough to persuade the majority of participants to progressively increase the level of shock given to the learner to a massive 450 volts. Essentially these participants were conforming to the demands of an authority figure – in this case a university professor in a prestigious US university, Yale – and inflicting (or at least believing that they were inflicting) pain and suffering on another human being.

Applying this to the issue of collaborative knowledge generation, if individuals conform to an authority figure they may refrain from questioning decisions or refrain from sharing their own knowledge, if this conflicts with the ideas of a leader. Thus, the group will not utilize the collective knowledge of its members, and the potential synergies arising from having people with different 'thought worlds' working together will not be exploited. For example, imagine a team of people with diverse backgrounds (engineers, accountants, natural scientists, social scientists, ethicists and IT professionals) brought together from within an organization to explore options for reducing energy waste. These individuals will likely have rather different ideas about how to do this, based on their different backgrounds. But if the team leader is perhaps an accountant who has for some reason decided that the best thing to do is turn down the temperature in offices and does not allow any real discussion of other options, then the team's diverse expertise will go unused. In this case the team fails to operate even multi-disciplinary (i.e. does not look at the problem or opportunity from different perspectives), never-mind trans-disciplinary (i.e. does not integrate these different perspectives to come up with novel solutions); but instead 'agrees' with the ideas of the authority figure. Of course, an authority figure may have good ideas and his/her knowledge base may itself be broad, but this may not necessarily be the case. Moreover it is likely that the collective would have the potential for even more creative solutions, were conformity not an issue.

In a group situation, the problems of conformity can be particularly acute, as evidenced by the phenomenon of 'groupthink', considered next.

Groupthink

Perhaps the most well-known team-working problem is the problem of groupthink identified by Irving Janis, who studied high-level strategy teams in the United States which had made some seemingly non-rational decisions in relation to crisis situations, for example the Cuban missile crisis (Janis, 1982). He found that this was related to excessive conformity pressures that built up within these teams who had worked together over time. He labeled this phenomenon 'groupthink' and identified a number of symptoms associated with it:

1. *Illusion of invulnerability*: members believe that past successes guarantee future successes and so take extreme risks.
2. *Collective rationalization*: members collectively rationalize away information that contradicts their assumptions.
3. *Illusion of morality*: members believe that they are all moral and so could not make a bad decision.
4. *Shared stereotypes*: members dismiss evidence that is contradictory by discrediting the source of that information.
5. *Direct pressure*: sanctions are placed on members who do dissent from the majority opinion, for example, using assertive language to enforce compliance.
6. *Self-censorship*: members keep quiet about any misgivings they have so that they do not voice concerns.
7. *Mind-guards*: members screen out information from outsiders where this might disconfirm the group's assumptions and beliefs.
8. *Illusion of unanimity*: given these other symptoms, it appears that there is consensus within the group, even though there are many of those involved who do not agree with the group decision.

Groupthink has been found to develop where there is a powerful team leader who makes known his or her preferences at an early stage, and where this is coupled with a strong drive to reach consensus because of pressures of time, which means that a decision needs to be reached quickly. In this situation, conformity to this leader's preference (i.e. to the leader's knowledge) is likely to occur. The tragic launching and subsequent explosion of the Challenger Space Shuttle has been analysed as an example of groupthink (Moorhead et al., 1991) as has, more recently, the Columbia Space Shuttle disaster. Again, as noted above, conformity can restrict the knowledge sharing and so knowledge creation in a team. Moreover, such group conformity – that is, groupthink – may be particularly relevant in the context of organizational project work because projects often work to very tight deadlines, which encourages the time pressures that have been found to encourage this type of restricted knowledge sharing. This helps to explain why projects often work to a logic of consequentiality (what is most expedient), rather than a logic of appropriateness (what is best), as discussed in the next chapter.

Group polarization

Another problem that we can identify from the literature on team-working in relation to knowledge creation is that teams tend to make more extreme decisions than individuals working alone. Originally research suggested that teams tend to make more risky decisions (Stoner, 1968). The experimental design to study this was as follows: an individual is provided with a brief scenario which describes a situation in which a decision has to be made; the individual is given a series of decision options, ranging from a very safe decision but with a low pay-off to a very risky decision but with a high pay-off; the individual is asked to say which level of risk they would be prepared to take; individuals are then put together in groups to discuss the scenario; once this group discussion has finished the individual is then asked to say whether they would like to change their original risk-taking decision option. In general, research using this type of study design found that, following the group discussion, individuals tended to increase the level of risk they saw as appropriate.

Subsequent research has also demonstrated that a team can produce a cautious shift following group discussion. The important point, however, is that research suggests that groups tend to make more extreme decisions, sometimes with a fatal outcome as with the Challenger Space Shuttle disaster, and more recently the Columbia Shuttle disaster. One explanation of this suggests that group polarization occurs through a process of social comparison. During the group discussion we compare our decision with the decision of the others in the group. At the outset we tend to think of ourselves as being fairly risk-taking, because this tends to be a valued personal attribute, at least in many societies and in relation to many situations. When, during the group discussion, we discover that we are not particularly risky compared to others, we then increase the level of risk in relation to our decision when asked to reconsider the decision. The cautious shift occurs in situations where caution rather than risk is the socially valued option. For example, making a risky investment decision may be admired if the individual involved would simply be a rich individual if the decision turned out to be successful and would not suffer significantly if the money invested was lost. However, if the risky investment decision will impact a person's ability to pay for a life-saving operation of a spouse, a cautious shift is more likely.

Applying this to knowledge creation, we can see how this group dynamic might influence some teams to generate very risky solutions that do not adequately take account of the various downsides associated with the solutions. This is why risk management has become such an important part of all project management methodologies.

Collaboration and power and control

Many of the problems of team-work and collaboration discussed above are related to fundamental issues of power and control in teams. Thus, an essential feature of successful knowledge-creating teams is the relatively free-flowing, sharing of ideas. After all, that is the rationale for bringing together particular individuals – the notion that all team members can contribute their knowledge or their intellectual and social capital. However, in most knowledge-creating teams in organizations, there are power differentials between those participating.

In particular, there is often a team leader who may have power to reward and punish team members, for example, by being able to influence their appraisal or promotion outcomes. In such situations, where there is personal risk involved in disobeying the authority figure, conformity, groupthink or group polarization may be very likely to occur. For example, Nadler, Hackman and Lawler (1979) note that the quality of interpersonal relationships among group members in real work settings often leaves much to be desired. They conclude that people fall too readily into patterns of competitiveness, conflict and hostility, and that only rarely do group members support and help one another.

Thus, teams (or projects) are not necessarily the organizational panacea that they are sometimes presented as being for knowledge creation. Sinclair (1992) goes as far as to say that the ideological assumptions of the prevailing team paradigm are naïve, in particular because power has been treated as 'a regrettable and regressive tendency exercised by individuals who fail to identify with the collective task' (Sinclair, 1992, pp. 618–619). Thus, while there is a clear recognition that political pressures exist within groups, the dominant response to this is to seek to minimize this impact 'through training and containing or banishing power-seekers or by creating an organizational environment in which a spirit of egalitarianism renders power and conflict irrelevant' (Sinclair, 1992, p. 619).

In contrast to this view, Sinclair (1992) advocates treating individual power-seeking within groups as endemic. Group behaviour from this view is seen as essentially conflict between individuals seeking to exercise power in different ways in order to advance their own individual ends. The outcome of team-work is, then, the result of the successful assertion of some individuals' power-seeking efforts over others. Where consensus is achieved this simply conceals conflicts and power discrepancies. This implies that groups with a clear and accepted distribution of power are most likely to be *judged* as productive because the output of the group conforms to expectations, even though the actual team-working effort may be very limited, judged in terms of the level of knowledge exchanged, the quality of group interactions, the level of creativity and so on. Indeed, from this perspective, effective group work, which involves substantial levels of information exchange, group interactions and creativity, actually depends on achieving some redistribution of power at least during team-working. Only with a redistribution of power will conflict be allowed to emerge so that the false consensus (as with groupthink) is eroded. In the Research Team case presented at the end of the chapter, these issues of false consensus and the attempt to ignore conflict were very apparent.

Ironically perhaps, while the redistribution of power is central to the team-working philosophy, in reality power becomes quickly formalized within team-working situations and leads to high levels of team control and coercion over individual members, even in the absence of an authority figure. Power is passed from the hierarchy to the team members themselves, so that they become self-managing teams. This power is used by the team members to police and control each other's behaviours. Barker (1993) demonstrated very vividly how a team comes to use its power to increase control over individual team members. Barker describes a manufacturing organization that changed from a system of bureaucratic control to a system of self-managed teams. Senior management at this organization set out a vision for these teams, which the teams accepted. This vision enshrined values such as team autonomy, responsibility and achieving objectives. These shared values led the teams to develop a set of norms to guide their behaviour (e.g. we need to be at work on time). Over time, these simple norms were turned into highly formalized and objective rules (e.g. if you are more than five minutes late, you will lose a day's pay). Other team members censored individuals who failed to abide by these rules. Sewell (1998) has subsequently demonstrated how this team surveillance can also develop through electronic communication as well as where those involved are interacting face-to-face.

The Barker (1993) case demonstrates very clearly how a new form of control emerges very quickly within the context of self-managed teams. He refers to this new form of control as 'concertive' control. Concertive control shifts power from management to the workers themselves. The individual team members collaborate to develop their own ideas, norms and rules that enable them to act in ways that are functional for the organization. Essentially, teams can create a system of control that is more powerful and repressive than traditional bureaucratic systems of control. In the Barker case the team control was far more powerful than had been the traditional hierarchical managerial control since team members could constantly monitor the behaviour of each other. In effect, the other team members had become peer managers. This can be stressful for individuals but can also detract from the creativity potential of the team; following team rules can become more important than finding the creative solution to problems or exploiting opportunities, again demonstrating the power of the logic of consequences as opposed to the logic of appropriateness.

These power issues become even more exaggerated when the knowledge sharing involves more than one organization. For example, if a small biotechnology company is working collaboratively with a large pharmaceutical to develop a very new cancer treatment, it may be the small biotechnology company that has the greatest expertise in relation to the science involved even though the large pharmaceutical company has the financial resources needed to move the development through the very expensive clinical trials stages. This creates competing sources of legitimacy, which can lead to complex dynamics with those involved having to constantly negotiate and bargain about what approach to take. These inter-organizational problems will be explored more fully in the next chapter.

>> ADVANTAGES AND DISADVANTAGES OF TEAM-WORK FOR EFFECTIVE KNOWLEDGE SHARING AND KNOWLEDGE CREATION

The sections above have demonstrated that while working collaboratively in teams can potentially create synergies so that those involved share knowledge and expertise which allows them to produce an output which is better than could have been achieved by any individual working alone, teams can also produce outputs which are worse than could have been produced by the most competent team

Table 4.1 Summary of the advantages and disadvantages of collaborative work

Advantages	Disadvantages
Potential for synergistic solution that integrates knowledge in new ways	Knowledge boundaries can restrict knowledge sharing
Increased pool of knowledge to draw upon	Conformity can stifle knowledge sharing
Increased acceptance and commitment of the selected decision	Groupthink can override individual judgement
Wider range of perspectives taken into consideration	Group polarization can lead to overly risky decisions
Novice team members can learn from more experienced team members	Diffusion of responsibility leads individuals to avoid feeling responsible
Greater understanding of the rationale of the selected decision	Satisficing so that the decision is acceptable rather than optimum
Learning opportunities are enhanced by learning from colleagues in different departments	Peer surveillance exerts normalizing control that stifles creativity and innovation

members (Hackman, 1990), as demonstrated by the groupthink phenomenon. West et al. (1998) provide a useful review of the advantages and disadvantages of team-working. Drawing on this work, Table 4.1 provides a summary of some of the most important advantages and disadvantages of collaborative work.

>> COLLABORATION AND INTEGRATION MECHANISMS

Grandori and Soda (1995), recognizing this problem of achieving collaboration, identify a number of what they describe as integration mechanisms that, they argue, can encourage cooperation. They list ten such mechanisms and suggest that in teams or networks where the objective is the joint production of knowledge, all ten mechanisms need to be employed. These mechanisms include access to communication channels, social coordination through agreed norms, providing individuals with particular role and responsibilities for linking individuals together, assigning authority and control to particular individuals, careful selection of individuals to ensure an appropriate mix of skills and expertise, and utilizing incentive systems.

More generally, there is a whole literature, and accompanying practice, that deals with project management. This literature stresses the importance of using formal project management methodologies that supposedly help to ensure that those involved work effectively together and share their knowledge as appropriate. Formal project management methodologies focus on:

1. Defining a clear and explicit vision, with associated goals and objectives;
2. Defining and following a formally defined project plan that sets out milestones and defines roles and responsibilities for all those involved;
3. Ensuring that necessary resources are available and allocated as necessary.

The assumption is that these formal, structured processes will guide the project work. However, what such formal processes ignore is how plans can never predict everything that is going to happen in practice, especially when the project is focusing on creating something new through collaborative knowledge generation. It is therefore the informal, emergent processes – the improvisation and muddling through – that are as important for project success as the formal project management processes, allowing those involved to make-do with the resources at hand, including knowledge, even when not ideal or not those that were planned for. These informal, often ad-hoc, processes, depend very significantly on the social milieu within which the collaborative work is being undertaken. Ciborra (1998), for example, talks about the importance of care taking, hospitality and cultivation in encouraging the type of improvisation often necessary in project contexts to overcome obstacles and challenges.

Dodgson (1993, 1994) also focuses on the social problems of collaboration, and argues that it is crucial to create and sustain personal relationships between the team members. He goes on to claim that for the exchange of knowledge and resources to be effective, a high-trust relationship needs to be developed. Partners need to trust one another to be 'honest, capable and committed to joint aims' (p. 291). In a similar way, Von Krogh et al. (2000) argue that an effective enabling context, allowing for a network of interactions, must be characterized by care and trust among the participants, if it is going to encourage knowledge sharing and knowledge creation. These authors delineate five aspects of an enabling context for knowledge creation – mutual trust, active empathy, access to help, leniency in judgement and courage. Trust has also been shown to be important in relation to knowledge transfer between organizations (Faems et al., 2007). The aspect of trust, therefore, seems to be central to understanding team knowledge sharing and knowledge creation. We need therefore to look at what is meant by trust and consider how trust can be developed and sustained.

>> THE IMPORTANCE OF TRUST IN COLLABORATIVE WORK

It is argued, then, that trust can lead to, and is a necessary condition or enabler for, cooperative behaviour among individuals, groups or organizations. High levels of trust are considered necessary in order to facilitate the type of communication and dialogue that is needed for people to share tacit knowledge and generate learning that can lead to knowledge creation. In many articles on the management of knowledge work the importance of trust for knowledge sharing and knowledge creation is indeed recognized. In such a context, knowledge can be created spontaneously, as conceptual insight and practice are merged in action. However, in most cases there is little more than a simple statement that 'trust is necessary'. In this section we consider the issue of trust in more detail and illustrate that while trust is indeed important for knowledge creation, it is also difficult to establish – individuals will not necessarily 'grow to trust each other' simply because they are told to work together in a team. Understanding the different types of trust that exist and the processes influencing trust development is crucial for considering the strategies that are likely to be effective for stimulating team knowledge creation.

>> DEFINITIONS OF TRUST

Trust is defined in different ways in the literature, although two issues seem central: first, that trust is about dealing with risk and uncertainty; and second, that trust is about accepting vulnerability. Luhmann (1988), for example, sees trust as an attitudinal mechanism that allows individuals to subjectively assess whether or not to expose themselves to situations where the possible damage may outweigh the advantage. This attitude develops where individuals choose to accept vulnerability to others. In other words, to trust someone there must be a situation of uncertainty in which there is an element of perceived risk on the trustee's part: 'the willingness of a party to be vulnerable to the actions of another party based on the expectation that the other will perform a particular action important to the trustor, irrespective of the ability to monitor or control that other party' (Mayer et al., 1995, p. 712). There are many sources of vulnerability that may be 'at risk' in collaborative situations, for example, reputation, financial resources, self-esteem, conversations. Where tasks are interdependent and there are goods or things that are valued, vulnerability and the need for trust are higher. This will be precisely the situation in a knowledge-creating team within an organization.

While we can have a generally agreed broad definition of trust, the literature also makes it clear that there are different types of trust, based either on different sources of trust or on different processes of trust development. For example, Sako (1992) considers three different reasons for being able to develop trust, that is, different reasons for being able to predict that another will behave in a 'mutually acceptable manner': first, because of a contractual agreement that binds the parties in the relationship; second, because of a belief in the competencies of those involved; and third, because of a belief in the goodwill of those involved. This is very similar to the typology developed by Shapiro et al. (1992), which distinguishes between deterrence-based trust, knowledge-based trust and identification-based trust.

Other writers have concentrated on understanding how trust is developed and maintained. In terms of development, Zucker (1986) depicts three central mechanisms of trust production – process-based (i.e. based on reciprocal, recurring exchange), characteristic-based (i.e. based on social similarity) and institutional-based (i.e. based on expectations embedded in societal norms and structures). In terms of maintenance, Ring and Van de Ven (1994) distinguish between fragile (easily developed but easily broken) and resilient (hard-won and less likely to break) trust. Similarly, Jones and George (1998) distinguish between conditional and unconditional trust. Conditional trust is established at the beginning of a social encounter as long as there are no obvious indications that the other has different values and so should not be trusted. This is because it is easier to assume trust than distrust. Over time, as one becomes more confident that the other person shares one's values, this trust will be converted into unconditional trust. Unconditional trust, they argue, is more enduring and is the basis for the development of synergistic relationships, which can lead to increased knowledge creation and superior performance. In other words, Jones and George (1998) argue that unconditional trust leads to more effective cooperative behaviour than does conditional trust.

Other research has focused on trust-building when there is a time pressure. Meyerson et al. (1996), for example, argue that in temporary groups working on short-lived complex tasks that require the specialist skills of relative strangers (the essential characteristics of much project work in organizations), trust needs to form very quickly if the group is to make any progress at all. They suggest that this 'swift trust' has unusual properties in that its development is driven more by contextual cues than by personalities or interpersonal relations. Thus swift trust is a pragmatic strategy for getting on with the job at hand involving 'artful making do with a modest set of general cues from which inferences are drawn about how people might care for what we entrust to them' (p. 191), The concept of swift trust is particularly useful in relation to knowledge-creating collaborative contexts. In many cases those involved in the projects, put together in order to share knowledge and develop new products or processes, have never worked together before. At the same time they often have very tight deadlines – just the situation where 'wading in on trust' may be more likely and indeed necessary.

Drawing these different ideas about trust together, a threefold typology is presented below. This typology pulls together the typologies that already exist in the literature.

Companion trust: This refers to trust that is based on judgements of goodwill or personal friendships. The trust rests on a moral foundation that others will behave in a way that does not harm other members of the network. The parties will expect each other to be open and honest. Such trust will be process-based in that it will develop over time as people get to know each other personally (and possibly become friends) through continuing, reciprocal exchange. This trust should be slow-forming and resilient. It has a strong emotional component and is important for the maintenance of social networks. Partners should be relatively tolerant of others' (well-intentioned) mistakes. However, if eventually broken, this trust is also likely to cause the greatest rift between the parties involved.

Competence trust: This trust is based on perceptions of the others' competence to carry out the tasks that need to be performed and will be important where the skills needed to perform a task are not able to be found within one person. In other words competence trust is based on an attitude of respect for the abilities of the trustee to complete their share of the job at hand. The truster feels that they can rely on the trustee. The development of this form of trust thus relies on perceiving the competences of the other partners. This may not necessarily need to occur through interpersonal exchange – competence judgements can also be driven by contextual cues such as the reputation of the institution that the person works for or the status of the professional group to which they belong. This type of trust can therefore develop much more swiftly but it is also likely to be more fragile since if the trustee does not quickly demonstrate the competences which were expected, the trust breaks down.

Commitment trust: This trust stems from the contractual agreements between the parties. In this case, the trust is developed on an institutional basis. Each party is expected to gain mutual benefit out of the relationship, and so can be relied on to be committed to deliver according to the details of the contract. While the contract itself embodies formal obligations on the part of the signatories, the important element as regards risk and uncertainty is that it allows those involved to believe that those others with whom they are working will demonstrate commitment trust; that is, that others can be trusted to put in the effort necessary to complete the joint work. This commitment trust means that only rarely will the contract itself be used to settle conflicts between the parties. Indeed, resorting to 'the contract' would be a sign that the commitment trust had broken down. This type of trust probably falls in between the first two in terms of how resilient it is. It is more resilient than competence-based trust because the contractual agreement underpinning commitment trust will still encourage a continuation of the alliance even if those involved stop respecting each other's abilities (they know they can resort to 'the contract' if all else fails). However, it is not likely to be as resilient as goodwill or companion trust. Partners that fail to demonstrate their commitment by delivering their share of the work on one contract are likely to be dropped from any future joint collaboration.

These different types of trust can all influence the ability of those involved in a team to create knowledge. For example, imagine that you have been put in a team to undertake a college assignment on where you have to identify opportunities in your own college for reducing waste and improving sustainability of operations. You have never worked with any member of the team before, but you have heard, through a friend, that one of your team members – Colin – always tries to dominate, even though he is not very clever, always wanting others to do the actual work; another team member – Jenny – so you have heard, is simply not very nice and will always try to undermine colleagues if provided with the opportunity; and finally, you have heard that the fourth team member – Scott – is not really interested in getting the degree because he is going to work in the family business where his qualifications simply will not be relevant. It is not hard to imagine that this team is not going to be very successful, lacking all three types of trust across different members. Nevertheless, perhaps the four of you decide to go to a bar after a not-very-successful first meeting. You have a few drinks and start to talk to each other. You learn from Colin that he really disliked the experience of a former class team assignment that he was involved in (the one your friend was also in) because none of his peers were willing to make any decisions; he therefore found that he had to be more pushy than he would ordinarily like to be and also try not to do all the work himself but delegate so that the others contributed at least something. You learn from

Jenny that she also had a bad experience in a previous team assignment because one of her peers tried to set-her-up by telling the professor in charge that Jenny was being destructive behind the backs of her team-mates even when this was not true. Finally, you learn from Scott that while there is a family-job waiting for him, this is not really what he wants to do and that he is really keen to get a good degree in order to open his options once he graduates. The next meeting that the team has is noticeably more productive and the team, at the end of the semester, comes out with a good grade. The moral of this story is, of course, that one should not rely too much on second-hand information, especially as it relates to personalities and dispositions, and also that socializing and getting to know those with whom one must work can be extremely helpful in setting the trust context for collaborative work. As the final case in this chapter illustrates, such socializing might not always be effective, especially if it cannot be sustained over the duration of the project work, but without it, it is difficult for a team to go beyond a mechanistic approach to the task which is unlikely to generate much collective knowledge.

>> CONCLUSIONS

In conclusion, this chapter has demonstrated the centrality of collaboration for knowledge creation. However, it has also illustrated that putting individuals with different backgrounds together will not automatically and inevitably generate the synergy that will result in knowledge creation because there are powerful knowledge boundaries that exist. Moreover, in certain situations power differentials and conformity pressures will impede the collective so that a false consensus is generated which is certainly not the result of the collaborative involvement of individuals with different knowledge sets. In order to overcome these problems of collaboration, this chapter has emphasized the importance of developing trust between the various parties involved.

Different types of trust have been identified that help us to consider in more depth the relationship between trust and knowledge creation. This can be explored in more detail as you consider the Research Team case next. This case also demonstrates the difficulty of actually creating trust when there is a lot of heterogeneity. Where those involved have very different backgrounds and perspectives, considerable time needs to be devoted to providing shared experiences so that some mutual understanding (knowledge redundancy) and trust can be developed. As we shall see in the Research Team case, the failure to provide sufficient time in project plans for the development of trust and to consider obstacles to knowledge sharing is likely to result in reduced rather than enhanced creativity.

This chapter has focused on the micro-processes of knowledge creation, providing an overview of the conditions that can facilitate knowledge integration within a team. In the next chapter we focus on how organizations may exploit knowledge that is created within a team setting (or more specifically within a project setting), whether this is within or across organizations.

CASE STUDY 4.1
RESEARCH TEAM

A university research team was working on a project to develop new knowledge in a particular subject area. The team consisted of four principal investigators (PIs), who wrote the original proposal, four research officers (ROs), and one full-time administrator. These individuals worked at three universities (with two PIs and two ROs and the administrator working at one university and one PI and RO at each of the other two universities), which were geographically separated, although all in the United Kingdom. The PIs and ROs also had different disciplinary backgrounds and experience to offer to the project (including, e.g., experience in engineering, operations management, marketing and organizational behaviour). The project was supported by a research grant from a government Research Council together with funding from a major industrial partner.

The case is described in relation to three phases of the project: Phase 1, where the PIs worked together to submit a project proposal to the potential funding body; Phase 2, where the ROs and administrator had been appointed and were working together with the PIs on the project; and Phase 3, which considers the outputs from the project.

>> PHASE 1: SUBMITTING THE PROPOSAL

Initially the project team consisted of the four PIs who came together as a result of a complex set of interrelated contacts; in particular through their joint membership of an expert panel, but also because of contacts made at conferences and other academic networking. In addition, two of the PIs were professors who had been friends since their university days together. The team decided to work together when they learnt that the Research Council was prepared to sponsor a large project in the research area they were all involved in, albeit from different disciplinary perspectives. The four PIs thus identified a potential mutual benefit from winning the research contract and started to work together collaboratively to put together a proposal.

While two of the four PIs knew each other well, the other two PIs had no prior 'history' other than casual acquaintance. Yet trust had to be established quickly if this group was to meet the deadline for the proposal specified by the funding body. This was achieved since competence could be inferred from the fact that each of the four PIs had published in credible journals and each belonged to a reputable university. There were no grounds for expecting harmful behaviour from others. The only cues available signalled expectations of high levels of competence that would allow them to put together, and subsequently deliver on, a creative research project.

The outcome of this phase was a proposal for a research project which included a list of 'deliverables' that the research team would produce jointly. This proposal then became the contract, which bound the team of four together and against which they would be judged by the funding body once the project was completed. While there were no real sanctions that would apply if the team failed to deliver, there was a potential that their reputations could be tarnished, especially with the funding Research Council. This was clearly significant since this body was a major source of research income for all of them. Unfortunately, the proposal was subsequently interpreted differently by the PIs, and so became a source of continuous tension and conflict (see below). This occurred largely because, in the rush to meet the deadline, the detail in the proposal, in terms of the stated objectives and how they would be achieved, had not been clearly negotiated and defined at the outset.

Once the research contract had been awarded, the PIs started working on the project. This involved several meetings to work out how they would operate as a team (e.g. establishing who would be responsible for what) and also to flesh out more precisely the nature of the research problem (e.g. which theoretical perspectives and empirical approaches would inform the research). Once the team actually started to work together, however, the swiftly made assumptions of competence trust started to break down. It became apparent that at least some of the PIs had in reality known very little about the academic work of some of the others. Indeed, one of the PIs eventually commented in exasperation that she would in future always read at least three articles by anyone she was considering working with; implying that if she had done so in this case she would not have gone ahead. This deterioration in perceptions of competence trust occurred because the PIs had fundamentally different theoretical and epistemological positions, which meant that the possibility of ever reaching a consensus on how the research should be done was remote, despite their genuine attempts to do so. The written contract (i.e., the research proposal) also became a problem during this phase. In retrospect at least some of the PIs felt they had committed themselves to a proposal that had not been mapped out well in the first place.

>> PHASE 2: ENLARGING THE TEAM

Once the proposal had been accepted and the grant awarded, the research team was enlarged with the recruitment of four ROs and one project administrator. The four individuals initially recruited as ROs were total strangers to each other. They were geographically dispersed across the three universities but were told that they needed to collaborate in order to undertake the research. They were encouraged by the PIs to work together, and several coordination mechanisms were introduced by the PIs to encourage this integration. For example, the project was divided into a series of work packages, which essentially laid down a formal project plan. At first these work packages were each led by one of the ROs. However, this did not work very effectively as the ROs found it difficult to demand action from their more senior PIs. Moreover, the work packages proved too inflexible for the inevitable complexities of a large-scale research project. Deadlines for the different work packages were never adhered to and the planning framework was therefore largely redundant.

Meetings were spent revisiting the plans and making new plans that were then never followed.

In terms of more general and informal social integration mechanisms, the ROs were largely left to 'make sense' of their role and their relationships with each other by themselves. On the first day of the project they telephoned each other to 'say hello' and subsequently met at a meeting of the whole research network that had been arranged by the PIs. Thereafter, they were expected to coordinate between themselves.

One of the first problems to emerge among the ROs occurred very quickly and related to the process of recruitment. Three of the ROs recruited were young (under 30), having just finished, or being in the process of completing, either Master's or doctoral degrees. They applied for the particular job because they wanted to pursue an academic career and were selected through a conventional process where they had to apply and be interviewed for the job in competition with other applicants. The fourth RO selected (we shall call him Pat) was older and was appointed without any competition on the basis of a single PI's personal opinion. Pat did not have a conventional academic background and had also failed to complete a postgraduate qualification. However, the PI who recruited him had decided that Pat would be better able to take over more of the work than would typically be expected of an RO. This was despite the fact that Pat already had a consultancy business which put considerable demands on his time. While the other ROs tried to be accommodating, Pat himself felt uncomfortable with the situation. He was also action-oriented and frustrated with what he felt was 'overtheorizing' by the others. Pat therefore soon tired of his new post, becoming irritated with the convoluted nature of much academic debate, together with the emphasis on rigorous process rather than on the generation of results. Within months he had left, an event which had significant effects in the context of a three-year project.

After Pat had left the project, no one was recruited to replace him for six months, so the three remaining ROs worked as a smaller team, dispersed at the three different universities. The work was divided up between them. Initially, the ROs recognized the need to coordinate their different tasks and they agreed to meet regularly. However, over time their meetings became less and less frequent. Thus, from weekly or at least fortnightly contact among this group, there was a period when they did not meet for almost six months. The reason for this increased estrangement was that trust did not develop between two of this group of three. The repeated contact actually led to a distrust based on a belief in the other's *in*competence. Again, as was the case with the PIs, these two individuals came from very different disciplinary backgrounds and each was simply not able to respect the other's contributions to the project. The two individuals were also quite different in terms of their personalities and interests. Their only common ground was the research project so that companion trust was difficult to develop in the absence of competence trust. This situation was uncomfortable for all the ROs, particularly these two. The outcome was that one of the pair left the project.

Much later, once the two departing ROs had been replaced, meetings between the new set of four ROs were once again instigated. These meetings were more successful and would run on into an evening meal and became a valuable integrative event, at least among the ROs. However, despite this early success the ROs eventually became discouraged from holding such gatherings, in part because the conceptual frameworks they developed during these meetings were heavily criticized by the PIs at whole team meetings (although the ROs claimed that their work surfaced again later in PI analyses). The low importance attached to RO contributions was reinforced at the whole team meetings, in which their involvement was limited to presenting some previously prepared findings from their local universities. They took little part in discussion and when they attempted to join in their contributions were generally disregarded. The low point in their marginalization from these meetings occurred when the PIs decided to split the whole team meetings into two parallel streams, holding a separate PI meeting in an adjoining room.

An important tension for the ROs, then, was that the espoused consensual approach to the research – we are all equal and the contributions from PIs and ROs are of equal importance – cut across the more hierarchical department structures, which were particularly apparent at one of the universities. Here the autocratic leadership style of the PI was reinforced by the layout of the building, in which all the professors, including this PI, were housed separately in a luxurious suite of rooms at the top of the building, commonly referred to as 'Prof. Corridor'. This PI preserved a remoteness from most aspects of the project, not taking part in the research and minimizing contact with the ROs. At full team meetings, to which he travelled first-class, he regularly employed a mocking and dismissive approach to the younger male RO working at his university. He clearly placed his departmental needs above those of the project, insisting that the project coordinator spend one day a week working for the department and 'not just the project'. However, such role expectations (of a superior, distant and 'figurehead' status) were not shared by the PI from one of the other universities, whose approach was to get considerably more involved in the project and to work closely with her RO.

>> PHASE 3: OUTCOMES

The emergent solution to the tensions and frustrations that were being experienced by both the PI and the RO groups within the project was a division of the project into three fairly autonomous 'bits', which therefore reduced the interdependencies between the project team, so that conflict could be more easily avoided. Essentially the project was run as three separate projects, broken down along disciplinary lines (which happened to also coincide with the geographical dispersion of the project team). This move to a federated approach completely undermined the initial explicit intention to ensure a synthesis across the team; indeed such an integration of the three disciplinary areas had been a major part of the academic rationale for the project. However, throughout the life cycle of the project two of the PIs continued to argue for the need to fulfil this early commitment to an integrated project. They tenaciously opposed the emerging tendency for the project to develop into three 'federated' sub-projects; arguing, for example, that all four ROs should carry out research fieldwork together. However, in reality the low synthesis across the team emerged very rapidly and quickly became strongly embedded so that a return to a synthesized approach became impossible.

The team did continue to have fairly regular face-to-face meetings where those working on the now independent projects came together to share experiences and analyses. However, these were never as frequent as originally intended because of the difficulties of actually finding dates when all the PIs could attend. There were, in the event, few meetings where all the PIs were present. This fluctuating membership was a problem because a lot of time had to be spent in bringing those absent from meetings up to date. More problematical still was the lack of follow-through and building on what was agreed at these meetings. One PI described it as 'the syndrome of hitting reset at the end of the meeting'. They tried to resolve this problem by having one of the PIs summarize the key points from the meetings and then circulate this to the others using e-mail. However, there were frequently problems in this process as individuals had interpreted the same meeting very differently.

Between meetings the team relied on e-mail communication to share experiences across the three federated projects. This created problems because some of those involved were lax in responding to their e-mails. Moreover, this mode of communication was found to be ineffective where conceptual and methodological issues needed to be resolved. The team then moved to using telephone conferencing to try and resolve differences between the various subgroups. Observing these conferences at any particular institution revealed how those at one site would ridicule those taking part from other sites. Mocking gestures and written comments, invisible to those on the other end of the telephone line, were clearly well-practised by the local group. This disdain towards team members from other departments was similarly seen in the distinction between e-mails circulated around a university group and those disseminated throughout the whole team.

The main formal outputs from this project were publications. The first publication from the project caused considerable conflict because one of the PIs decided to publish some of the research outputs without consulting, or crediting, team members from the other departments. The other PIs argued that they should all be jointly involved in publications, since this would provide the opportunity to synthesize across the different disciplines. Following this first publication, therefore, there was a standing item on the agenda of every project team meeting so that they could discuss this as a group. Thus, at every meeting they talked about writing papers jointly, albeit the ROs were typically excluded from this discussion. However, the reality was that virtually all output was written by team members from only one of the universities, in other words by individuals from the same disciplinary background. The only real output that was jointly produced was the final report that was written for the sponsoring Research Council. This had to be written jointly and present an integrated conceptual framework and analysis, in line with the initial project proposal. However, those involved were relatively dissatisfied with this output, feeling that it did not do justice to the richness of the independent parts of the research conducted at the separate university departments. While it is difficult to clearly evaluate the creativeness of such research, the grading of this final report, given by independent peer reviewers, did not rate this research project highly.

>> QUESTIONS

1. What knowledge boundaries existed between the members of Research Team?

2. How did interaction affect the development of trust in this project team? Was this different among the PI and RO groups?

3. What impact did integration mechanisms have on the development of trust?

4. How did power and conformity affect knowledge creation within this project team?

5. What does the Research Team case teach us about knowledge creation in multi-disciplinary/transdisciplinary contexts?

Summary of key learning points

>> Knowledge creation within organizations, leading to the development of new products, services or processes, typically occurs within teams and projects.

>> Both the intellectual and social capital of team members is important.

>> The process of knowledge creation within teams depends on achieving a synergy between members so that, through 'creative abrasion', something new and useful will emerge.

>> Knowledge sharing within a team will only be successful if there is some shared understanding or knowledge redundancy among team members such that the team develops an absorptive capacity for new ideas – this is not always easy to achieve in practice.

>> Syntactic, semantic and pragmatic knowledge boundaries exist between people from different backgrounds and these boundaries make it increasingly difficult to share knowledge, so that knowledge needs to be either transferred, translated or transformed depending on the type of boundary that exists.

>> Boundary objects (concrete objects or abstract concepts) play an important role in helping to overcome knowledge boundaries but the boundaries are often multiple and so difficult to overcome in practice.

>> Teams should not, therefore, be seen as a panacea for all organizational problems; nor should the problems of enabling effective team-working be underestimated.

>> Teams essentially consist of individuals, each of whom has his or her own agenda, and individuals may use their power to attempt to satisfy personal goals. Some individuals, however, have more power than others and so can more easily persuade the team to work in a way that satisfies their agendas.

>> Teams thus suffer from many potential problems, including a propensity to conformity, groupthink, social loafing and group polarization effects.

>> To overcome some of these problems there is a need to consider implementing integration mechanisms and in particular encouraging the development of trust between team members.

>> There are different types of trust that are important, including companion, competence and commitment trust. These three types of trust do not develop through the same mechanisms nor do they necessarily develop simultaneously.

>> Trust is not easy to develop, especially where team members come from very different backgrounds and so have different knowledge and understanding. In such situations, prolonged interaction and common experiences are necessary to develop the shared understanding necessary for trust to develop and knowledge sharing to be possible.

5

PROJECT-BASED ORGANIZATIONS AND KNOWLEDGE WORK

Chapter Outline

Learning Outcomes

At the end of this chapter you should be able to:

⇒ Understand why exploiting knowledge from projects is often difficult
⇒ Understand what is meant by learning boundaries
⇒ Understand why mechanisms used to facilitate the exploitation of knowledge from projects are often not very successful
⇒ Understand complex project contexts
⇒ Recognize why it is difficult to achieve high levels of project interactivity in some contexts

---

>> INTRODUCTION

As discussed in the previous chapter, much organizational work today takes place in projects, especially in relation to knowledge work and where the focus is innovation. We look at innovation more specifically in Chapter 9. Here we simply need to note that innovation processes in knowledge-intensive sectors are often described as being 'open' (Chesbrough, 2003a, b), or 'networked', especially where radical innovation is concerned. This emphasizes how, in the 'knowledge era', innovation increasingly relies on the production of knowledge through use, and involves knowledge integration across scientific, professional and organizational boundaries via multiple stakeholder groups (including users) involved in collaborative and reciprocal modes of working (Castells, 1996; Hardy et al., 2003; Okhuysen and Eisenhardt, 2002). Such collaboration across professional and organizational boundaries often occurs in projects.

In this chapter we explore some of the problems of working in projects – thus even while project-based forms of organizing allow for the kinds of collaboration that may be essential for innovation, these forms of organizing also create problems, in particular in relation to the sharing of knowledge across projects (we looked at some of the issues related to sharing knowledge within projects in the previous chapter on teams and knowledge creation). Thus, working in projects requires overcoming significant knowledge boundaries but the actual overcoming of these boundaries creates knock-on problems for the ability to exploit this knowledge in other contexts. Thus, while in the previous chapter we focused on the conditions that supported knowledge exploration (creation), including overcoming knowledge boundaries, in this chapter we look at the problems associated with knowledge exploitation arising from the very fact that most of the knowledge exploration activity within organizations (and indeed across organizations as we shall see) occurs within projects.

>> TEAMS VERSUS PROJECTS

In the previous chapter we focused on teams and knowledge creation. Projects are certainly a form of team-work in the sense that they involve multiple individuals working together to achieve some kind of objective. However, projects are also in some ways different from teams as we discuss in this section. These differences are important to understand as they influence some of the problems that are often experienced in projects, in relation to both problems within projects and problems across projects. We first consider the key characteristics of teams and then identify how projects are different to teams. This allows us to then explore some of the problems of working within and especially across projects.

Proehl (1997) reviewed articles written between 1992 and 1995 and concluded that the following were commonly defined characteristics of a (psychological) team:

- Shared identity – all members perceive themselves as part of a unit
- Common goal – all members are working towards a common goal

- Interdependence – all members have to contribute towards the task in some way
- Personal interaction – members communicate and share information with each other
- Mutual influence – each member influences every other member.

These features of teams are important in order to encourage effective knowledge sharing and so facilitate knowledge creation. However, these features of a team are often not present in the context of projects and it is projects that are typically used by organizations to create new products and services or to effect organizational change. Thus, even though we might talk about project *teams* the reality is that a project in an organizational context often does not have a fixed membership and the work undertaken in a project is often very temporary, fluid, interrupted and distributed. For example, innovation projects often involve a range of individuals (and organizations) who enter and leave the project at different points in time, depending on particular issues that arise, so that project members often work on several projects at once and may not identify themselves with the success of a particular project. As such, individuals involved may not necessarily see themselves as part of a (psychological) team and group goals, mutual interests and common understanding may be difficult to develop because there is no shared practice that unites project team members. Moreover, the tight deadlines that are often imposed on projects can mean that creativity is curtailed at the expense of expediency. Projects may, thus, operate to a 'logic of consequentiality' (i.e. which actions will produce the quickest acceptable outcomes) rather than a 'logic of appropriateness' (i.e. which actions will produce the optimal outcomes in the long term – March and Olsen, 1995). Lindkvist (2005), thus, suggests that 'collectivity' – that is a constellation of groups and individuals who temporarily share insights in order to achieve particular objectives – can sometimes be a better descriptor of project work than is 'community', which brings with it connotations of shared understandings and identity constructed and negotiated over time, as per a psychological team. This lack of a sense of 'community' (that is encouraged by shared practice) in project work can impede the development of trust that we saw in the previous chapter is so crucial for knowledge sharing.

Despite this caveat, projects can stimulate knowledge creation and be fertile sites for learning, precisely because they bring together individuals from different backgrounds to work collectively to achieve some kind of common objective, with the objective typically having something to do with creating something new – something that would not neatly fit within the mainstream organization, where routines are established to take care of day-to-day business. In achieving this learning, teams will need to overcome the various kinds of knowledge boundaries considered in the previous chapter and actually develop some level of community around a shared practice, at least if they are going to create knowledge. Ironically, however, the very ability of projects to develop new shared practices to overcome the knowledge boundaries created by organizational specialization also limits the extent to which projects are able to share what has been learnt with the rest of the organization. We consider this next before turning to other problems which inhibit learning from projects to the wider organization.

>> LEARNING BOUNDARIES VERSUS KNOWLEDGE BOUNDARIES

In understanding the problems associated with exploiting knowledge that has been created within a project, it is helpful to draw a distinction between knowledge boundaries (discussed in the previous chapter) and learning boundaries. Projects can facilitate flexible organizational responses to environmental contingencies, precisely because in projects, individuals are brought together to work collectively on a particular problem in ways that help them to overcome knowledge boundaries, integrate knowledge and so generate new ideas (albeit projects may not always be successful in overcoming these knowledge boundaries and creating knowledge, as we saw with the case at the end of the previous chapter). However, the more radical is the problem-solving and knowledge creation within a particular project, actually the more difficult will it be for the organization to learn from the project. In other words, the more knowledge boundaries within a project have been overcome to generate new shared practices at the project level, the greater will be the learning boundaries between the project and the organization. This is because the new shared practices at the project level are now very different from the practices elsewhere in the organization. In this sense, learning (i.e. knowledge creation) at the project level may actually inhibit learning at the organizational level. This illustrates how learning within organizations is 'nested' – occurring at different levels simultaneously, albeit the different levels of learning may not feed into each other. Thus, knowledge boundaries operate horizontally, reflecting divisions in practice and knowledge between specialized groups. Learning boundaries, on the other hand, operate vertically, across nested levels of learning (see Figure 5.1). We can unpack this further.

At the organizational level, the focus of learning is on establishing repeatability – ensuring that people follow the same practices in relation to the various customers, whether these customers are internal or external. Thus, no organization of any scale could survive for long if every situation was treated as an opportunity to learn and experiment to do things differently. Thus, at a university there are a multitude of routines that people follow to attract new students, register students, confer degrees, discipline students and so on. While routines can and do change over time, often through a gradual process of structuration, for those involved in a particular ongoing practice, there is little opportunity to experiment and create new ways of doing things. Indeed, not following the established procedure is often a disciplinary offense, even if the new practice may appear to be more effective. This is not to deny that much improvisation occurs within the context of individuals carrying out their daily work activities (Suchman, 1987); however, the degree of learning and improvisation is likely to be much higher for those involved in a project as compared to those engaged in routine work assignments.

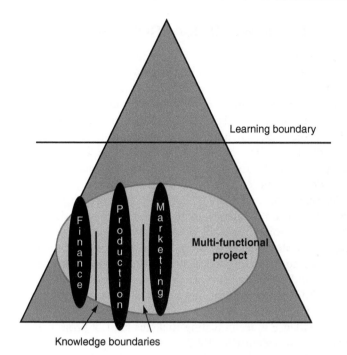

Figure 5.1   Learning and knowledge boundaries

At the project level, on the other hand, experimentation and knowledge creation is exactly what is required, because a project is trying to create new solutions to problems or opportunities. If nothing new was required, a project would not typically be set up. This then creates a learning boundary between the project and the organization – the new practices that are developed within the project are often so different to the ongoing practices within the organization; this makes it very difficult for the organization to learn from the project. For example, in a university setting, a project may be set up to design a new programme and new methods may be developed to recruit students to the programme; perhaps involving faculty members who were involved in the development of the programme actually doing a lot of the recruiting themselves, rather than relying on a central administrative team. However, other faculty who have not been involved in the project to develop the new programme are not going to easily accept and learn that they should be playing an active role in student recruitment – this is therefore a learning boundary. Such learning boundaries help to account for some of the difficulties of transferring knowledge across projects or more generally from projects to the wider organization.

Noting these difficulties of sharing knowledge across projects or from projects to the wider organization, many organizations have attempted to institute mechanisms to facilitate this sharing, we take a look at this next.

>> SHARING KNOWLEDGE ACROSS PROJECTS

The above indicates that exploiting knowledge that arises from projects is not easy. However, this does not mean that organizations do not try hard to facilitate this. Thus, organizations have recognized the importance of cross-project learning, and most project-management methodologies include practices aimed at exploiting knowledge that is created within a project. This typically involves maintaining project documentation and conducting project learning reviews. In these, project members are asked to capture the knowledge and learning from their project in the form of 'lessons learned' (Raelin, 2001). Often these reviews are done at the end of the project or when a project has met a particular milestone (Kotnour, 1999). Once the knowledge has been captured, the reviews are entered on databases, alongside other project documentation. The idea is that other project teams or organizational members more generally can then search these documents by project title, staff or keywords, assimilate the knowledge they contain, and so learn from them. These databases are typically computerized and, in larger firms, accessed via a corporate intranet. In this way, it is assumed, knowledge and learning can be shared across projects and reinvention can be avoided (Sharp, 2003).

However, evidence is accumulating that this kind of project review practice is not very helpful (Von Zedtwitz, 2002). For example, Keegan and Turner (2001) studied 18 project-based companies and found that all had post-project review practices in place. They also report that: 'In no single company did respondents express satisfaction with the process' (p. 90). These authors highlighted the main problem as a lack of time. Clearly if no 'lessons learned' are placed on the database because of pressure of time, then the exploitation of the knowledge will not occur as anticipated. It is also apparent that, even when databases exist, and time is available, there are limits to the extent that 'lessons learnt' are actually used (Kotnour, 1999). This suggests that we need to consider problems with the actual practice, not just the time available. For example, there is accumulating evidence that the medium for capture and transfer – that is through databases and intranets – is limited in terms of how far such technology can actually facilitate knowledge sharing (e.g. Walsham, 2002). We cover this more fully in Chapter 7, where we look at the use of ICT to share knowledge (i.e. Knowledge Management Systems – KMS). Here, we focus on the more general problems associated with sharing learning across projects, over and above, the problem of the existence of learning boundaries between projects and organizations, already discussed.

There seem to be a number of reasons why sharing learning across projects is often problematic, even when there are specific mechanisms in place to facilitate this:

Belief in uniqueness of context: It is not unusual to find several projects of a very similar nature going on in different parts of the organization but, typically, individuals do not necessarily see the connection between projects. The perceived uniqueness of projects means there is often a view that learning in the project is too specific to be relevant to the rest of the organization.

Standardization: While some teams see their project as unique other projects are seen as standard. Knowledge transfer is also restricted in these situations. Thus, in a construction company, many projects are repeat projects, such as warehouses where design routines are well established. These routines may work well when a project fits the normal template. However, where a project is different in some way, then this standard procedure becomes an inhibitor rather than a facilitator of the successful accomplishment of the project. Moreover, where new knowledge has been created in the context of these projects that do not fit the standard routines there is a reluctance to try and share this learning precisely because the particular project was deemed to be different and unique and so not relevant to the ongoing 'standard' projects, even though in reality most projects deemed 'standard' face unique circumstances so that this sharing of responses to the non-standard could be very useful.

Ability to capture and access 'softer' lessons: Project members also often find it difficult to capture and share what has been learnt about the process of actually doing the work; this is often referred to as 'softer learning'. For example, imagine a project has experienced problems dealing with an external consultant because they failed to specify their requirements clearly. Most projects do not attempt to capture and share the lessons that they have learnt about this process although they may capture what was actually achieved (or not) by the consultant.

Project reviews and milestones: Even where project reviews are part of the methodology, they are often not done systematically or with any real emphasis on learning. One reason why end-of-project reviews are often not very effective is because there is often a time lag between the completion of the project and the final review meeting, by which time people have moved on to other projects and so are not really interested in spending time reflecting on what was learnt in the previous project.

Lack of awareness that knowledge transfer is needed: Generally, people seek out knowledge only when they recognize they have a problem. For example, a software project may go wrong because it is implemented with insufficient testing. However, if those involved in the project are not aware of the importance of testing, they are not going to seek out knowledge about how much testing to do!

We can condense these issues and identify three important criteria in relation to successful knowledge exploitation from projects. First, there must be some knowledge actually created at the project-team level. Second, the team must be knowledgeable enough to realize that there is indeed knowledge that exists beyond the confines of the project that could be useful to help to improve progress on their project. Finally, the knowledge that exists in documents that have attempted to capture 'lessons learnt' must actually be useful to others. Importantly, in the context of exploiting knowledge from projects, these criteria are often not satisfied – there is limited project-level learning, there is a lack of awareness that there is knowledge available that could be helpful and the knowledge that is captured is often not the most useful for other projects to learn from.

Relating to the first criterion, where those involved in projects approach the tasks mechanistically (Knights and Wilmott, 1997) – each project member working independently on a set of clearly defined tasks or processes with which he/she is familiar using his/her existing knowledge – then there is no real project-level learning. We defined this as a multi-disciplinary mode of working in the previous chapter. Individuals may learn through this process but there is no collective level of learning and so there is no project-level knowledge to exploit. We will discuss this issue a little further below. Suffice to say now, where projects are approached in this kind of mechanistic way, the level of creativity that is actually fostered is likely to be negligible. It is like a group of students being given a project assignment, but instead of working together they divide up the assignment and each does a little piece and then they add the pieces together. Individuals may have learnt from their small piece of the assignment but they will not have learnt from each other or created any collective level of knowledge. You can also see that approached like this, knowledge boundaries are not confronted, even though they may well exist.

Relating to the second criterion, project team members typically only seek out knowledge beyond the confines of their project when they are experiencing a problem that they cannot solve with their existing knowledge. As long as things go 'more or less to plan' there is typically no attempt to learn from others. The supply of knowledge on intranets therefore often goes unused because the corresponding demand for this knowledge does not exist. The lack of demand for knowledge is particularly acute at certain points in the project life cycle, for example, when deadlines are approaching. So while milestones and review points are potentially opportunities for reflection regarding process, in reality many project only focus on deliverables at these points.

Given this common problem of failing to seek out prior knowledge that may be helpful in relation to avoiding previous mistakes that have been made, intermediaries can play a very useful role. For example, programme managers can operate as important intermediaries – they over-see several projects and, so, can identify how knowledge created on one project might be useful to another project, even when the other project does not recognize that it could usefully use prior knowledge.

Intermediaries can, thus, act as the bridge for exploiting knowledge arising from a project across an organization. However, they are more likely to connect people personally rather than connect people to documents. It is not that the project team members lack the tacit knowledge or the 'absorptive capacity' (Cohen and Levinthal, 1990) to make use of explicit knowledge, but rather that the explicit knowledge is typically simply of the wrong type to be useful. This is because the documents that exist tend to focus very much on what has been achieved by a project team (we can call this product knowledge) rather than how this has been achieved and/or why it either worked or did not work (i.e. process knowledge). Yet product knowledge concerns the specific objectives of a project (what we do/did) and is unlikely to be helpful in other contexts precisely because project objectives tend to be unique. What might be more useful is knowledge about the process (how we do/did things) since this has a potentially much wider relevance for others in an organization. For example, referring to the project described above to design a new academic programme in a university. The project members will create documents about the new programme, but are much less likely to create documents that articulate what worked well and what worked less well in terms of the actual processes they used to get to the point of being able to create the new programme – whether they started with too big/small a group, whether the division of tasks was effective, whether the frequency of meetings was adequate and so on.

In the chapter to this point we have stressed the problems of sharing knowledge from projects to the wider organization. In reality, the problem is actually even more acute than this, because actually the sharing of knowledge will often require inter-organizational sharing and will often involve not merely 'nice to transfer' types of knowledge but essential transfer to keep an innovation process going. We turn to this next.

>> DIFFERENT TYPES OF PROJECT CONTEXT

Existing research on project-based organizing assumes that projects have certain characteristics. In particular, they are described as relatively autonomous, with project work being more or less detached from the history and context of the host organization (Hobday, 2000); indeed we examined this issue above in relation to the learning boundaries that exist between a project and the wider organization. Thus, Engwall (2003) describes projects as 'lonely phenomena'. From this perspective, projects are viewed as being initiated to accomplish pre-specified goals and objectives, within a defined period of time, and in a relatively autonomous way, unencumbered by established organizational routines and practice. Indeed, it is this relative autonomy, and the degree of decision discretion that this confers on project members, that is seen to promote innovation, by allowing organizations to respond more flexibly and speedily to external demands and to work across organizational and disciplinary boundaries (even though, as we have seen, this can also make it difficult to exploit knowledge created from a project more widely across an organization). This emphasis on project autonomy has led researchers to focus on how to organize and manage work within projects and project teams – that is at a project level of analysis – seeing projects as an important locus for knowledge creation and innovation.

However, it is now being recognized that single, stand-along projects are not the only type of project-context. Thus, Desouza and Evaristo (2004) recently distinguished between three types of project, other than the traditional single project:

1. Projects that are part of a co-located programme; here multiple projects run concurrently at one location. For example, designing a new car typically involves multiple projects that each work on a different part of the design. Traditionally, this work has been done at the development site of a car company,

with each project reporting to a programme director whose role is to coordinate the different projects to ensure that they are developing solutions that are compatible. Being co-located there is also a lot of potential opportunity for those involved in the different projects to communicate with one another.

2. The distributed project; which is a single endeavour conducted from multiple locations, often involving different organizations. For example, a software development project is often now undertaken at different locations, with certain parts of the development work, outsourced to a different organization. India has obviously been the prime site for this kind of outsourcing software work, although today there are several other countries where outsourcing is becoming common, including China and Eastern Europe. In this type of project, members in the home country would typically do the requirements definitional work, while members in the outsource company would do the development and maybe the testing work.

3. Multiple projects run at multiple locations. This type of project context is the most complex because it requires managing multiple interdependencies across time and space. For example, in developing a new drug, the initial basic research is typically initiated in a project in a PRO (public research organization, e.g. a university). Here, the focus of the project work is to discover and isolate biological agents and mechanisms that, for example, cause disease. 'Breakthroughs' are patented in the hope that they might facilitate the development of new treatments. Since the role of PROs is not, primarily, product development, patents are commonly acquired and commercialized by private firms who will actually acquire intellectual property (IP) from several different projects in order to develop a drug through the lengthy clinical trials process. The knowledge from all these various projects must be integrated to allow the innovation process to continue.

This typology suggests that managing across projects (not just sharing knowledge across projects to limit reinvention) is as important as managing within projects because knowledge often needs to be brought together from multiple projects.

>> COMPLEX PROJECT CONTEXTS

The above indicates that there are different types of project context. Two aspects of this project context appear to be most significant in terms of our understanding the issues that are likely to arise in the management of projects – the complexity of the project context and the degree of interdependence across projects, as depicted in Figure 5.2.

Looking first at the complexity of the context, along the vertical axis, the distribution of project work can vary to a greater or lesser degree along three main dimensions: organizational, spatial and temporal. That is, there can be one or many organizations involved; projects can be co-located or spatially distributed; and/or projects can be worked on simultaneously or distributed across time.

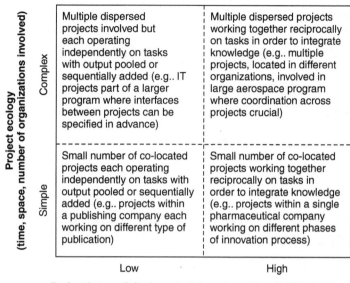

Figure 5.2   Complex project contexts

Thus, the complexity of the project context can vary from low to high. We refer to this dimension as the project ecology as it represents the ecosystem of the different projects that are linked in some way.

The second dimension of the figure, along the horizontal axis, represents the degree of interdependence between projects, which can also vary from high to low. Thus, in some complex project contexts there may be few interdependencies – for example, where projects are merely encouraged to share 'lessons learned' in order to reduce 'reinvention' and encourage exploitation of knowledge (Prusak, 1997). However, in projects involved in an ongoing innovation process, interdependencies are likely to be significant. In such situations, interdependence between projects is the result of the dual requirements to divide knowledge (and labour) in order to complete specialist work and to integrate different knowledge domains (e.g. scientific, technological, commercial) in the innovation process. It is these differences in the respective knowledge resources of each project that create interdependencies, with each project often conducting a particular type of specialist work that produces knowledge that must be integrated with the knowledge produced by specialists in another project. How these interdependencies are handled is crucial to the ongoing sustainability of the innovation process in a complex project context.

Thompson (1967) identified three different types of interdependency – pooled, sequential and reciprocal. Whilst Thompson (1967) viewed task interdependence as deriving from the technologies deployed, others argue that interdependencies are not technologically determined but, rather, are characteristic of the way people behave and act in designing and carrying out tasks. For example, assembly-line workers who help each other in a lean production 'cell' are more task interdependent than those who do not (Wageman, 1995). Viewed in this way, a key difference between forms of interdependence is the degree of collaboration among the parties involved. In pooled and sequential interdependence there is little collaboration as tasks are handed over; whereas, in contrast, reciprocal interdependence involves continuous collaboration and knowledge flows to and from projects. We, thus, refer to this dimension as project interactivity as it represents the degree of interactivity between the different linked projects.

>> RADICAL INNOVATION AND HIGH PROJECT INTERACTIVITY

In some contexts radical innovation is the goal; that is, innovation processes are aimed at creating very different and sometimes disruptive ways of doing things (Christensen et al., 2000), as for example, the development of selling music over the Internet to be downloaded to a device rather than selling CDs. In these contexts, reciprocal interdependence (i.e. high project interactivity) is likely to be necessary. This is because, as Carlile (2004) notes, where tasks are knowledge-intensive and high in novelty, and where outcomes are unknown (or unknowable) in advance (as in radical innovation), there is a need to transform, and not simply transfer knowledge, across the parties involved because knowledge boundaries will be greater. In other words, one would predict that objectifying or 'blackboxing' (Scarbrough, 1995) the knowledge produced and, so, passing it from one more or less independent project to another, in a pooled or sequential way (e.g. simply acquiring a patent from a previous project), will not allow for the kinds of transformation that are necessary. Rather, knowledge produced across projects would need to be mutually constituted through a more continuous, reciprocal form of collaboration between the parties involved. In this sense those involved in the different projects would need to work in a transdisciplinary, rather than a multi-disciplinary way. Actors, thus, are required to engage in negotiating and bargaining in order to create common rules of action, in particular where different groups have something to lose if a practice changes, as is the case with disruptive technologies.

This indicates that in complex project contexts, where knowledge is produced from multiple, distributed projects, a high level of project interactivity is required in order to manage the interdependencies and keep the innovation process moving forward, as depicted in Figure 5.2. In other words, in knowledge-intensive domains, where innovation is characterized by relatively long, complex, systemic and high-risk product development cycles (e.g. biomedical, aerospace), high project interactivity needs to be the norm. However, this type of context also poses distinctive challenges for the coordination of project work and knowledge integration.

One response to these challenges could be to coordinate projects through an umbrella programme (Evaristo and Van Fenema, 1999). However, in the early development episodes of some kinds of innovation projects, such as medical innovation or complex engineering programmes, there is much that is unknowable in advance and interacting projects are often not governed by a programme with pre-defined super-ordinate goals to coordinate project tasks. Instead, projects are brought together in a rather more haphazard, opportunistic way as different 'pieces' of the scientific and commercial 'jigsaw' converge or collide over time. Product development often follows what Lampel (2001) describes as a 'switching' strategy, with those involved 'seeking high quality opportunities wherever they might be found; trying to capture these opportunities, and then turning their attention to transforming these opportunities into revenues' (p. 480).

At the same time, however, complex project contexts pose significant barriers to knowledge integration because there are often pragmatic knowledge boundaries (see previous chapter) that are encountered which can impede project interactivity. We look at these special problems next.

>> PROBLEMS ENCOUNTERED IN COMPLEX PROJECT CONTEXTS

In complex project contexts pragmatic knowledge boundaries are likely to be acute. For example, taking a medical example, there may be an opportunity to develop a medical innovation that potentially allows a patient to be treated by their GP in a local practice rather than by a surgeon in a hospital. However, the surgeons in the hospital may refuse to work with the GPs in order to bring this innovation into reality. Two issues thus become relevant in dealing with these contexts. One is related to power dynamics in the inter-organizational context and its effect on knowledge integration, and another is related to the knowledge regime (in particular the Intellectual Property or IP framework) of many high-tech industries.

With respect to the latter, it is not always clear what part of a discovery can be patented and whether and how this knowledge can be protected. For example, in relation to medical innovation, it is often not the molecule itself, but knowledge about how to use it and what its effects are, that is of most value; knowledge which cannot be easily protected via a patent. Similarly, in software development, it is difficult to protect the software because it is so easy to work around the code, as evidenced by Apple's difficulties in protecting its iPhones from being unlocked and so used on any network. This makes knowledge sharing problematic as the financial transactions between the parties involved are based on the value of IP, and this can be diminished if too much information is shared, even between formal partners. Given the often fragmented nature of the development process, organizations will guard their knowledge (e.g. in the form of IP), meaning that 'pieces' of knowledge and technology tend to be transferred on the back of economic transactions. Each party will be focused on obtaining maximum value from the knowledge derived from a particular project. In this way, instead of taking a collaborative, more trust-based, approach that might maximize the chance of success in future development, firms adopt a 'black boxing' strategy focused on securing a good return on the investments already made. We see this issue very clearly in the two cases at the end of this chapter.

The issue of the value of knowledge derived from IP protection is closely related to inter-organizational power dynamics. Hardy and Phillips (1998) identify three important aspects of inter-organizational power dynamics: formal authority, critical resources and discursive legitimacy. Formal authority refers to the recognized, legitimate right to make a decision. In a complex project context, however, such power is often ambiguous – it can rest with one particular project or be distributed across projects and/or shift over time. This can create problems for knowledge sharing across projects.

In the case of critical resources, if one project relies on another for such resources as information, money, equipment, the dependent project is at a power disadvantage, as depicted by resource dependency theory (Pfeffer and Salancik, 1978). Thus, by having power based on resources (including knowledge), one organization can exercise power over its partner by controlling resources. This can create problems for knowledge sharing as the more powerful partner project may be able to withhold resources from the less powerful partner project, if this is in its interests. Thus, although complementarities between knowledge resources may bring partners together, ultimately the effort placed on knowledge integration may be restricted by these power-dependency relationships. In this way, aligning interests and, more importantly, sustaining alignment of interests when the inevitable twists and turns of fortune occur become crucial but also very difficult to achieve.

Finally, discursive legitimacy arises from the ability of one interest group to legitimize their demands and 'de-legitimize' the demands of others by the management of meaning (Pettigrew, 1973). For instance, having a scientific reputation may afford one project team more influence over decisions than its resource-rich partner. In this way, knowledge integration in complex project contexts should be seen as involving a range of actors negotiating and bargaining between different perspectives and identities within shifting relations and domains of power. This is likely to mean that in many cases knowledge from the interdependent projects will not be effectively integrated because interdependencies between projects will be managed sequentially or in a pooled fashion, without the level of reciprocity that is required. This is illustrated in the case at the end of this chapter.

>> CONCLUSION

Exploiting knowledge that is created within a particular project – so that it can be reused in other contexts or integrated with knowledge created in other projects – is not easy. In this chapter we have examined a number of reasons for this. One particular problem occurs because of the nested nature of the learning within organizations, which creates what we have called 'learning boundaries'; that is boundaries between learning that happens at one level (e.g. during knowledge creation in projects) and learning at other levels (e.g. following routines that standardize organizational processes). While organizations have recognized that this is a problem, the mechanisms that have been introduced to try and facilitate this knowledge exploitation from projects are not always very effective. We identified three particular issues that help to account for this – because sometimes little collective knowledge is created because of the way tasks are divided up; because sometimes those involved in projects do not realize that there is or that they could usefully use knowledge that has been produced in previous projects; and finally because often the knowledge that is codified from projects is product (what was produced) rather than process (the processes that accounted for the creation of this product – whether successful or unsuccessful) knowledge, which is actually less useful, given that projects are often focused on developing unique products.

These problems related to the exploitation of knowledge arising from projects become even more acute in contexts where the knowledge is not just potentially useful, but essential, for example in complex project ecologies which demand high levels of interactivity among projects. In such contexts, reciprocal approaches to managing interdependencies between projects are more likely to be successful. However, we also examined the reasons why it is often difficult to manage interdependencies more reciprocally, in particular because of the short-term need to maximize the return from the IP that is produced in a project and because of the power dynamics that complicate all kinds of inter-organizational relationships. The opportunity to explore these issues is provided below in the two cases that are described.

CASE STUDY 5.1
THERAGNOSTIC AND SKIN CASES

Below you will find two different cases that each describe different approaches to managing across projects.

>> THERAGNOSTIC

DiagnosticLabs is a small private company in the United Kingdom specializing in the development, manufacture and distribution of diagnostic assays for a number of diseases. In early 2004, DiagnosticLabs initiated a new 'THERAGNOSTIC' development project, where they hoped to combine one of their diagnostics with a new therapeutic, the logic being that availability of a drug would increase the market for the diagnostic, and vice versa. They had multiple options in terms of the disease area to go for, and in the end decided on a specific inflammatory disease characterized by a high mortality rate where currently there is no approved treatment.

The new project aimed to build upon a diagnostics kit that had been developed through an earlier project within DiagnosticLabs. Whilst DiagnosticLabs' development team continued to develop this diagnostic, at the same time its strategic team, championed by the CEO, began to look for a partner to develop the associated therapeutic. There were again multiple options here and the CEO used her personal connections to identify a company (TherapeuticCo) that held IP that could be used to develop this therapeutic. However, being traditionally a diagnostics company, DiagnosticLabs lacked clinical trials and regulatory experience and so, again via the personal networks of the CEO, formed an alliance with a third organization, Bioclinical, who specialized in clinical trials consulting and services, to conduct 'due diligence' on the therapeutic. The THERAGNOSTIC project was therefore initiated, bringing together IP from projects previously conducted at DiagnosticLabs and TherapeuticCo, with a team at Bioclinical providing the regulatory and commercial expertise. The logic of the alliance between the three companies was based on their complementarities in terms of resources and expertise:

> It could be an interesting conglomerate of a company that has IP and availability of a diagnostic with a therapeutic company that wanted to out-license some of their non-core technology and a group that can actually bring the two together and make it work.
>
> (CEO, Bioclinical)

It was originally believed that the IP from TherapeuticCo was supported by sufficiently robust pre-clinical data to allow the THERAGNOSTIC project to go straight to human clinical trials. However, the Bioclinical due diligence project revealed that whilst the preclinical data seemed reasonable, there were anomalies in the ways the trials were conducted (some years previously by TherapeuticCo) that they believed would cause problems in getting FDA approval (e.g. notes from the original experiments were sub-standard and only a single dose study had been done). Bioclinical concluded that an additional investment in multiple-dose pre-clinical trials would be required, especially if they were to convince venture capitalists to provide the investment needed. That this had not been picked up earlier reflected DiagnosticLabs' lack of regulatory expertise, rather than a lack of scientific expertise – the DiagnosticLabs scientific team had to understand biological mechanisms underpinning the disease in order to have developed their original diagnostic. Nevertheless, it implied significant additional financial investment, with Bioclinical estimating an extra nine months of work costing around $1 million. TherapeuticCo's intentions were not distrusted by DiagnosticsLabs. Rather, the problem was put down to the fact that the IP development project in TherapeuticCo had happened some time before and that this particular project had never been core to their product portfolio, so TherapeuticCo were unaware themselves of the problems.

> [TherapeuticCo] represented what they had as best they could. Everything we did was picking up somebody's technology that they decided not to commercialize. You know, it's a little bit like this box here. You've got to look through the boxes and find out whether you've got something that's good, and until you've actually got the boxes in your possession, you know, you don't come across the Rembrandt and find that the Rembrandt's a fake.
>
> (CEO, DiagnosticLabs)

From TherapeuticCo's point of view, making additional investments in pre-clinical development of a non-core area did not meet their interests, which were to license out the available IP at minimum additional cost. Up to this point the different projects had interacted largely informally (Bioclinical having conducted due diligence on a 'goodwill' basis in anticipation of a future share in the project), and none of the partners were willing to make the additional investments needed to move the project forward. Therefore, THERAGNOSTIC was eventually abandoned.

>> SKIN CASE

Cell is a medium-sized biotechnology company located on the US west coast, which started as a university spin-out. The foundational project for Cell was to develop a product called 'SKIN' in the area of regenerative medicine based on tissue engineering. Internal development work on SKIN resulted in an IND application to start clinical trials. At that time, however, the Cell team realized that they did not have the commercial expertise to market the product, so they licensed out the global sales and marketing rights of the product to GlobalPharma, which had a division that sold immunosuppressive drugs to support transplantations. GlobalPharma believed that organ transplantation would ultimately be replaced by tissue-reengineering and so wanted to move into this technology area, despite the fact that it was (and remains) an as-yet unproven technology commercially. The idea was that Cell would continue to do the development project work and conduct the early phase clinical trials, using the money from the license agreement from GlobalPharma, as well as commission a new project to scale up manufacturing capacity. GlobalPharma committed to setting up a project to commercialize the product and, later, a project to conduct the final phases of clinical trials.

This collaboration involved projects being conducted in two very different companies. Cell was described as 'a small research lab...There wasn't even a person here could spell the word "marketing". There were 250 PhDs (this number was used figuratively) doing cutting-edge research and some of that research was at the level of Nobel Prizes'. Meanwhile GlobalPharma was described as 'a huge, multinational corporation...high complexity, a lot of management layers, a lot of politics, not particularly agile in reacting to your partners' needs'. Soon after closing the deal, major problems began to emerge. For instance, the products manufactured by Cell were being sold to GlobalPharma at a price that was below what it was actually costing Cell. This was because Cell had not known, when the deal to work with GlobalPharma was agreed, what the actual cost of its production was. The GlobalPharma project team also began to realize that their initial sales projections were unrealistic because the clinical trials had led them to appreciate that selling SKIN was very different to selling a 'pill'. SKIN, they came to realize, was actually more similar to a medical device in terms of its adoption curve because of the need for GlobalPharma sales representatives to work intensively with the clinicians, teaching them to use the product; while selling a 'pill' merely required them to get the clinicians' attention and so persuade them to prescribe this – not easy but not requiring the same level of one-on-one work as teaching clinicians to use a new medical device.

Moreover, GlobalPharma had assumed that they would market the product to dermatologists with whom they had strong sales links. However, it transpired that it was surgeons who were treating the ulcers SKIN was being used for in the trials.

> We had to build up those networks with surgeons. Besides that, you need to understand the reimbursement environment; you need to understand how a doctor or a medical center can make money or at least not lose money by using the product; how to use it; when to use it; you also have to understand the underlying disease. [GlobalPharma] simply did not have the sales force to cope with this level of complexity.
>
> (Project Manager, Cell)

This led to tensions between the respective product development teams with sceptics in GlobalPharma pointing out: 'it's going to be 0.01% of our revenue; it's 20% of our headaches; Why don't we just get out of it?' Others were still supporting the project: ' this is very innovative; it's good for our PR; it's still a pilot project, and we have certain obligations to our contractual partner, [Cell]'. At about this time, the Cell team started to request a renegotiation of the contract because they realized that they could not go on losing money on every sample of SKIN that they were supplying to GlobalPharma. This request allowed the sceptics to gain the upper-hand and so accelerated GlobalPharma's decision to abandon their project, leaving Cell at significant financial risk. However, because the clinical trials had involved using the product in some life-saving operations, Globalpharma could not be associated with letting Cell simply collapse, so they agreed a significant financial settlement with Cell and gave them back the global marketing and sales rights for SKIN. In this way, Cell continued the development of SKIN, albeit without the continued support of GlobalPharma.

>> QUESTIONS

1. Describe the project ecology that is depicted by each of these cases.
2. What type of project interdependency is represented by each case?
3. What influenced the organizations involved in each case to adopt the particular approach to managing their project interdependencies?
4. What might they have done differently to have encouraged a more successful outcome in each case?

Summary of key learning points

>> Projects are often used to facilitate knowledge creation within organizations and they can be successful at this (as attested by the multitude of innovative products and services that are created by organizations) even though they can lack some of the characteristics of psychological teams that facilitate creativity.

>> Exploiting knowledge that is created within projects can be difficult because of learning boundaries that can exist between projects and the broader organization.

>> Most project-management methodologies include mechanisms that are aimed at facilitating knowledge exploitation from projects, but these are often not very successful.

>> Knowledge exploitation from projects can be difficult because of a deficit of collective knowledge, because of a lack of awareness that useful knowledge is available and because the knowledge that is available is often not very useful because it focuses on product and not process knowledge.

>> Problems of sharing knowledge across projects are especially pertinent in contexts where there are significant interdependencies between projects.

>> How such interdependencies are managed is often crucial to the success of an innovation process, with high levels of project interactivity important.

>> High levels of project interactivity are often thwarted by pervasive knowledge regimes and by inter-organizational dynamics.

6

HUMAN RESOURCE MANAGEMENT AND KNOWLEDGE WORK

Chapter Outline

>> Learning Outcomes
>> Introduction
>> Challenges for HRM
>> Existing HRM Approaches to Knowledge Work

>> Conclusions
>> Case Study 6.1: Buckman Labs
>> Summary of Key Learning Points

Learning Outcomes

At the end of this chapter you should be able to:

⇒ Analyse knowledge work within the context of the employment relationship.

⇒ Identify the major Human Resource Management (HRM) challenges created by knowledge work.

⇒ Evaluate the potential impact of HRM policies on the performance of knowledge worker groups.

⇒ Review the HRM problems of ensuring both commitment and control in the management of knowledge workers.

⇒ Identify major trends towards outsourcing and contingent work in the employment of knowledge workers.

⇒ Analyse the major HRM approaches to knowledge work.

⇒ Understand the contribution of HRM factors to knowledge sharing and innovation within organizations.

>> INTRODUCTION

One recurring feature of all the chapters in this book – even those chapters dealing with more technical issues – is the central role played by human activity and potential in the development of knowledge work. Put simply, knowledge work depends on the capacity, motivation and performance of knowledge workers. This chapter will explore this human dimension further by highlighting the 'worker' aspect of knowledge work – the fact that most of those doing knowledge work are employees of organizations. Now, as we will show, in some settings knowledge workers are a distinctive group who are treated differently from other groups of employees. Nonetheless, setting aside the self-employed ranks of freelance workers, consultants and partners, most knowledge workers are still *employees*. As such, an important strand in the way they are managed comes from the Human Resource Management policies and practices of their employing organization. These not only influence the recruitment, selection and training of knowledge workers, but also the rewards provided to motivate good performance and the development of career tracks designed to retain them within the firm.

This aspect of knowledge work is sometimes neglected in existing debates because there is understandably much more interest, in what is new and different about knowledge workers. This deflects attention away from what they share with other groups, namely, their status as employees who are hired by an employer to do a particular job. Of course, the employment relationship is only one of the ways in which firms can access the services of knowledge workers. Indeed, other ways of contracting for such services – as, for example, in 'outsourcing' arrangements – are discussed later in this chapter. However, the employment relationship remains dominant and can be highly flexible, giving the employer the ability to direct knowledge workers' expertise according to the shifting needs created by customer demand, technological innovation and market requirements. As such, it still has many advantages, especially for forms of knowledge work which are difficult to specify in a formal contract, such as team-based skills and non-standardized or tacit forms of knowledge.

The management function which is principally responsible for designing and regulating the employment relationship is often labeled the 'Human Resource Management' or HRM function. The label itself reflects some of the effects which the increasing number of knowledge workers is having on organizations. The term 'HRM' was to a significant extent spawned by high-tech organizations in the United States, notably firms such as IBM, Xerox and Hewlett Packard (Guest, 1990). These companies had found that previous labels used to designate the management of employees – 'Personnel' or 'Labour Relations', for instance – did not do justice to the role which a new group of knowledge workers played in the organization. Previous approaches tended to define the role of employees essentially in terms of their effort or labour – just 'pairs of hands' as Henry Ford famously put it. However, as these firms discovered, the role played by knowledge workers extended some way beyond this description. Where other workers were seen as labour costs to be minimized, knowledge workers were seen more positively – they were *human resources* not costs. It followed that the recruitment, training and development of this group could actually be seen as an investment for the firm because these knowledge workers had the potential to be a productive resource.

While the HRM label has been widely adopted, actual policy and practice can vary enormously from one organization to another. In some organizations, for example, the HRM function has little more than an administrative role, handling the paperwork associated with processes of recruitment and selection, appraisal and reward. In others, it may play a more important role in helping to deliver business strategy. There are relatively few boardrooms, however, where the HR function has a strong voice in influencing the direction of business strategy.

This is not to say that top managers can only develop effective HRM policies and practices where the HR function is powerful. Wherever businesses recognize the value of their employees' contribution – and this is often where the employees are knowledge workers – there is likely to be more attention to recruiting, motivating and retaining employees as a vital part of the organization's strategy. This is certainly reflected in the experience of the knowledge-intensive firms discussed in Chapter 2. Given this experience, the emphasis in this chapter is not on the HR function itself but on the HRM policies and practices which organizations can apply to knowledge workers as a an employee group in order to nurture an effective environment for knowledge work.

>> CHALLENGES FOR HRM

As discussed in previous chapters, knowledge work can take many different forms and can therefore pose a wide range of challenges for organizations. In discussing HRM for knowledge workers then, we need to be wary of generalizing too far about what knowledge workers want from employers, or how employers treat them as a group. As highlighted by the Baron et al. framework in Chapter 2, for instance, knowledge workers can develop many different kinds of attachment to their organizations – everything from 'love' to 'money'. This being said, however, once we allow for this variation across organizations and societies, existing research does suggest some recurring challenges arising from managing knowledge workers.

One consequence of the knowledge worker's expertise, for instance, is that such workers tend to operate in tight labour markets where demand from employers exceeds supply. As the discussion of 'gold collar workers' in Chapter 2 underlined, this gives knowledge workers a degree of labour market power. In other words, because they have more ability to pick and choose their employer, they enjoy greater bargaining power than many other employees. Such power is important in allowing knowledge workers to resist changes in work practices, as we saw in the Uni case in Chapter 3. It also helps to explain the high level of expectations which knowledge workers are seen as bringing to their jobs. Enhanced by their educational background, but – crucially – reinforced by their labour market power, knowledge workers typically expect to be given interesting and varied work rather than follow a prescribed routine (Davenport et al., 1996).

As discussed in Chapter 2 – and again closely intertwined with the scarcity of their expertise in the marketplace – is the degree of autonomy which knowledge workers enjoy in their work compared to other groups. In most other areas of organizational life, control is exercised either directly over the work process itself, by specifying the standards, methods and pace of work (*behavioural control*), or by specifying and measuring the outputs of work (*output control*). But knowledge work is difficult for managers to observe, and its outputs are unpredictable and hard to specify. As a result, knowledge workers enjoy a good deal of autonomy. They may have to account for their time (as, e.g. with the use of detailed timesheets for consultants, professionals and technical staff) but they do not have to account for their actions in the detailed way that other employees do. The result is that whereas other workers are often tightly controlled through technological systems or behavioural routines, knowledge workers have more freedom to determine their own work practices.

We need to be careful not to overstate how much autonomy knowledge workers have. They do not typically enjoy the 'strategic autonomy' to set their own goals. These are defined by top management and the needs of the organization's strategy. But, within this framework, they do have more 'operational autonomy' to decide how they will achieve these goals (Bailyn, 1988). What this means in practice is that the knowledge worker is able to exercise a good deal of discretion over key behaviours affecting their performance. Behaviours such as cooperating with others, protecting the organization, and self-development have to be volunteered by knowledge workers and cannot simply be commanded by managers. Crucially, knowledge sharing, which we have highlighted as a vital process in knowledge work, is also a voluntary behaviour, and needs to be distinguished from the reporting of information which is mandated by organizational routines (Davenport and Prusak, 1997).

This autonomy enjoyed by knowledge workers has been shown to be an important ingredient in individual and group performance (Amabile et al., 1996). It is underpinned not only by their own personal expertise but also by their ability to acquire and exploit sources of knowledge and legitimacy which are external to the organization. These external sources sometimes take the form of professional associations or other formal bodies, but they are more often informal, occupationally based networks which may span many organizations or even sectors. In some instances, these networks can be just as important to knowledge workers as their employer organization, providing them not only with a defined professional identity but also with access to a knowledge base and a wider range of job opportunities, as discussed more fully in Chapter 8.

Control and commitment

From the employer standpoint, one of the most important consequences of the relative freedom enjoyed by knowledge workers is a heightened need to ensure that their autonomy and discretion is applied for the benefit of the organization.

This challenge was one of the important, if sometimes, unspoken, ingredients in the development of HRM as a management discipline. Early writers on HRM contrasted the traditional emphasis on control with HRM's pursuit of 'commitment'. Control involved tightly prescribed job designs, a focus on stable, measurable performance and direction through rules. In contrast, an emphasis on employee commitment required flexible, team-based job designs, the pursuit of improvement and change, and direction through shared values and culture (Walton, 1985).

Commitment can take a variety of different forms. Continuance commitment, for example, simply denotes an intention to carry on in an existing job. This may have little or no implications for the individual's motivation and behaviour. Where commitment is affective, however, and embraces a positive attitude towards the organization, it may be an important factor in eliciting the voluntary behaviours highlighted earlier. Knowledge sharing, in particular, is more likely to occur where employees view their organization positively (Thompson and Heron, 2006).

The emphasis which the early HRM literature placed on commitment tended to locate it at the opposite end of the spectrum to management control. While it is certainly true that commitment can be an alternative to control for employers seeking strategies to achieve high performance, more recent work has tended to see these strategies not as mutually exclusive but as complementary. Thus, the development of the kind of supportive organization culture highlighted in Chapter 2 is sometimes seen not simply as a way of gaining employee commitment but as another form of control which seeks to shape the identity of the employee (Kunda, 1992). Some critical writers argue that this form of cultural, indirect control is one of the most insidious aspects of HRM because it shapes the employee's identity and enlists their autonomy in the pursuit of corporate goals (Willmott, 1993).

Even if we see this as too Machiavellian a view of HRM, it is clear that control and commitment tend to co-exist in the management of knowledge work, because organizations are unwilling to rely wholly on the voluntary commitment of their employees to ensure good performance. This co-existence is always precarious, however, because of the contradictory logics of commitment and control. A good example of this is what has been termed 'the vicious circle of control'. As Crozier describes it, this cycle operates as follows: attempts to impose new controls on employees reduce their commitment, with the result that performance deteriorates. Faced by deteriorating performance, managers impose even greater controls, leading to a downward spiral of further loss of commitment, declines in performance and so on (Crozier, 1964).

Outsourcing and offshoring

The difficulties of pursuing control and commitment simultaneously have led many organizations to see-saw back and forth between different kinds of policy for their knowledge workers. Within the last decade or so, though, we have seen a decisive shift away from managing such workers within the conventional hierarchy of the firm, as organizations have made increasing moves to develop alternative, and less costly forms of control. These include the re-engineering of work and the use of IT systems to monitor knowledge workers' activities. Re-engineering involves a shift away from functional silos and towards an integrated, cross-organizational work process, as described in Chapter 3. This approach was adopted by many organizations as a way of gaining greater transparency of the work process, and thereby increasing the accountability of knowledge worker groups to both managers and customers (Davenport et al., 1996). Similar motives lay behind the extensive deployment of ICT-based monitoring systems, described in Chapter 7.

More radically, however, some sectors have moved beyond these strategies by 'outsourcing' knowledge work altogether. This involves subcontracting knowledge work functions to external service suppliers. IT professionals and HR managers have been particularly affected by the outsourcing of their work. In some sectors, outsourcing also increasingly means 'offshoring' as work is relocated offshore (e.g. from the UK or USA to sites in India and China).

As explicit management strategies, outsourcing and offshoring have really gathered pace in the last decade or so, spurred on by the example set by leading multinational firms such as Kodak and American Express. Over time, the emphasis has shifted away from simple cost reduction towards a desire to re-focus the business on its core competencies. Activities which are 'non-core' thus become candidates for outsourcing (Lewin and Peeters, 2006).

The kinds of knowledge work most vulnerable to these strategies include those which are highly reliant on a codified knowledge base, and which can be delivered from remote locations. One obvious candidate has been the delivery of IT-based services. IT expertise is in some ways the victim of its own success in that developments in ICTs combined with the great spread of IT applications have combined to make it a vital service, but one which can be readily provided from remote sites or by external suppliers. In some ways, this is a classic example of knowledge becoming a commodity, but with the caveat that the challenges of outsourcing work seemingly reliant on codified knowledge are often underestimated (David et al., 2008).

HRM work itself has also increasingly been subject to outsourcing as firms look to external 'shared service centres' to provide HR support. Though a softer form of expertise than IT, HRM work is vulnerable because it is codified procedurally in the form of standardized and centralized service offerings. Moreover, when the shared service centre model is combined with Internet-based self-service functions for staff, the costs of HRM can be dramatically reduced; hence making the outsourcing of HRM an attractive option.

The overall result of these changes has been that hierarchical forms of organization have given way in many sectors to more market-based forms, where knowledge work is directed through explicit target-based contracts. For some groups, these trends may even mean that their work role shifts to what is termed 'contingent employment' where they move from one temporary job to another (Redpath et al., 2007). This form of employment can have some benefits. 'Contingent workers' such as freelance IT experts can sometimes be paid at significantly higher rates than other staff. They can also get the opportunity to develop a richer variety of skills due to the range of projects that they work on. Their working hours and place of work are also more flexible. On the other hand, contingent worker status also has significant disadvantages due to the lack of job security, and lack of access to higher levels of the career ladders within firms.

The impact of these different trends in employment are quite unpredictable as far as particular groups are concerned. Developments in the marketplace or in technology can contribute to the rapid de-skilling or upskilling of different groups, such that no group of knowledge workers can ever be fully confident about their long-term role and status in the economy (Attewell, 1990; Braverman, 1974). It is certainly true, as noted above, that codified forms of knowledge work are probably the most vulnerable to these new patterns of employment and control. However, in some areas even more tacit and context-dependent forms of knowledge have become subject to greater market discipline. This applies, for example, even in specialized arenas such as R&D (Research and Development), where the advent of Open Innovation, as discussed in Chapter 9, may be indicative of not only a new mode of innovation, but also of new ways of sourcing and controlling R&D activities.

Table 6.1 summarizes the characteristics of knowledge workers as discussed above, and highlights the challenges which these create for HRM policy. As the table outlines, HRM policies in one area almost invariably have implications for policies in other areas. One obvious effect of operational autonomy, for example, is to make it more difficult to control the work practices of knowledge workers. At the same time, this affects the kind of rewards which can be applied to this group; the outputs from their work can be complex and hard to measure, so

Table 6.1 The challenges posed by knowledge work for HRM policy

Knowledge worker characteristics	Challenges for HRM policy
Operational autonomy in work practices	Gaining knowledge workers' commitment to the organization.
	Controlling knowledge worker behaviour.
	Designing work and reward systems that encourage required knowledge processes.
Labour market power	Recruiting and selecting employees to ensure the best fit with other staff.
	Retaining highly valued employees who are in demand from other organizations.
High expectations of work	Creating work satisfaction through interesting and challenging work.
	Developing career systems that enable knowledge workers to gain promotion and higher level jobs.

linking rewards too closely to one kind of output may undermine the overall contribution that they make. Similar comments apply to the challenge of dealing with the labour market power and higher expectations of knowledge workers where responses often centre on better ways of selecting and retaining employees.

Chapter 2 has already illustrated some of the ways organizations respond to these challenges. It is precisely because knowledge workers are hard to control and reward through the usual means that organizations tend to adopt softer management approaches, including attempts to gain employee commitment. Chapter 2 highlighted some of the structural and cultural features of such approaches. In the remainder of this chapter, however, we will focus on the management practices where HRM policy and practice has greatest influence.

Creating an attractive employment package for knowledge workers

One important area of HRM policy and practice in relation to knowledge workers is that of performance management and rewards. Here employers face some complex challenges because the financial reward of the monthly pay cheque is certainly important in recruiting and retaining knowledge workers, but is rarely the most important factor in motivating them to apply their expertise. As noted above, knowledge workers' expectations of their job extend beyond having a good salary, to include interesting work and opportunities to develop their expertise and status. This means that they are likely to evaluate their current job not only on its own merits, but as part of the wider package of benefits coming from the employment relationship. Because of this, employers who over-emphasize pay compared to other aspects of employment actually risk undermining employee motivation. One recent study, for example, found that performance pay had a negative effect on the performance of R&D staff because it narrowed perceptions of their work responsibilities (Thompson and Heron, 2006) – a finding which is in line with previous work highlighting the motivational consequences of extrinsic rewards (Amabile et al., 1996).

Another important element in the employment package is the career development opportunities afforded by a particular employer. Knowledge workers typically view their current job as one step in a longer term career that will take them into more senior and highly paid roles over time. One HRM response to this expectation is to develop specified career tracks within the organization that will allow the employee progression based on achieving specified performance and competencies. These tracks will normally involve a move into more managerial roles over time to gain higher status and rewards. But, where the organization values highly specialized expertise, it may also support the so-called 'dual career' tracks where knowledge workers can progress to more senior positions without taking on such management responsibilities.

Only larger, more established organizations can offer these kinds of career track opportunities because, to be meaningful, they involve providing a high level of job security over a sustained period. In sectors dominated by smaller firms or where job security is threatened by market and technological change, long-run careers with a single organization may be rare. In such contexts, knowledge worker careers will normally involve jobs in a number of different organizations, and even in different industries. Expectations will shift correspondingly towards opportunities for developing portable forms of expertise that offer 'employability' across a range of employers rather than employment with a single employer.

Translating these challenges into possible managerial responses, we can see that HRM policies need to take account of a number of different factors if they are to succeed in recruiting, retaining and motivating knowledge workers. The *tangible* financial rewards of the job, which are determined through company remuneration policies, are important because employers are often operating in competitive labour markets for these workers, and they need to be able to offer attractive inducements. At the same time, these financial rewards need to be complemented by the *intangible* rewards created by work design, training and development and the social and cultural environment of the firm. The latter are crucial if managers are to succeed not only in recruiting this group, but also in motivating and retaining them.

This analysis explains why managers often see knowledge workers as a difficult group to deal with. If HRM is to create an enabling context for knowledge work, it needs to be capable of developing joined-up policies across the different areas of reward, careers and work design. Given the limited power of HRM functions noted earlier, this kind of integrated approach to HRM policy is often difficult or impossible to secure, despite the advantages of doing so.

>> EXISTING HRM APPROACHES TO KNOWLEDGE WORK

Having discussed the challenges which knowledge work creates for HRM policy and practice, in this section we turn to the existing approaches which are available to respond to these challenges. We focus on four major approaches – briefly labeled as 'best practice', 'best fit', human capital and psychological contract approaches – which aim to give managers better frameworks for developing effective HRM policies in contexts where knowledge work is important.

Best-practice approach

One major strand of HRM research has focused on identifying 'best practice', that is a set of HRM practices which are universally effective across a range of settings in producing high levels of performance from employees (Wood, 1995). One of the problems with applying this approach to knowledge work, however, is that such work involves a number of different processes, depending, for example, on whether workers are sharing, creating or integrating knowledge and the context in which this work is being undertaken. As a result, a range of 'best practices' can be identified depending on the knowledge processes we wish to support. For example, a recent review of the literature (Cabrera and

Cabrera, 2005), identified a number of HR-related factors which are said to promote knowledge sharing, as follows:

- Work designs that encourage collaboration among employees, interdependency and cross-functional interactions.
- Selection of employees driven by person–organization fit and the assessment of communication skills.
- Extensive training programmes geared towards increasing participant self-efficacy and developing team-work skills.
- Formalized orientation and socialization programmes, as well as more informal communities of practice and social events.
- Developmental performance appraisals that recognize knowledge-sharing behaviours.
- Incentive programmes that reward effective knowledge sharing and emphasize intrinsic rewards.
- Group and firm-based compensation systems.

As this example indicates, however, it is by no means clear how all these different practices will interact or whether they are mutually consistent. One example here is the tension between emphasizing 'extrinsic' rewards such as pay and promotion, over the 'intrinsic' rewards which have to do with the fulfilment that comes from the nature of the work itself. Thus, in the above list we can note the possible contradiction of rewarding knowledge sharing through incentives, yet also emphasizing 'intrinsic rewards', such as job satisfaction. Putting a financial value on knowledge sharing risks reducing its intrinsic value as something which gives workers a sense of fulfillment and recognition in their work. There is a significant body of research which suggests that tying individuals to a formal contract to do a particular task significantly affects the motivation which they bring to that task. Their approach becomes more narrowly instrumental and less influenced by their intrinsic interest in the task. The creativity they bring to it is greatly reduced (Amabile et al., 1996).

In the same vein, it does not follow that the HRM practices which promote knowledge sharing amongst employees will necessarily help to motivate key groups of sometimes highly individualistic knowledge workers. Such groups often rightly see their expertise as their best guarantee of future rewards and job security. They are unlikely to see 'sharing' it with others as serving their best interests. These kind of problems leave managers with the problem of selecting which of a range of 'best practices' is actually the best for a particular situation.

Best-fit approach

In response to the limitations of best-practice approaches, some studies have attempted to develop a more tailored approach which focuses on finding the 'best fit' between HR practices and a particular organization's needs. Unlike the best-practice idea, this approach suggests that there is no 'one best way' to manage employees. The important thing is to find the right fit between management practices and the characteristics of knowledge work processes.

One of the most important contributions to this approach comes from Hansen et al. (1999) who argue that there are basically two strategies for managing knowledge. These strategies they term 'codification' and 'personalization':

- *Codification*: 'Knowledge is carefully codified and stored in databases where it can be accessed and used readily by anyone in the company' (p. 107).

- *Personalization*: 'Knowledge is closely tied to the person who developed it and is shared mainly through direct person-to-person contacts' (p. 107).

Although they do not claim that organizations pursue these strategies exclusively, Hansen et al. argue that competitive success involves pursuing one strategy predominantly. Attempting to 'straddle' both strategies leads to failure, they claim. The codification approach to knowledge demands well-trained people who are able to exploit ICT databases and communication systems. The IT consultancy, Accenture, represents a good example of this kind of firm.

With a personalization strategy knowledge is closely tied to the person who developed it, and it is shared informally through person-to-person contacts. Again a different kind of employee is required, one able to creatively develop and apply knowledge to unique business problems. The Bain & Co and McKinsey consulting firms are cited as good examples of this different kind of organization; and the case in Chapter 2 can also be seen to rely more heavily on personalization than codification.

The Hansen study focused on consulting firms, of course, and, as subsequent chapters will make clear (see in particular Chapter 8), it is possible to question whether their analysis emphasizes the role of individual experts at the expense of the role of groups and communities in creating and sharing knowledge. It may be relevant for consultancy firms employing talented individuals, but it is doubtful whether it applies to all organizations. As far as HRM is concerned, however, this study does make several useful contributions. First, it links both the management of knowledge and HRM to the competitive strategy of the organization. This analysis shows that it is not knowledge *per se* but the way it is applied to strategic objectives which is the critical ingredient of competitiveness. Second, this analysis highlights the need for 'best fit' between HRM practices such as reward systems and the organization's approach to managing knowledge work. The relevant fit is outlined as follows:

> In the codification model, managers need to develop a system that encourages people to write down what they know and to get those documents into the electronic repository... companies that are following the personalization approach... need to reward people for sharing knowledge directly with other people.
>
> (Hansen et al., 1999, p. 113)

It is important to note that getting the best fit between HRM practices and different kinds of knowledge work has two facets (Fombrun et al., 1984) – internal and external fit. Internal fit means that management practices are consistent with each other and pulling in the same direction. Thus, in the personalization strategy, the kinds of people that are recruited needs to be consistent with the way those people are rewarded. External fit has to do with ensuring that outcomes of HRM practices fit with the strategic needs of the firm. Thus, with the personalization strategy we can see that the kinds of knowledge produced by the consultants in companies like Bain & Co fit well with those companies' business strategies and their approach to solving client problems.

Human capital approach

The best-fit approach may be more tailored to individual organizations but it is also limited in some respects. This approach is essentially *managerial* in its focus. That is, it is concerned with getting management practices aligned with each other at one point in time. By doing this, the right kinds of knowledge will theoretically *flow* amongst employees, and from employees to clients. What it does not do, however, is address the long-term factors which influence the development of the *stocks* of knowledge within an organization. These stocks can be accumulated in a number of different ways. They can come from organizational learning, for instance, where organizations develop highly efficient routines for dealing with problems. They may also be developed through good relationships with suppliers and customers, which extend the firm's knowledge base. Crucially, because such stocks are difficult to acquire and copy, they are seen as vital sources of the organizational capabilities through which firms compete (Barney, 1991).

Conventional systems of accounting – balance sheets, profit and loss accounts – have difficulty in dealing with the intrinsic value of these stocks of knowledge. They are not a tangible asset of the firm, and cannot be as easily quantified as, say, the value of capital equipment. Nonetheless, for organizations within the growing knowledge economy, these intangible assets are often the most important assets they possess. Their increasing importance has been reflected in the growing interest in what has been called the 'intellectual capital' of the organization. Such capital is normally seen as being made up of three principal forms of intangible asset:

- Human Capital – the ability of individuals to contribute to organizational performance based on their personal competencies, and mindsets.

- Customer Capital – the strength of the customer relationship as reflected in superior customer-perceived value, and the increasing customization of business solutions.

- Organizational Capital – the capabilities of the organization which are accumulated from its knowledge base, business processes, shared culture, values and norms.

In this perspective, the expertise applied by knowledge workers represents the human capital component of the organization's intellectual capital. Viewing knowledge workers in this way can provide a more strategic approach because it highlights the links between the way people are recruited and managed and long-term organizational performance. It also helps organizations identify the distinctive contribution which its employees make to performance compared to other sources of intellectual capital.

The concept of human capital itself derives originally from work by economists seeking to explain the impact of learning and education on economic growth (Becker, 1975). More recently, it has been used to explain the employee contribution to organizational performance. In this context, researchers have suggested that the formation of human capital within an organization may be a source of competitive advantage because it is difficult to replicate in other firms. Studies have also emphasized that human capital is about more than the expertise possessed by individuals. It also has to do with the organization's ability to motivate those individuals to apply their expertise to organizational goals. For example, Ulrich defines human capital simply as 'competence x commitment' (Ulrich, 1998).

In recent years, there have been efforts to measure the human capital of the firm in the same way that other assets are measured. However, they often fail because of what has been termed the 'paradox' of human capital (Scarbrough and Elias, 2002). In other words, human capital is valuable to the organization because it is developed and applied according to the needs of a particular context. Much of the most important human capital, for instance, accrues through learning by doing and is closely related to successful performance by individuals. The value which this creates encourages organizations to try to measure human capital so that it can be managed more effectively. The paradox, however, arises because the very same qualities – dynamic, context-dependent and so on – which make human capital valuable also make it hard to measure. Because managers are driven by their own performance targets to focus on things which can be measured (often the financial numbers of the firm), one outward sign of this paradox is managers paying more attention to measurable, but short-term, financial targets than to the long-run value of human capital.

This tendency to marginalize human capital is particularly risky where its contribution to organizational performance is ambiguous or hard to identify. This is often the case in complex, knowledge-intensive organizations where human capital is more about teams than a few outstanding individuals, and where its impact on performance is longer term rather than immediate. If managers in these settings take decisions on business strategy, as they often do, which overlook the human capital of their knowledge workers, they risk damaging or destroying their firm's major competitive asset. This risk is enhanced because human capital is also a fragile asset. Organizations do not 'own' their human capital in the same way they do other assets. Knowledge workers, in particular, are highly mobile, and can move to other employers, so any major change in strategy can result in the rapid exit of highly valued expertise. A good example is when takeovers of high-tech and professional service firms are followed by the departure of many of the highly skilled staff who made the company valuable in the first place.

Even though measures of human capital are always likely to be imprecise and context-dependent, the risk of losing this asset has prompted some firms to develop more systematic ways of managing it. In such cases, managers often recognize that the *process* of developing and using measures may be valuable in itself regardless of the measures developed because it provides vital insights into key areas of employee skill and motivation (Elias and Scarbrough, 2004).

Where measures have been developed, they can help to guide managers' decision-making by highlighting the impact which different decisions are having, or are likely to have, on the human capital of the organization. This risk can be mitigated to some extent by reducing dependence on a few individuals and emphasizing team-based skills. Equally, the organization may seek to turn knowledge workers' expertise into a corporate resource by developing routines and systems based on the codification of knowledge. However, for organizations in fast-moving industries, the role of human capital is so great that such measures can do little to mitigate the risks.

Psychological contract

The approaches outlined above tend to adopt a top-down view by taking the organization's strategy as their starting point. This can make a lot of sense where managers find it difficult to see the links between knowledge workers' contribution and overall corporate goals. What these approaches lack, however, is the knowledge worker's perspective on that contribution. This is important because, as discussed, the motivation and commitment of this group comes not from management but from the knowledge workers' own perceptions of their role and rewards.

One promising approach for gaining the knowledge workers' perspective has been developed by scholars working on the so-called 'psychological contract' between employer and employee. This term is used to distinguish it from the formal contract of employment. It describes the unspoken but psychologically significant agreement which employees feel they have with their employing organization. This framework is valuable in developing a more integrated approach because it presents the employment relationship in the way that knowledge workers themselves see it. Thus, knowledge workers do not respond to their pay packet in isolation from the kind of work which they get to do, or the career opportunities which their employer provides for them. They look at the employment relationship as a whole – the complete package – and respond to it accordingly. If their employer succeeds in meeting the full range of their expectations, they are much more likely to be motivated and committed in their job.

The concept of the psychological contract is useful here because it draws managers' attention to the implicit nature of this exchange. Knowledge workers become committed and motivated in return for the employer's ability to meet their expectations. Commitment and motivation are not a given, and even good salaries do not always secure them. Recent studies have underlined the importance of this implicit contract and the kind of things which employers need to deliver if knowledge workers are to see it as a fair exchange. Thus, a study by Flood et al. (2001) found that knowledge workers were more likely to leave employers who were seen as breaking the psychological contract. Particularly important here was the employer's ability to meet the worker's expectation of interesting and challenging work:

The findings reinforce the importance of continuously attending to the work-design side of the employment contract. Knowledge workers remain with employers who provide interesting and challenging assignments which allow workers to build a portable portfolio of skills.

(p. 1164)

Flood and his colleagues argue that the importance of the psychological contract is such that organizations should seek to make it more 'transparent and tangible'. Such transparency involves an open discussion of the expectations which both employer and employee bring to the job at every stage from recruitment through to performance review.

>> CONCLUSIONS

This chapter has highlighted the challenges which knowledge work poses for HRM, and the different policy responses which firms have developed for dealing with these challenges. It is clear that the autonomy enjoyed by knowledge workers has prompted a range of responses from organizations. Some have developed soft HRM policies which attempt to gain the commitment of knowledge workers by creating a supportive organizational context. Such policies can be highly effective where they succeed in gaining real affective commitment and thus help to realize the full potential of highly skilled groups and individuals. On the other hand, such policies are also difficult to develop and sustain. This may be because they require consistency across the different areas of culture, rewards, careers and work design. It may also reflect the relatively bureaucratic character of HRM where policies are often standardized for the organization as a whole. These factors help to explain why such HRM policies for knowledge work are often more effective when the organization is relatively small or is composed largely of knowledge workers itself – as in the ScienceCo case described in Chapter 2.

Meanwhile, however, other organizations have resolved the tensions between control and commitment not through HRM policies but through major changes in organizational form and focus. The spread of outsourcing and offshoring underscores the vulnerability of knowledge work to wider changes in the global division of labour – a vulnerability which is increased by the very developments in IT and communications which have accelerated the growth in knowledge work.

The radical solution of simply outsourcing activities is not available or appropriate for many organizations, of course, and for managers still struggling to develop supportive HRM policies, we outlined the wide range of approaches currently available. Each of these approaches emphasizes different ways of improving the links between knowledge work and business performance. But, all depend to some degree on managers' ability to shape the employment relationship in a way that best serves the needs of the particular context within which the knowledge work is being undertaken. This underlines the importance of managers and business leaders' actions in shaping the context for knowledge work – a factor which is amply underlined by the case study outlined below.

CASE STUDY 6.1
BUCKMAN LABS

Buckman Labs was established in 1945 as a family-firm engaged in the production of specialist chemicals for aqueous industrial systems. The business grew rapidly under the hard driving leadership of Dr Stanley Buckman. The management philosophy was to change radically, however, in 1978 when Stanley died from a heart attack at his office. His son and successor as CEO, Bob Buckman had a new vision for the company. This involved, first, a change in management style away from centralized control. As he later commented, 'I knew I didn't want to do it Dad's way. Every single business decision had to be approved by my father. I thought, this is too much work.' Second, he aimed to develop a new strategy for the business that would allow it to compete not on cost alone, but by exploiting its knowledge base more effectively.

By the end of 1992, Buckman Laboratories had invested $8 million to lay the groundwork for a new knowledge transfer system. For a total investment of $75,000 per month in access charges and the provision of an IBM ThinkPad 720 with modem to each employee, all Buckman staff were able to make a single phone call that established online contact with headquarters and provided the necessary real-time access to global information services. With this infrastructure in place, management developed a global knowledge transfer network which they termed K'Netix. Seven discussion forums were established (three customer-focused forums and four regional-focused forums) to allow employees to share experience in particular areas. By March 1993, every employee was able to access K'Netix, and this made it possible to deliver knowledge-based services to customers in over 90 countries worldwide.

The K'Netix Knowledge Management system was divided into two basic parts: organizational forums and codified databases. The focus, however, was very much on connecting individuals rather than stockpiling knowledge for its own sake. The system enabled the electronic sharing of knowledge both between associates themselves and between associates and customers. The most knowledgeable experts at all levels of the organization were therefore kept in touch with each other, encouraging group problem-solving and the sharing of new ideas and knowledge (Buckman, 1998).

While the technological infrastructure was being established, an equally important development was the attempt to foster a knowledge-sharing culture at Buckman Labs. In many respects, this attempt to change 'hearts and minds' was an even bigger challenge as established ways of thinking and working tend to be both culturally and politically embedded within organizations. Bob Buckman sought to overcome such resistance within the firm, by seeking to create a culture in which employees who shared their knowledge would be the most influential and sought-after individuals within the company.

Resistance to this knowledge-sharing vision came in large part from middle management who had been traditionally perceived as information gatekeepers in the company. The radical cultural change introduced by Bob Buckman had major implications for the power structure of middle management. In the past, middle management had sought to control the flow of information to employees in order to protect their own roles in the organization.

It took some years for these attitudes to change – learning the new norms and values involved painfully unlearning the old culture. To help associates understand the expected behaviour, Buckman sought to put in place a new Code of Ethics which was presented as the 'glue' that would hold the company together. It was seen as providing the basis for the respect and trust that are necessary in a knowledge-sharing environment. Buckman asked his employees to think about the company as a ship, with the Code of Ethics as the waterline of the ship. The message to associates was simple: 'You do not shoot below the waterline, because you can sink the ship. However, you are free to be as innovative as you wish in changing the superstructure of the ship to meet the needs of the customer'. Buckman thus sought to ensure that creating and sharing knowledge was no longer seen as the exclusive responsibility of the R&D department but rather a responsibility of all employees.

>> BUCKMAN LABS' CODE OF ETHICS

Because we are separated – by many miles, by diversity of cultures and languages – we at Buckman need a clear understanding of the basic principles by which we will operate our company. These are:

That the company is made up of individuals – each of whom has different capabilities and potentials – all of which are necessary to the success of the company.

That we acknowledge that individuality by treating each other with dignity and respect – striving to maintain continuous and positive communications among all of us.

That we will recognize and reward the contributions and accomplishments of each individual.

That we will continually plan for the future so that we can control our destiny instead of letting events overtake us.

The cultural change at Buckman Labs was also driven through by Bob Buckman's stern resolve to 'manage the managers'. The experience here arguably highlights another side of leadership: the selective use of sticks as well as carrots to reinforce certain kinds of behaviour. This led Bob Buckman to write personally to all of those associates who were deemed to be unwilling to participate in the sharing activities. These letters conveyed a blunt message about the consequences of refusing to share knowledge.

The result of these efforts was to marginalize the middle management who had previously acted as the gatekeepers for knowledge flows within the company. Many employees positively embraced the new opportunity to voice their contributions outside the chain of command. As one manager observed, 'With the global network in place, it does not matter if you are a sales associate, a regional or district manager or a corporate VP [Vice President] – everybody talks to everybody.'

The new IT systems supported and facilitated this new, egalitarian approach to knowledge sharing. This was particularly evident with the development of online forums where individual employees can post requests for advice and support in dealing with specific for work problems. These forums, which are accessible only to company associates, are each divided into sections based on Buckman's lines of business, such as water treatment and leather.

>> ROLE OF COMMUNITIES

As seen in other companies, various forms of communities were developed within Buckman to facilitate the sharing of knowledge across organizational boundaries. Initially, such communities evolved informally as individuals contacted each other to seek and to share knowledge for specific problems. These communities developed around the problem-solving forums that were established through the K'Netix system. Over time, communities became more formalized as Buckman began to provide support through the development of 'forum specialists'. The role of forum specialists was to respond to requests for help posted on discussion forums and to codify the responses to make them available over a longer time period and to a wider audience. Forum specialists worked to organize, validate and verify the responses to requests before uploading them into a database to be available for re-use. This work allowed front-line employees to continue serving customers while the specialists devoted their time to capturing their knowledge in a re-usable form.

To illustrate this cooperative knowledge sharing, we can take a fairly typical example of how the system operated in practice. This example has to do with a need for specialist knowledge on 'pitch control'. Pitch control involves working on removing or minimizing the effect of pitch in the paper-making process. Pitch is made up of sticky materials left over in the pulp fibres used in the paper-making process or derived from adhesives or plastics in recycled fibres. Given the range of Buckman Labs' technical activities, there were frequent demands for knowledge of new or esoteric domains. In this instance, knowledge of pitch control was required for a work programme in an Indonesian pulp mill. When Dennis Dalton, who is based in Singapore as Managing Director of all company activities in Asia, was proposing this programme, he circulated a message through the K'Netix system requesting help on how he could go about preparing it: 'I would appreciate an update on successful recent pitch-control strategies in your parts of the world', he wrote.

A response came within a matter of a few hours from Phil Hoekstra in Memphis, including a suggestion for the specific Buckman chemical to use as well as a reference to a Master's thesis on the pitch control of tropical hardwoods, written by an Indonesian student attending North Carolina State University. A further response came only 50 minutes after the first, this time from Michael Sund in Canada. This offered his experience in solving the pitch problem in British Columbia. Then in quick succession Nils Hallberg logged in with examples from Sweden; Wendy Bijiker offered details from a New Zealand paper mill; Jose Vallcorba cited examples from Spain and France; Chip Hill in Memphis contributed scientific advice from the R&D Department; Javier del Rosal included a detailed chemical formula and specific application directions from Mexico; and Lionel Hughes wrote about his experience in South Africa. In total, Dalton's request for suggestions generated 11 replies from six different countries. It stimulated new discussions, generated new knowledge, and put him into a position to secure a $6 million order from the Indonesian pulp mill (Buckman, 1998).

>> THE ROLE OF LEARNING AND REWARDS

This ready flow of knowledge through dialogue amongst associates was underpinned by the efforts which Buckman Labs made to promote learning and employee development. In 1996, the Buckman Laboratories Learning Center (Bulab Learning Center) was established to help associates manage their own personal and career development. This involved using information technology to give associates opportunities to participate in learning events electronically. The Learning Center's content ranged from short training and reference materials to advanced academic degrees. The content was drawn from leading universities, and also included custom-designed tools to help with employees' day-to-day duties. The responsibility for personal development was thus transferred to the individual associate, reinforcing Buckman's concern to make the individual accountable for their own performance.

While the company stressed the individual's responsibility for their performance, it drew back from linking individual rewards to knowledge sharing in a systematic way. Rather, rewards were used in a very selective way for specific purposes. Thus, a one-off event at a fashionable resort was arranged for the 150 employees who had contributed the most widely used knowledge to the forums. At the event, employees helped to plan the future of the Knowledge Management initiatives. Those chosen also received new laptop computers and participated in a number of Knowledge Management-related discussions. Thus, the reward here was more intangible – the recognition and status of attending the event – than financial. This helped to symbolize and reinforce the cultural changes within the company. Although some of those who were not selected for the event were left feeling disappointed, overall participation in the knowledge-sharing forums rose immediately.

Evidence for the success of knowledge-sharing activities is sometimes difficult to provide because so many of the benefits are intangible. Knowledge sharing has the effect of supporting innovation within the organization, but as discussed earlier, this effect is difficult to validate and measure. Top management at Buckman Labs, however, believed that the impact of their strategic initiatives was reflected in company performance. This saw a major increase in the contribution of new products, and overall sales increased by upwards of 250 per cent within a few years following the introduction of the K'Netix system.

>> QUESTIONS

1. What were the major factors which encouraged the development of knowledge sharing and innovation at Buckman Labs?

2. How influential were HRM policies around culture, rewards and job design, in supporting the development of knowledge sharing?

3. How far did the role of HRM reflect the best-practice approach discussed previously?

4. Compare the relevance of the HRM approaches outlined above (best practice, best fit, human capital, psychological contract) to the experience at Buckman Labs. Which of these approaches best explains the ways in which Buckman sought to make better use of employee knowledge?

We gratefully acknowledge the authorship of Shan Ling Pan in relation to the original version of this case study.

Summary of Key Learning Points

>> HRM policies have an impact in several areas of management practice which influence knowledge work directly: rewards, work design, corporate culture and organization careers.

>> There are a variety of HRM approaches to supporting knowledge work. We have described them here as best practice, best fit, human capital and psychological contract approaches.

>> The best-practice approach suggests that there is a specific set of HRM policies which are effective for knowledge workers in all types of organizations.

>> The best-fit approach suggests that HRM policies are only effective in managing knowledge work when they are tailored to fit the strategy and context of the individual organization.

>> The human capital approach focuses on the long-term development of skills, trust and personal relationships within the organization.

>> The psychological contract approach emphasizes the knowledge workers' own views of the costs and benefits of working for a particular employer.

>> The deployment of HRM policies reflects some employers' continued dependence on knowledge workers. Other organizations, however, are seeking to reduce their dependence by outsourcing and offshoring this kind of work.

7

KNOWLEDGE MANAGEMENT SYSTEMS

Chapter Outline

Learning Outcomes

At the end of this chapter you should be able to:

- Understand two types of ICT that influence knowledge work and knowledge workers – Knowledge Management Systems (KMS) and Enterprise Systems.
- Understand how Enterprise Systems have evolved from earlier approaches that attempted to capture and standardize 'best practices'.
- Recognize the constraining and facilitating influences of Enterprise Systems on knowledge work and knowledge workers.
- Differentiate between channel/network and platform/repository KMS.
- Develop a critical appreciation of the role of ICTs as 'Knowledge Management Systems'.
- Recognize the difference between structural/possession manifestations of ICTs to support knowledge work and processual/practice approaches.
- Appreciate the potential of new forms of ICT that can expose knowledge processes as well as knowledge content.

>> INTRODUCTION

In Chapter 3 we considered how ICTs do not, in and of themselves, change the way work is done on a daily basis, nor the knowledge that is processed across an organization. Unfortunately, as we will see in this chapter, many organizations assume that ICT *does* drive organizational change and assume that introducing some type of ICT will more or less automatically improve Knowledge Management processes. Thus, organizations interested in improving the management and flow of knowledge focus typically on two types of ICT: Knowledge Management Systems (KMS) and Enterprise Systems. KMS are the dominant type of 'KM' initiative and are used to capture, store, search, connect, transfer and, so, reuse information and knowledge across individuals, for example using intranets or e-mail (Alavi and Tiwana, 2003). Enterprise Systems are a different type of ICT but are still important in relation to understanding the role of ICT in knowledge work. The case study in Chapter 3 provided an introductory example of this kind of technology. Thus, Enterprise Systems are used to support (and control) all types of work, being designed to ensure that standardized and integrated work processes are used across a distributed organization. The idea is that Enterprise Systems embed knowledge about 'best practice' in a software package, so that when an organization adopts an Enterprise System they are also adopting the industry 'best practices' in relation to how best to organize work (Wagner et al., 2006). Below we will explore these technologies, and their historical roots, and also identify their constraining and facilitating impact on knowledge work and knowledge workers and more generally, their effectiveness in supporting Knowledge Management processes.

The deployment of both types of technology is usually based very much on what was described in Chapter 1 as an 'epistemology of possession' approach and are structural in nature – knowledge is viewed as a cognitive resource, a possession, that can be captured and transferred across people using ICT (Schultze and Leidner, 2002). KMS/Enterprise Systems try, then, to transfer knowledge, assuming that it is an entity that can be captured and moved fairly easily across people, places and time. Thus, organizations rely on codifying knowledge that can either be transferred to the particular individual(s) who needs it – typically using e-mail – or put into a repository of some kind – an intranet, for example – where it can be stored and searched, and hopefully found, by those who will find it useful. Or they may rely on embedding knowledge in an Enterprise Systems package that then dictates how work shall be completed to ensure maximum efficiency. Much effort, therefore, goes into codifying knowledge (converting tacit to explicit knowledge, for example) that can be used in distributed locations (transferring it from the individual to the collective), rather than relying on personal networks and collaborative practices (discussed more fully in Chapter 8).

The dominance of these structural KMS/Enterprise Systems approaches is perhaps not surprising, given that many organizations today are very large and/or geographically distributed. As we saw in Chapter 3, new organizational forms often make it challenging or impossible for organizations to rely on face-to-face communication and personal networks for the sharing of information and knowledge. This is the case whether this be:

1. General communications for the whole organization (e.g. the organizational vision, goals or values) that are communicated through platform technologies, or,

2. Communications for a sub-group of employees (e.g. the budget statement for all VPs, or information about progress for all those involved in a large software project) that are communicated through channel technologies.

While KM initiatives are often structural in nature, there are also new forms of ICT that can potentially accommodate a more processual/practice orientation. These allow observation of the processes and practices through which knowledge is created, and accept that the same content can be interpreted differently across communities. With the advent of what is sometimes called Web 2.0 or Enterprise 2.0, for example, it is now possible for documents to be created collectively using technologies like google.doc, sharepoint and wikis of all kinds. These technologies crucially allow people to engage in a process of joint knowledge creation and as well as to observe the product of that effort (McAfee, 2006). Moreover, with social networking software applications (including Facebook, Myspace LinkedIn, various kinds of blogs and YouTube), it is now possible for people to conduct online discussions and share a variety of multimedia content. These technologies, in other words, can facilitate interaction and expose practices of knowing as individuals create and recreate content in cyberspace. We will explore these practice-based KMS at the end of this chapter once we have discussed the dominant structural approaches of KMS and Enterprise Systems.

We illustrate in this chapter the problems of an exclusively structural KMS-approach to managing knowledge through exploring the ICC case at the end of the chapter. This consulting company had introduced a KMS in order to facilitate knowledge sharing between people geographically distributed across its global network. However, it did not produce the results that were anticipated.

>> THE HISTORICAL ROOTS OF CURRENT ENTERPRISE SYSTEMS

Enterprise Systems (a more generic term for the kind of Enterprise Resource Planning or ERP systems, introduced in Chapter 3) are currently very popular in organizations because of their potential ability to streamline business processes across the value chain (Davenport, 2000; Kumar and Hillegersberg, 2000). Enterprise Systems (also based very much on an epistemology of possession) assume that knowledge about successful organizational practices within a particular industry can be identified, captured and embedded in software and so transferred across organizations. From this perspective, current Enterprise Systems initiatives can be seen as a direct descendant of the much earlier Scientific

Management tradition developed by F. W. Taylor, introduced in Chapter 1. Thus, while Taylor sought to transfer the knowledge that existed in worker's heads to their managers, and the Ford production system sought to transfer workers' and to an extent managers' knowledge to the assembly-line technology, Enterprise Systems seek to transfer knowledge of presumed 'best practices' across an industry sector by embedding the knowledge in a software package (Gratton and Ghoshal, 2005). Moreover, like Scientific Management and Fordist production, an Enterprise Systems seeks to impose the same kind of standardizing control on the ways work gets done, even in the context of knowledge work.

As we saw in Chapter 1, Taylor's so-called Scientific Management philosophy can be understood as an early attempt at Knowledge Management. Taylor believed that it was necessary to extract the knowledge from the workers and give it to managers who would then devise standardized work processes that each worker would be forced to follow. In this sense, Taylor supposed that there was 'one best way' to accomplish tasks – very like the current philosophy behind Enterprise Systems packages. We also saw in Chapter 1 how Scientific Management and the related Fordist production system had negative effects on the workers. More importantly, perhaps, such approaches also restrict flexibility since it is much more difficult to change workflows when control is embedded in complex production technologies that cost a lot, in terms of time and money, to change. This is demonstrated today very clearly with many very large car companies, especially in the United States, being very slow to respond to what has been a fairly dramatic change in customer preferences for cars – changing production lines from producing gas-guzzling SUVs, which customers no longer want because of high fuel costs, to small cars, which are more attractive because they are energy efficient, takes several years to accomplish, for example. Dramatic losses in market share are occurring in those companies that did not foresee this change and that, therefore, are not able to make adjustments quickly enough. These limitations on work and workers can be similarly recognized in today's very popular Enterprise Systems, discussed next.

>> ENTERPRISE SYSTEMS AND THE SPREAD OF 'BEST PRACTICE' KNOWLEDGE

While some of the underlying assumptions about human nature were clearly naïve in these early Scientific Management/Fordist approaches to managing work, the general idea of standardizing work practices through the use of technology remains dominant, only today standardization covers not just manual work but also a lot of non-manual work, including what might be considered knowledge work, and occurs through the use of ICT rather than through designing specific work tools, like spades, or machines, like assembly lines. Enterprise Systems exemplify this trend.

Enterprise Systems have their roots in earlier technologies for managing production processes – Manufacturing Requirements Planning (MRP),

Manufacturing Resource Planning (MRP2) and Enterprise Resource Planning (ERP) (Wallace and Kremzar, 2001). The generic term 'Enterprise Systems' is used to describe, then, a range of ICTs that are designed to support workflows across an enterprise. All are based on the same assumption about the importance and efficacy of integrating and standardizing work practices for all types of workers.

The standardization of practices within an Enterprise System begins, so the rhetoric goes, with the capture of knowledge of 'best practices'. This is typically done by consultants working for software companies, and is based on their interpretation and benchmarking of how particular types of work are performed (e.g. the process of accounts payable or goods received) in what they define to be leading firms. This knowledge of 'best practices' is then embedded in the software packages that, when implemented in a given organization, will theoretically mean that the adopting organization acquires this 'best practice' knowledge (Gratton and Ghoshal, 2005). This is because the Enterprise System controls workflows by requiring data is input in a particular way and also requiring that data move in a certain way across a work process. Such Enterprise Systems packages are thus marketed as knowledge processing systems – a way for any given company to learn (i.e. acquire knowledge) to operate in the same way as the very successful companies in their industry, since by adopting the package the organization will be forced to reorganize its workflows to fit the work process models in the Enterprise System.

This is why there is so much emphasis from Enterprise Systems software companies, and the consultants involved in supporting implementations, on sticking to a 'vanilla implementation'. A 'vanilla implementation', as we saw in Chapter 3, means that the adopting organization should not customize the software to support different work processes to those embedded in the software because, if they do this, then they are losing the advantage of using the Enterprise System to support their adoption of the 'best practice' knowledge. Typically, however, there are configuration options which can supposedly accommodate important differences between firms, for example, in terms of their structure or geographical and so language and legal environments. However, such options are to be kept to a minimum so, in principle, when an organization adopts the Enterprise System, they will supposedly be adopting 'best practices' as defined for their particular industry. In this sense, context is not seen to matter that much, since it is assumed that there are 'best practices' that are broadly applicable across a wide range of situations. The problem with this underpinning notion of 'best practice' is an issue that we will return to in Chapter 9 when we consider the nature of innovation processes.

The central idea behind an Enterprise System is that there should be a single database that stores data from across functions of a business (Gattiker and Goodhue, 2005). For example, all sales data will be stored in the single repository in the same format so that it is possible to integrate data from distributed sites as well as compare data across sites. This, it is claimed, provides a powerful system infrastructure for a business based on codifying 'best practice'. For example, in a consultancy organization a Customer Relationship Management (CRM) system might be used to standardize customer data used across departments; in a healthcare setting, an Electronic Health Record (EHR) system might be used to standardize patient data to be shared across different doctors; while in a university, an e-learning system might be used to create a standard learning environment for sharing information with students. Achieving this integrated system infrastructure depends on instituting standardized business/organizational practices so that the same processes are followed, meaning the data is consistent and standard across the organization.

Knowledge workers are certainly not immune from the influences of such standardizing processes. For example, university teachers are often required to use an e-learning course management system or some other kind of educational repository to communicate with their classes. 'Blackboard', for example, is designed around a particular 'best practice' vision of what a 'class' consists of and what type of information needs to be communicated between a teacher and their students. So, there is a button for announcements, syllabus, course documents, assignments, communication and so on that presumes a particular type of lecturing practice. Of course, individual professors will use this functionality somewhat differently, but nevertheless, the material design of the ICT constrains what they can do. Moreover, the system may well be a mechanism used by administrators to control the behaviour of knowledge workers – the Blackboard website can be looked at, for example, by a chair of department to ensure that an individual faculty member is conforming to expectations around norms of 'good teaching practice'.

>> THE FALLACY OF 'BEST PRACTICE' KNOWLEDGE

In the section above we considered the rhetoric of Enterprise Systems as carriers of 'best practice' knowledge. In this section we look at the limitations of this view. These limitations relate to:

1. the ways users enact (rather than simply adopt) technologies;
2. the myth that 'best practice' can be defined independently of the specific context;
3. the restrictions on flexibility and;
4. the creation of competitive value.

Taking each in turn, first, research has shown that individuals often find ways to work around the restrictions imposed by Enterprise Systems (or indeed other types of standardizing KMS). As we discussed in Chapter 3, users enact a technology, they do not simply adopt it. For example, sales people often maintain their legacy Excel spreadsheets to organize their customer leads and only input into the Enterprise System information that they want their boss or their colleagues to know about. For example, they may not record every sales contact (as the system says they should) because they do not want to share potential sales opportunities with colleagues. Similarly medical doctors maintain paper records on their patients but may only record partial information on the EHR system – the equivalent of an Enterprise Systems in a healthcare setting – either because they find this easier or because they do not want to record all of the information for wider consumption (Orlikowski, 2002). This demonstrates one of the limitations of assuming that the adoption of an Enterprise Systems will automatically embed 'best practice' knowledge in an organization.

Second, there is considerable debate and criticism of the very notion of 'best practice' given the very different history and culture of each organization. Crucially, you should be thinking about how the process and practice approaches to knowledge work, introduced in Chapter 1, would suggest that the very idea that an Enterprise System embeds knowledge of 'best practice' ignores the importance of context and disregards the processes through which knowledge is negotiated. Thus, Wagner et al. (2006) illustrate that the definition of a 'best practice' is a socio-political process of negotiation, rather than an objective reality. In this sense, implementing an Enterprise System is an organizational change project. Organizational change, however, is never straightforward, as we saw in Chapter 3. Thus, research has shown that during an Enterprise System implementation there is often conflict with some end-users resisting the technology (as in the case in Chapter 3) as they fight over what is 'best practice'. This is because individuals in different locations will carry out ostensibly the same practice (e.g. medical doctors making a diagnosis) somewhat differently. The introduction of an Enterprise System poses constraints on these localized work practices, with the software's integrated design encouraging the institutionalization of one approach to practice while silencing other ways of working. This is why the introduction of an Enterprise System to manage knowledge work (and knowledge workers) is often fraught with difficulties, as individuals and groups (perhaps in different locations or different departments) fight to get their existing practices imposed as 'best' and fight against the standard 'vanilla' processes (Wagner and Newell, 2004).

Third, questions have been raised about how, in attempting to manage knowledge work, Enterprise Systems may restrict the very organizational flexibility that such work requires, so becoming the 'legacy' systems of the future (Galliers, 2006). Thus, it now seems clear that organizations need to be able to differentiate between what is standard and what is their unique 'value added'. One estimation is that around 75 per cent of work processes can be considered standard so that following 'best practice' workflows by instituting the 'vanilla' Enterprise Systems may be most efficient (Davenport, 2000). Nevertheless, even in these 'standard' cases (referred to as commodity processes) it may be possible to use knowledge of what will create added value for a customer to differentiate the process and provide some competitive edge to knowledge work (Huang et al., 2007). For example, wake-up calls in hotels today rely on a fairly standard technology – everything is automated and hotel staff do not usually make the wake-up calls in person. However, some hotels have slightly modified this technology to influence greater customer satisfaction. Thus, some hotels in Disneyland now allow guests to select which Disney character will wake them up in the morning! Customizing some commodity processes may, therefore, be useful.

However, and fourth, deciding the 25 per cent of processes that can differentiate an organization is extremely problematic, especially because the software companies and consultants who sell Enterprise System technologies have a vested interest in trying to ignore this aspect of an Enterprise System adoption because their main selling point is that *all* 'best practice' knowledge is embedded in the software.

All of this suggests that the notion of 'best practice' knowledge that underpins Enterprise, and other Knowledge Management, Systems is more about convenient rhetoric than about actual practice. Despite this, it is important that we recognize both the constraining and facilitating influences of Enterprise System on knowledge work and workers. Enterprise System do constrict the way knowledge workers carry out their daily work tasks (as with the example of Blackboard given above) but they also potentially assist such workers by providing them with information on what is happening across an organization that feeds into their decision-making processes. For example, before the advent of Enterprise System it was very difficult for a senior manager of a large company to be able to compare business units because each business unit collected data in a different format. Today, with the integrated database, it is easier for managers to compare business units and to draw distinctions about which is doing relatively better or worse. This ability to draw distinctions is a core feature of what it means to have knowledge – as seen in our definition of knowledge in Chapter 1. However, we also need to recognize that the system in itself does not automatically draw these distinctions – these rely on the managers' prior experience and interpretation of the context. In this sense, Enterprise System do not, in effect, constitute KM systems, despite claims to the contrary. They are actually information systems (Galliers and Newell, 2003) – the individual uses knowledge of the context and processes to make sense of the information that is provided by the Enterprise System.

Nevertheless, Enterprise Systems are often marketed as systems that can support Knowledge Management – they are sold as systems which embed knowledge of 'best practice' and as systems which facilitate the production of knowledge. We have discussed the fallacy of such an idea. These limitations are also relevant to the second group of technologies that we will look at in this chapter which are actually often described as 'Knowledge Management Systems' – that is they are systems that are specifically designed to transfer information and knowledge across an organization. We turn to look at these KMS next.

>> THE POSSESSION VIEW AND KNOWLEDGE MANAGEMENT SYSTEMS AS REPOSITORY

Like Enterprise Systems, KMS also assume a possession/structural view – valuable knowledge, located inside people's heads (i.e. the input) can be identified, captured and processed via the use of ICT tools so that it can be applied in new contexts (i.e. the output) (Tseng, 2007). The aim is thus to make the knowledge inside people's heads or knowledge embedded in successful routines widely available. Indeed, 'Knowledge Management' is frequently reduced to the implementation of ICTs for knowledge transfer (Jennex and Olfman, 2003; Scarbrough and Swan, 2001). Thus, surveys of firms introducing what they describe as 'Knowledge Management initiatives' show that these are dominated by ICT implementations. For example, Ruggles (1998) reports on a survey of 431 organizations and describes what firms are actually doing to 'manage knowledge'. The four initiatives that were the most popular were all related to ICT developments – creating an intranet, data warehousing, decision-support tools and groupware. Similar findings were reported by Alavi and Leidner (1999). A more recent survey in Australia (Xu and Quaddus, 2005) found that nearly 70 per cent of the 1500 participants indicated that they had some type of KMS. The range of what is defined as KMS has been expanded over time, but the same technologies still dominate. Thus, Xu and Quaddus identified the following as examples of KMS (with the % in brackets indicating their popularity):

E-mail (92%)	Video conferencing (43%)	Electronic bulletin boards (29%)	Best practice database (22%)	Extranet (17%)
Internet (90%)	Online discussion systems (40%)	Electronic meeting systems (26%)	Corporate yellow pages (22%)	Issue management systems (16%)
Databases (86%)	Workflow systems (39%)	Learning tools (25%)	Online analytical processing systems (21%)	Knowledge directories (15%)
Intranet (80%)	Data warehousing/ mining (37%)	People information archive (23%)	Knowledge repositories (21%)	Expert systems (8%)
Document management systems (60%)	Search and retrieval tools (36%)	Decision support systems (23%)	Knowledge portals (19%)	Artificial intelligence (5%)
Customer management systems (48%)	Executive information systems (34%)	Groupware (22%)	Lessons-learnt databases (18%)	

Alavi and Tiwana (2003) categorize these different KMS in terms of the knowledge processes that they aim to enhance (knowledge creation, storage, transfer and application), as depicted below:

Knowledge process	Knowledge creation	Knowledge storage	Knowledge transfer	Knowledge application
KMS	– E-learning systems – Collaboration support systems	– Knowledge repositories (data-warehousing and data-mining)	– Communication support systems (e-mail) – Enterprise information portals (intranets/internets)	– Expert systems – Decision support systems

This is helpful in the sense that it recognizes that different types of ICT will be more or less useful for different knowledge processes. At the same time, the Xu and Quaddus (2005) study demonstrates that it is the storage and transfer technologies which are most popular in terms of the types of KMS that are used in practice.

In relation to the storage and transfer processes, we can contrast two different types of KMS: McAfee (2006) describes these as 'platform' and 'channel' technologies; while Alavi (2000) distinguishes between 'network' and 'repository' technologies. Channel or network technologies (e.g. e-mail) can be used where it is clear that a particular individual or group needs specific information and knowledge from another individual – for example, a software project manager needing information from sales about the client requirements for a new system. Channel technologies are thus used to pass information and knowledge from a source to one or more recipients. In other cases, however, it is not known in advance who will need, or find useful, particular information and knowledge, either right now or in the future. In this situation some kind of platform or repository technology (e.g. an organizational intranet) is used so that people can store and search/retrieve information and knowledge as they need it. The fact that so many organizations have adopted these two types of KMS implies that decision-makers believe that sophisticated ICT tools can help in the capture, storage and transfer of knowledge.

Many commentators, however, are more sceptical about the utility of new ICTs for delivering organizational performance improvements (Blair, 2002). Thus, many organizations have put a lot of effort into putting content on to their intranets – a type of platform technology (McAfee, 2006), where documents can be stored and searched – but research has found that users do not always find these platform technologies useful. Davenport (2005), for example, found that only 44 per cent of survey respondents felt that it was easy to find information they needed by looking on the company intranet. The other very popular type of KMS involves channel technologies, such as e-mail (McAfee, 2006), which allow the sharing of documents between particular individuals, either one-to-one or one-to-many. This research finds that those involved in knowledge work rely more heavily on the channel (e.g. e-mail) than the platform (e.g. intranets) technologies, reflecting the extent to which knowledge work is a social activity dependent on joint production of knowledge. However, even the channel tools have problems with regards their ability to enhance knowledge processes. For example, Davenport (2005) found that 26 per cent of people in a survey felt that e-mail was over-used in their organization; 15 per cent felt that it reduced their productivity; and 21 per cent actually felt overwhelmed by the amount of e-mail that they received.

One reason for the limitations of these KMS, goes back to the earlier discussion in Chapter 3 about the mutual relationship between technology and organization. A KMS *per se*, will not in itself, improve the capture, storage and sharing of knowledge. It depends on how the KMS is perceived and used as part of people's everyday work practices. From all the many studies that have been done on the implementation of all kinds of ICT in an organization, we know that adoption of technology and its subsequent use are not straight-forwardly linked.

Another issue in understanding the problems with this kind of KMS is to reflect on why some knowledge may not readily lend itself to capture and codification. There are a number of reasons for this, including:

1. *Difficulty*: Some knowledge may just be too difficult to express in written form and so may be more effectively communicated through face-to-face interaction or learning by doing. For example, it may be far easier to simply show a person how to set up, log on and use a computer than to ask them to follow a set of detailed written instructions on how to do this. The complexity of computer manuals and the continued attempts by designers to create 'user-friendly' help services attests to this. The telephone helpline where knowledge can be communicated through two-way interaction is often preferred to the text-form help databases available on the computer itself.

2. *Uncertainty*: Some knowledge may be too uncertain. For example, I may feel that I 'know' that the best way to design a training course is to include humour and anecdotes. However, this is based on personal experience and intuition, and so I am uncertain of its accuracy. I am therefore not likely to write it down (in case it is wrong), although I may well share this 'knowledge' informally.

3. *Dynamism*: Some knowledge may be subject to continuous change. For example, 'process mapping' attempts to articulate and represent in written form the underlying processes involved in work tasks. However, organizational routines are subject to almost continuous change such that by the time the processes are mapped they are almost immediately out of date or wrong in some detail.

4. *Context-dependency*: Some knowledge may be highly context-dependent. For example, knowledge about how customers react to a particular new humorous marketing campaign is likely to be unique to a particular country, given what we know about national predispositions in humour. Reusing the same campaign in a different country, ignoring the importance of context, is likely to prove ineffective and may even produce the opposite effects to those expected.

5. *Cost*: Some knowledge may cost more to codify than to learn by trial and error. For example, writing down in detail instructions about how to use a simple mechanical device, like a stapler in an office environment, is not likely to prove very useful. This may sound like a trivial example, but it does not take much imagination to realize that there is an awful lot of material 'written down' in an organization, which is rarely if ever referred to.

6. *Politics*: Some knowledge may be politically too sensitive to codify. For example, very important knowledge when managing a project relates to who is a good team player and who is likely to be obstructive and difficult. It is very unlikely that someone will formally share this knowledge with others, stating on a database that 'Sue is a pain to work with!' (and in any case it might well be considered libelous if it were formally codified).

All these issues mean that what is actually available on the organizational KMS may be trivial and unhelpful while the really important knowledge continues to reside in everyday practices. Moreover, not only are there problems in actually codifying some knowledge, but also it must be recognized that people may be reluctant to even attempt to 'brain dump' what they 'know' onto a database because knowledge, or knowing, is also a key source of personal power within organizations. Ironically, in cases where knowledge really needs to be shared – that is, where it is both in short supply and central to the organization – there may be a particular reluctance amongst people to share it with others. This is because knowledge, or knowing, confers personal advantages – it means that some people can do things that others are not able to – and so is kept secret by the 'knower'.

More fundamentally, the practice view of knowledge suggests that KMS are limited by the very possession view of knowledge that they assume. Thus, the practice approach views knowledge (unlike data) as something that cannot simply be possessed and transferred; rather it is continuously recreated and reconstituted through dynamic, interactive, and social, action and interaction.

>> THE PRACTICE VIEW AND KNOWLEDGE MANAGEMENT SYSTEMS AS NETWORKING

As seen in Chapter 1, the epistemology of practice – that underpins both process and practice-sensitive accounts of knowledge work – starts from the premise that, truth, and so knowledge, is contestable, which means that knowledge cannot be transferred between people through ICTs in any straightforward way. A particular version of 'truth' can be transferred but, were this to be understood by the intended recipients (and this in itself is problematic), it may not be accepted given alternative 'justified true beliefs'. Knowledge, or rather knowing, cannot, therefore, be disassociated from the beliefs and experiences of those people that use it. ICTs marketed as 'Knowledge Management Systems' obscure and/or deny this socially constructed nature of knowledge. Instead, those promoting such systems imply that, by introducing standard processes and ICT-supported communication channels which link people and groups, 'best practice' knowledge can be shared throughout a global organization. However, unlike data, knowledge cannot be simply transferred from a sender to a receiver. Data can be directly transferred but their interpretation, which involves the process of 'knowing', may be highly variable (Galliers and Newell, 2003).

The knowledge-as-practice view highlights the importance of relationships, and shared understandings and attitudes to knowledge formation and knowledge sharing (Kofman and Senge, 1993). It is important to acknowledge these issues since they help to define the likely success or failure of attempts to implement KMS. The knowledge-as-practice view suggests that it is likely to be fairly easy to share knowledge between individuals who are relatively homogeneous in terms of their practice, because they share a common understanding and meaning/belief system. For example, globally distributed software engineers, with a similar training and understanding, may be able to work collaboratively without much difficulty and to share information via a KMS. However, it is extremely difficult for such globally distributed collaboration to occur where the individuals have heterogeneous beliefs and understandings, as in the Research Team case in Chapter 4. Yet, the sharing of knowledge across functional, organizational and/or national boundaries is precisely the goal of most KMS initiatives. Paradoxically, then, this means that attempts to manage knowledge using KMS may actually be most problematic in the very conditions where the need is greatest – that is, where there are significant divisions of practice.

Developments in ICT do, however, open up opportunities for knowledge work and knowledge workers from a practice perspective. In particular, new material properties of ICT, in particular the development of the so-called Web 2.0 and Enterprise 2.0, can facilitate the types of interaction that support knowing in practice. These developments led *Time* Magazine in 2006 to nominate the person of the year as 'You'. This was to celebrate how all kinds of content – news, entertainment, information of all kinds, reviews and so on – was being created, not by dedicated corporations who would then transmit this content to passive recipients, but by everyone using Web 2.0 technologies. Web 2.0 is a term used to describe the new type of software that allows users themselves to create content and share directly with each other, whether through social networking sites like Facebook, MySpace, YouTube and LinkedIn, or through wikis and blogs. The Internet has thus become a tool for collaboration and networking rather than a repository.

In the context of an organization, McAfee (2006) uses the term 'Enterprise 2.0' to define these same kinds of technologies, but used within the firewall of an organization. The key characteristic of these 2.0 technologies, according to McAfee, is that they not only allow the sharing of documents (i.e. outputs of knowledge work) but also make visible the *practices* of knowledge workers and interdependencies between practices (i.e. valuable process knowledge not just content or product knowledge – see Chapter 4). Thus, Web 2.0 technologies allow users to observe the processes of knowledge production, as well as the output – who adds/deletes/amends something over time and what they have added/deleted/amended. McAfee suggests that there are six key features of 2.0 technologies that differentiate them from traditional ICT:

1. Search – new tools that make it possible to search for information rather than having to rely on navigation options.

2. Links – dynamic links between content, reflecting how people have actually moved across pages and sites, make it possible to identify related content, thus facilitating users in finding useful content.

3. Authoring – blogs (enabling individuals to author content that others can add to), wikis (enabling groups to author content in an iterative fashion)

and YouTube (enabling individuals or groups to produce multi-media content for others to view) provide everyone the opportunity to author content that others can read or view – many people are now actively engaged in either producing or consuming this user-generated content.

4. Tags – allow individuals to have control of categorizing the content of their digital material (e.g. del-icio.us allows users to tag websites with bookmarks). These user-generated categorization systems are called folksonomies – a folksonomy emerges over time depending on what users find useful to group together based on the information structures and relationships that are actually used in practice.

5. Extensions – systems can also go beyond this tagging process to develop algorithms based on the pattern of use of different information which then allows for automatic referrals to individuals who have shown interest in a certain type of content. This is done by Amazon very effectively to make recommendations to their customers of other books they might enjoy reading, based on their pattern of consumption to-date as compared to the millions of other customers.

6. Signals – given the sheer amount of information that is digitally available, it can also be helpful to have certain information automatically pushed to users based on their interests. Signals are the means of doing this, alerting users to the fact that new information is available that they may be interested in. RSS (really simple syndication) is now a popular technology that provides this kind of signal.

All of these features of 2.0 technologies suggest a very different environment as compared to a repository environment. McAfee (2006), thus, argues, that

> Enterprise 2.0 technologies have the potential to let an intranet become what the Internet already is – an online platform with a constantly changing structure built by distributed autonomous and largely self-interested peers. On this platform, authoring creates content; links and tags knit it together; and search, extensions, tags and signals make emergent structures and patterns in the content visible and help people stay on top of it all.
>
> (p. 26)

In reality, however, many organizations have yet to take advantage of 2.0 technologies. A major reason is that they can reduce managerial control and may be used by some to express negativity, which many senior managers want to avoid. For example, individuals can use blogs to broadcast weaknesses in a company's strategy or to deride organizational decision-makers. Some may fear that chaos may rein if knowledge workers are allowed to add or change content on their departmental website without this being vetted by a central authority. Nevertheless, we can expect that KMS will change over time in organizations as the potential of these new 2.0 technologies become more fully understood, especially in support of knowledge work, and more accepted in practice. For now, repository systems remain dominant.

>> CONCLUSIONS

In this chapter we have considered the fallacy of assuming that the adoption of Enterprise Systems or KMS such as company intranets will allow an organization to painlessly improve the management of knowledge processes within an organization. We have recognized the importance of engagement in practice as an essential vehicle for developing, what Orlikowski (2002) refers to as 'knowledgeability'. Taking the position that knowledge is an outcome of participation in practice, and not just something possessed by individuals, we have indicated how traditional KMS systems do have a role but that their limitations must be acknowledged. In fact, we would suggest that it is a misnomer to call many of these systems KM systems – reverting to the, albeit less sexy, label of 'information systems' may in fact provide a more fruitful way forward in terms of thinking about how such systems can enable (or disable) knowledge work. Newer Web 2.0 and Enterprise 2.0 technologies provide promise for the future as tools that play a role in the generation of knowledge as well as supporting traditional sharing of documents. In particular, these newer tools are important because they can help to make visible ongoing practices of knowledge workers. The case of ICC, presented next, illustrates the major challenges of KMS outlined in this chapter.

CASE STUDY 7.1
INTERNATIONAL CONSULTANCY COMPANY (ICC)*

ICC is a medium-sized, private, US-based management consulting company, which operates out of 16 offices located worldwide in the American, European, Japanese, Chinese and Indian markets. It turns over approximately $250 million per year, employing around 800 employees, of which approximately 600 are consultants. Its core business lies in counselling established firms across different industry sectors on how to improve their operational strategy, and how to achieve product, supply chain, customer experience and business technology innovations. It claims to differentiate itself from competitors through its focus on implementation, driven by a highly engineering-oriented workforce and culture. Its client base includes many market-leading companies across a large variety of industry sectors, including healthcare, government, and electronics and computing. The company structure is organized geographically with one global managing director and three regional managing directors, who are respectively in charge of the Americas, Europe and Asia regions. The rest of the consultants can be classified into the roles of directors, principals, managers, associates and consultants, sorted in a hierarchically descending order. Directors are the owners and shareholders of the company.

The management consultancy grew steadily and reached a size and global span, which made it difficult to harness the knowledge that was being developed throughout the organization. Directors recognized that this situation would only worsen over the years, as plans to expand in new, emerging markets were already under way. In addition, other management consultancies had already implemented KMS and it was thought that such technology would be instrumental to stay abreast of the competition by providing clients with a better service in less time. Hence, in 2003, the company implemented the SharePoint KMS developed by Microsoft and built a team of two knowledge managers to handle it.

>> THE KMS AT ICC

The KMS at ICC functions as a repository of documents. In terms of the supply side, at the end of every project, consultants are encouraged, although never coerced, to upload what is termed a knowledge closeout. A knowledge closeout is a standard template document, which consultants fill in with information of the project they are

---

* This case was authored by Michael Vellat.

currently staffed on. The form requires them to input information about the type of project, the steps undertaken, the lessons learned and so on. Once this is done, consultants should go to a specific web-page on the KMS and upload the document onto the system. Before this, however, they are required to supply the metadata that will allow for the document to be searchable once it is on the system. The metadata to be input consists of name, date, type of practice, type of service delivered, document importance and so on. Document importance refers to the value of the document: consultants can decide to tag a particular document as 'premium content'. Knowledge closeouts are not the sole documents that are uploaded. PowerPoint presentations detailing common frameworks and processes applied throughout projects can be frequently found. Yet, the vast majority of documents are stored and presented from a project-perspective, as opposed to a topic- or time-perspective. What this means is that although you can search documents from different angles, when they are retrieved and downloaded, they always present knowledge in terms of the different steps and processes undertaken in a project, as dictated by the knowledge closeout template.

In terms of the demand side, consultants can go on the home page of the KMS and use the search facility to search for relevant articles. The site is tailored to the specific characteristics of the organization and allows consultants to perform searches according to authors (i.e. director who led the project), client type, practice areas, service areas and industry type. For instance, if you go into the industry areas and click on electronics and computing, then the KMS will display the titles of all the documents that pertain to that industry sector in order of importance (i.e. premium content is displayed first). Alternatively, if the consultant searches for a particular keyword, such as 'product development', the KMS will retrieve all the documents that have metadata matching that keyword.

There is also a special section termed the 'People Section' on the KMS, which does not possess content related to projects. Instead, it allows searching for the profiles of other consultants. Such profiles usually contain information on the education of the consultant, her/his work undertaken prior to joining the company, and the types of projects she/he has been involved in with the management consultancy so far.

The KM team is responsible for monitoring and fostering the use of the KMS. They publish a monthly KM report, which gives an overview of metrics aimed at assessing the performance of the KMS and the use made of it by consultants. Metrics most commonly used include number of monthly searches undertaken, number of monthly searchers and so on. These reports show that of the 600 consultants, about two-thirds use the KMS and most of the searches are directed to the 'People Section'.

Factors affecting the KMS use

Access: Most of the time, consultants are either on the road or on a client site. Only rarely do they come to the office. This forces them to access the KMS from the client location or over a wireless connection. The problems with this are threefold: first, the procedure is highly cumbersome; secondly, the connection is much slower; thirdly, the client may not always grant the consultants access to their network:

So, the big challenge we have is that as we try to keep the system secure we have to have some safeguards as to accessibility. On the flipside our ability to access the system is not always seamless based on where we are. For example, one of my main clients I have worked with almost continuously over the last 5 years and with whom the management consultancy has worked for over 12 years blocks our VPN from usage. So, we have alternative connectivity technologies around our portal software that do allow us to access the KM system, but quite frankly they are less convenient to use and they do somewhat inhibit the use of the KM system. So, for example if somebody sent me a link to a particular document in the KM system I cannot directly access that link going through our portal.

Uploading: Consultants find the process of uploading documents on the KMS highly cumbersome and complex. The reason behind this was the large amount of metadata that the system requires to be submitted along with the document. Consultants work in a highly pressurized environment where they have very little spare time. Coercing them to fill in lengthy metadata forms for the submission of every single document saps their incentive to contribute to the system:

> So, every time you want to upload anything, you got to put in your name, the day it was created, the category, and I understand why that information is important, but it takes a lot of time to upload a document. And people that are in this indus-try and people that work for the management consulting company are extremely busy and overloaded that no one is willing to take the time that requires to fill in all the additional information.

Layout: The problems do not merely plague the access to the system or the upload-ing process, but also the surfing of the KMS. The layout of the website is perceived by some as user-unfriendly:

> I also find it that sometimes it is not clear how I get back from where I came from. Sure, hit the back button, but from a structural perspective I wasn't clear how I could get back to a similar area to where I was before [...]. I wanted to go back and I wanted to find a logical way to go back, but for most areas the layout changes quite completely.

Search: Lastly, the searching facility provided by the KMS was perceived to do a bad job at ranking content:

> But one thing we found out is that when we put keywords into the searching sys-tem, usually the best results do not appear at the top, which means that we have to flip over different pages and then maybe you find something you want. Some-times the result is not accurate in reflecting the information you wanted to search for. I think that is an area that can be improved.

>> KMS USE AND CONSULTANT EXPERIENCE

The KMS is used differently by consultants with under two years of experience – referred to as less experienced consultants or LECs – and those with more experience (MECs). LECs tend to undertake what we can term a gap/synthesis analysis – they sift through the documents to learn how past projects have been undertaken and understand what common practice is. They seek to make up for their relative inexperience by acquiring knowledge about those activities that have been performed for years within the management consultancy and which are widely documented and similar throughout projects. The KMS is not necessarily used to solve a particular problem, but simply to familiarize and understand what will be required of them and what they are expected to do:

> I download typically more than 20 or 30 files, which are related to the topic or the kind of project we are working on [...]. We are addressing similar issues as the ones addressed in the documents even though they are not exactly the same. So, we use some of the approaches in the documents to help us. So, we use the documents to figure out which way is the best to deal with the particular client. [...] That helps us generate some ideas and understand what the traditional way is to approach a client.

MECs, on the other hand, use the KMS much less frequently, mostly because when they need knowledge it is new knowledge:

> If we've never done it, it would be really hard to find it, even if we have done something similar to it, because it would never be tagged appropriately, or no one would have ever thought about it. So, it is only the second or third time you are looking for something that you could rely on a system. And I find that most of the requests you get from people are new things, which we haven't done yet. You know, these are things that are on the edge of something. Like you have painted your room blue before and now you are painting it blue with stripes, but we've never done stripes. I can find something about painting blue, but I have no idea what to do about the stripes [...].

MECs make much more use of the 'People Section' on the KMS and sift through the backgrounds of other consultants in terms of the projects they have undertaken and what practice they belong to in order to select people who may help them with the new knowledge they are looking for:

> [...] The number 1 reason I go onto KM now is actually to go find people's profiles and look at the resumes of consulting staff, for instance for staffing a new project or get in contact with someone who knows about something I need. And that is a reason for me to log into the system, access the system, and get familiar with the system.

However, despite its existence, the 'people section' was never developed to fulfil this purpose and does not provide contact details, such as e-mail or phone number.

>> THE KMS AND COLLABORATION

All consultants expressed a strong need for direct collaboration, shedding light upon the limits of the collaboration capabilities of the current KMS. Even in this instance, however, consultants diverged in their opinions of what would provide an appropriate direct collaborative technology. In fact, MECs called for highly interactive and on-demand collaboration that would address their specific knowledge needs as they surfaced. LECs, on the other hand, requested more content-based and incremental collaboration through time, which relied less on human interaction. In fact, LECs seemed to be very enthusiastic about the possibilities from a wiki as a collaborative tool:

I think that a wiki could help us share ideas about a particular topic. For example, you might want to look at the issues surrounding product development or sourcing and supply chain issues and whilst you have some ideas, you don't know exactly how to solve the client's problems. So, if people all go to the same place and share some ideas with you, even if they are not on the same project that could be very useful. Yes, I think that if such a technology could be used that would be very useful.

MECs, on the other hand, thought wikis would be less of a panacea:

I don't see that playing a major role to be honest with you. [...] I don't want something else that I have to check every day. I read emails every day, I get a million phone calls every day, I don't need a new thing such as a wiki [...]. Maybe for some people that would be great, but for me that would not be helpful. It's not like working at an office [...].

>> QUESTIONS

1. What do you see as the main strengths and limitations of the KMS at ICC?
2. How would you describe the problems of the KMS at ICC – technical, organizational or a combination of both?
3. Why do you think there are differences between the MECs and LECs in terms of their use of the KMS at ICC?
4. What recommendations would you make to ICC to improve their KMS?

Summary of key learning points

>> Two types of ICT are often defined as supporting 'Knowledge Management' – Enterprise Systems, which supposedly embed 'best practice' knowledge, and Knowledge Management Systems, which supposedly facilitate the transfer of knowledge across individuals and groups.

>> Enterprise Systems follow the historical trajectory of attempting to standardize work and embed knowledge in systems (rather than in workers). However, the idea that they can embed 'best practice' knowledge is inherently problematic.

>> The most prevalent KMS initiatives involve the introduction of ICTs, for example, e-mail, intranets, databases, groupware.

>> The majority of current KMS can be described as either platform or channel technologies.

>> Both platform and channel KMS have limitations because they are based on a structural 'epistemology of possession' view and so neglect process and practice and the socially constructed, context-dependent nature of knowledge.

>> Newer forms of ICT – Web 2.0 and Enterprise 2.0 – have the potential to expose knowledge practices and so, potentially, can play an important role in the future in encouraging knowledge sharing and knowledge creation.

8

THE ROLE OF SOCIAL NETWORKS AND BOUNDARY-SPANNERS

Chapter Outline

Learning Outcomes

At the end of this chapter you should be able to:

⇒ Evaluate the contribution of networks and networking to knowledge work.

⇒ Discuss the role of different types of social network in enabling and constraining knowledge flows.

⇒ Assess the role of boundary spanners in connecting localized networks.

⇒ Identify different types of community relevant to knowledge work and analyse their impact on knowledge sharing between groups.

⇒ Discuss the positive and negative effects of social networks on change and innovation in organizations.

>> INTRODUCTION

Previous chapters have already touched on the importance of social networks in different aspects of knowledge work. In this chapter, the role that they play takes centre-stage as we explore the many different ways in which such networks – and there are many different types of network – can both enhance and sometimes hinder the management of knowledge work.

As we will discuss in this chapter, social networks play a variety of roles in knowledge work. These roles really arise out of the close interdependence which we noted previously between patterns of social relations and the creation and sharing of knowledge. As this interdependence is played out in different social and institutional contexts, we find that social networks may act variously as channels enabling the flow of knowledge amongst different groups; containers, limiting such flows through the divisions between different groups; creators of new knowledge as new ideas emerge from interactions within and across networks; and custodians of established forms of knowledge. Understanding the role that social networks may play in any particular context, therefore, involves appreciating the features of different types of network and how they impact the creation and flow of knowledge.

There are many different approaches to analysing the role which social networks play in knowledge work. Some of these approaches focus more at the industry and economy level and highlight the importance of underlying social networks that connect groups and individuals within a particular geographical area or industry sector. Because these networks connect individuals across organizations they are an important source of what are termed 'spillovers' by which knowledge somehow manages to flow between organizations below the radar of management (Owen-Smith and Powell, 2004). These spillovers help to explain the concentration of innovative activities in certain places – for example, Hollywood for movies, Silicon Valley for computing, London for the advertising industry and the United Kingdom's M4 corridor for motorsport.

Another less-developed strand in existing studies focuses on the level of the individual. Studies here have highlighted the importance of active networking by individuals in areas such as the development of innovations and for overcoming the limitations of existing networks. Although such networking is often seen as a purely selfish and exploitative activity, some recent work has suggested that the most successful networkers are generous in cultivating relationships and are quick to reciprocate the exchange of knowledge and information with others (Cross et al., 2003). New social networking sites, such as LinkedIn, thrive on the basis that networks can be personally rewarding, but only if those involved contribute to, as well as take from, the network.

The focus of this chapter, however, is firmly on the *organizational* impact of social networks. In this respect, we can identify two major theoretical approaches to such networks. One approach emphasizes the role of networks as *channels* for the flow of knowledge. In this approach, the benefits of the network are the connectivity it provides between individuals and organizations. This allows knowledge to flow across different groups and settings. The second major approach is to see social networks as *communities*. This approach emphasizes not so much the form and structure of the network as the quality of the relationships within it. In particular, it highlights the importance of shared practices and understandings amongst the members of the community. Where the first approach emphasizes the benefits of knowledge flow, a focus on community highlights the benefits of shared learning.

>> NETWORKS AS CHANNELS

Much of the research in this area focuses on the way social networks enable knowledge to flow between groups and organizations. This is certainly an important effect of such networks and well worth discussing. But, before we move on to this positive effect of networks, it is worth remembering that in some settings social networks can operate as exclusive clubs or 'old boy networks' which close down knowledge flows, restrict less privileged groups such as women and ethnic minorities, and generally hamper innovation and change. Thus, as Edelman et al. note, social networks are double-edged in their effects – sometimes supporting and speeding knowledge flows, but at other points, slowing or halting them (Edelman et al., 2004).

Turning to the more positive effects of networks, we can note first that their role in knowledge flows is to a large extent influenced by their shape and structure. Horizontal networks extending across multiple organizations, for example, enable the transfer of knowledge across organizational and inter-organizational boundaries (Alter and Hage, 1993; Conway, 1995). The network's ability to cut across such boundaries depends not only on its structure but also on the kind of social ties that it contains. The importance of such ties is revealed by studies based on the techniques of social network analysis. One of the persistent findings from such studies is the tendency for knowledge to flow only within the bounds set by existing networks. This was highlighted, for instance, by one such analysis of knowledge sharing within a major pharmaceutical company. This found that 70 per cent of knowledge sharing amongst the company's five R&D centres worldwide took place *within* the individual centres and only 5 per cent *between* centres: this despite the fact that groups within the five centres were working on a number of common problems. This lack of knowledge sharing between the centres was attributed not so much to geographical distance as to the lack of social ties between them. Levels of trust and social interaction were low because recent closures of some facilities had left the centres feeling that they were in competition with each other (Scarbrough, 2003).

As indicated above, the quality of the social ties making up a network is important because it helps to determine the network's capacity as a channel for knowledge. Here, we need to distinguish between 'strong' and 'weak ties'. Strong ties are trust-based and denote close personal relationships with family, friends and workmates (Granovetter, 1973). Weak ties, however, encompass the individual's relationships with a much wider group of contacts and acquaintances.

Subsequent work has suggested that networks based on strong ties have greater capacity in that they can enable the transfer of more tacit forms of knowledge (Grandori and Soda, 1995; Kreiner and Schultz, 1993; Oliver and Liebeskind, 1998; Ring and Van de Ven, 1994). However, this does not mean that networks based on strong ties are always the most effective. For one, strong ties take longer to evolve and therefore require a bigger investment in time. For another, as highlighted by Granovetter's original study, strong tie networks are more localized and therefore contain more redundant information. Weak ties are much more likely to be a source of new information. Granovetter termed this phenomenon 'the strength of weak ties'. One of the implications of this insight, subsequently reinforced by further empirical studies, is that weak tie networks may be much more efficient and effective for the transfer of explicit forms of knowledge (Hansen, 1999).

Role of boundary-spanners

One of the puzzling features of social networks is termed the 'small world' effect. We will often remark 'it's a small world' when we find that we share a link, such as a mutual friend or acquaintance, with a complete stranger in a totally different part of the world. This effect was given empirical support by a 1960s study which is said to have found that anyone in the world is connected to anyone else by only six links between existing social contacts – that is just 'six degrees of separation' (Milgram, 1967).

What is puzzling about the 'small world' effect, and why we tend to find it a bit uncanny when we experience it, is that it flies in the face of our everyday experience. We know from personal experience, as well as from research, that our individual networks are generally pretty localized, being based on our job, spatial proximity and family ties. Their boundaries act as cut-off points in social ties and information flows which keep different groups more or less separate from each other. How then can we be linked to people on the far side of the world or in totally different social groups? The simple answer is that our local networks become connected globally through a small number of links between highly connected people within each group. These highly connected people have been given a number of different labels but the easiest way to define what they do is to call them 'boundary-spanners' (Allen, 1977). These are people who enjoy membership of different groups and hence are able to span the boundaries of social networks.

Now, the role of boundary spanners has been widely discussed in research studies. For example, some studies highlight their importance in developing and maintaining inter-organizational links (Tushman and Scanlon, 1981). Most organizations can be analysed in terms of more inward-facing and more outward-facing groups, and it is often a few key individuals within the latter who are responsible for many of the links which a firm develops with other organizations.

Boundary-spanners can also be important within the organization in their ability to manage relationships across internal interfaces, such as between project groups, functional departments and divisions. A classic example of their importance is at the internal boundary between marketing and R&D (Rothwell et al., 1974). It may seem paradoxical to discuss boundary-spanning *within* an organization, but a repeated research finding is that different groups within firms often fail to share knowledge. Sometimes this is due to organizational politics. Frequently knowledge worker groups will exploit their knowledge as a power-base to influence other groups within the organization, including top management (Willem and Scarbrough, 2006). Equally, some individuals may exploit their position at the boundaries of different groups to derive personal power for themselves. Where this happens they act more as a 'gatekeeper' than a boundary-spanner, cleverly manipulating the flow of knowledge and information to pursue their own personal objectives (Pettigrew, 1973). A similar observation may apply to the way in which certain networks constrain the spread of new ideas (Swan et al., 1999a). This applies, for example, to professional groups who establish and control boundaries around specialized work. On other occasions, groups within the organization may find it difficult to share knowledge not because they are particularly resistant, but because they operate in different social worlds and are consequently incapable of grasping the value of other groups' knowledge (Boland and Tenkasi, 1995; Carlile, 2002). In this context, boundary spanning individuals become important in translating the experience of particular individuals or groups into the language understood by others in the wider organization (Cook and Brown, 1999).

While much of the research on boundary-spanners has focused on their *organizational* impact, in some situations they can also play a key entrepreneurial role by being strategically positioned between groups. Entrepreneurial knowledge workers can gain great benefits by positioning themselves in the so-called 'structural holes' which separate non-overlapping sources of information between networks (Burt, 1992). This allows individuals to act as 'knowledge brokers' by trading in the knowledge which is available in one network yet is in scarce supply in another.

>> NETWORKS AS COMMUNITIES

From a networks as communities perspective, social networks are seen as providing a vital context for the creation and sharing of knowledge. This places a different emphasis on the characteristics of such networks, with less focus on their structure and scope, and more on the way that network members engage with and form a community that is able to shape their thoughts and actions. The major differences between this view and the view of networks as channels are outlined in Table 8.1. These contrasting views show that significant differences can exist between social networks in their structures, benefits for participants and patterns of evolution. While the table presents these differences in a stylized way, it is important to recognize that social networks which operate primarily as channels have very different dynamics and effects compared to those which develop more as communities. Thus, a channel type of network will

Table 8.1   Contrasting views of social networks

	Channels	**Communities**
Basic unit	Individual	Social group
Supports	Information flows	Ways of knowing
Engagement	Personal ties	Shared identity
Benefits from	Connectivity (scale & scope)	Shared learning
Increasing bandwidth through	Trust	Shared practices
Growth through	Rapid via communications & resources	Slow via shared goals and identity
Structure	Open	Closed

be better at sharing information but poor at sharing learning. It is likely to be more open and less exclusive, because it connects individuals rather than groups. However, social ties remain important because they help to increase bandwidth (the carrying capacity of the network) by fostering trust. Channel types of network are often favoured by managers and policy-makers because they are easier to establish – requiring some investments in time and resources to support social interaction and communications.

In contrast, where the network is best viewed as a community, the structure is less open because members' participation is intensive and dependent on shared identities. The community is also more likely to support distinctive ways of knowing – for example, certain kinds of specialist and professional expertise – than the free sharing of information. Such communities are also slower to grow because they depend to a much greater extent on a feeling of shared goals. On the other hand, they can also be more robust over time because they are ultimately based on shared social practices rather than more fragile personal ties or communication links.

As we will see, a focus on communities gives us a number of fresh insights into the actions of knowledge workers which cannot be explained simply by their individual characteristics or by the tasks which they undertake. In many settings, the knowledge which is applied in knowledge work is as much a product of a wider community, as it is the individual worker's own thought processes (as we discussed in Chapter 3 when we were looking specifically at knowledge creation). Before we identify this important influence on knowledge work, however, we need to carefully disentangle the different meanings which have been applied to the word 'community'. This is a word which conveys a powerful and generally positive meaning. It is often used as part of a politician's or manager's discourse to enrol individuals into a shared enterprise. Developing a community in this self-conscious way can be an important manoeuvre in fostering innovation (Swan et al., 2002).

Setting aside the discursive use of the term itself, there are several different views of what constitutes a community in existing studies. One view emphasizes what we term *emergent communities* which develop from the bottom-up through informal interactions within a particular social group. A second view is concerned more with the formally defined groups which are established by organizations, often in a top-down way, to contribute to organizational performance. These we will term *managed communities*. Finally, the most recent development is the spread of the many communities whose members interact primarily or exclusively through information systems and the Internet. These *online communities* may have elements of both the emergent and managed forms (and vice versa) but are definable primarily in terms of their medium of interaction rather than the nature of their development.

Emergent communities

Research on emergent communities has tended to build on an early and highly influential study carried out by Lave and Wenger (1991). A key idea here was the proposition that knowledge is not simply a cognitive phenomenon – something which resides in the head of the individual. Instead, these authors saw knowledge as something which emerges out of the way people learn. Their study went on to argue that individuals learn by carrying out tasks within a specific social group which helps them make sense of their work. What they do individually is thus not an isolated activity, but part of a 'social practice' which they carry out and experience alongside other members of their group. This dual emphasis on social practices and the individual's identification with a community was reflected in Lave and Wenger's use of the term 'community of practice' to denote the social contexts that shaped individual learning. In its original formulation, the term was not really referring to specific, identified communities but to the emergent interplay between learning and socialization within localized groups.

Their study has two important implications for our understanding of knowledge work. First, it suggests that knowledge and learning are closely tied up with *social practices*. One important result of this, as we will see, is that people generally find it much easier to share knowledge with someone who is engaged in the same social practice as they are. The second is that knowledge work is very often shaped by the wider communities through which individuals learn. Lave and Wenger (1991, p. 51), for instance, describe learning in terms of 'legitimate peripheral participation'; a kind of informal apprenticeship through which individuals learn not so much how to mimic a particular practice but rather how to become a practitioner. Learning is thus seen as involving a change in the individual and is related to their socialization and identity formation within a particular community. This wider community helps to determine both what knowledge is relevant and how it should be applied to specific tasks.

Emergent communities of this kind are of interest for a number of reasons. For one, they are often important contexts for the sharing of knowledge across formal boundaries within and between organizations – helping to explain the knowledge 'spillovers' mentioned earlier. Also, because they emerge from the bottom-up, and out of the way people work and the groups they work in, they escape the usual forms of control and accountability. They do not appear on organization charts, and are responsible to no one but to themselves. Individuals only become involved voluntarily because they have something to learn and to contribute. This allows us to distinguish such communities from teams, which, though equally unlikely to figure on the organization chart, are much more explicitly linked into formal systems of goal-setting and accountability. Teams have goals and leaders, and they are accountable for delivering outputs – reports, new products and so on – within a specific timescale. The team disbands when the project is completed. In contrast, an emergent community is open-ended. It has neither deadlines nor specific 'deliverables'. Brown and Duguid (1998) define such communities by making a distinction between 'know-what' and 'know-how' (also termed 'explicit' and 'tacit' knowledge). They argue that know-how includes the ability to put know-what into practice and is typically found amongst work groups engaged cooperatively in the same work practices.

One further important dimension of emergent communities has to do with the way in which knowledge is shared. Wenger (1998) has suggested that knowledge sharing within communities is facilitated by three features. First, *mutual engagement* which has to do with the dynamics of interacting together socially, leading to the development of trust and a set of mutual relationships. Second, *joint enterprise* – in other words, some kind of shared norms and accountability in behaviour. And, third, *shared repertoire*, which has to do with the circulation of shared stories and concepts related to practice.

Communities exhibiting these features find that many of the usual barriers to knowledge sharing are lowered. For example, community members have typically developed a set of shared meanings deriving from their common experience. One consequence is that they can employ more specialized forms of language or technical jargon for their communication. They do not have to spell out the basic assumptions or contextual features that their insight and experience relate to – these are already understood (Bernstein, 1975). This knowledge sharing is facilitated by the norms of reciprocity – 'you help me and I will help you' – and the levels of trust generated amongst the community.

One result of these features of communities of practice is that story-telling is a more important way of communicating knowledge than codifying it in ICT systems (Brown and Duguid, 1991). Stories are important because:

- They present information in an interesting way – they have a beginning, a middle and an end, and they involve people behaving well or badly.
- They personalize the information – instead of talking about situations in the abstract, we hear about the doings of individuals whom we might know or have heard of.
- They bring people together, emphasizing a shared social identity and interests – we 'share' knowledge rather than 'transfer' it.
- Stories express values – they often contain a moral about certain kinds of behaviour leading to either positive or negative outcomes.

In this way, stories link information with interest, values and relevance, giving us a sense of the context in which experience has been developed and helping us to grasp the tacit nature of some of the knowledge being communicated.

Emergent communities can be seen as a vital ingredient in the individual organization's ability to learn – making knowledge a collective resource for the organization, rather than the property of a particular individual. A good example of this is provided by Orr's (1990) influential study of customer service representatives ('reps') who repair the photocopiers of Xerox customers. From the management viewpoint, a rep's work is well-defined and largely independent. Customers with problems call the Customer Service Centre, which in turn notifies a rep. He or she goes to the customer's site and, with the help of the error codes displayed and a problem-solving manual, diagnoses the problem and applies the specified fix. When Orr looked at the reps' work more closely, however, he found that they did not operate independently at all. Their working day typically revolved around informal meetings with other reps over breakfast, lunch and coffee. At these meetings the reps would swap war stories about malfunctioning machines that could not be repaired simply by going through the know-what of the repair manual. This sharing of stories was not a technical exercise, just part of their everyday socializing. Orr found that one of these informal conversations would be worth hours of training. While chatting, the reps posed questions to each other, offered solutions, laughed at mistakes and generally kept each other up to date about what they knew and what they had learned on the job. As a result, knowledge was shared extensively about the ways of dealing with unusual glitches and problems that were simply not covered in the photocopier repair manual.

While the Xerox case highlights the value of the emergent community as a forum for knowledge sharing, it is important to acknowledge some of the potentially negative implications of such settings for the management of knowledge work. In Chapter 3, for example, we highlighted the problem of 'groupthink' as one of the negative potential outcomes of team-working. Although emergent communities operate on a much more extensive scale and are not subject to the same group dynamics, the potential loss of objectivity can also be a problem where large numbers of people come to share a similar world-view or perspective (Locke, 1999). The danger inherent in such communities is for a more conservative outlook to dominate, creating barriers against external groups or new ideas. As we will observe in Chapter 9, this can frustrate innovation projects as it inhibits the kind of knowledge sharing and trust which such projects need to achieve across communities or professional groups.

Although there is much evidence for the value of a community approach to knowledge work, in the past organizations were reluctant to develop this approach. This is partly because management have tended to emphasize individual roles and the use of technology to 'capture' knowledge. The concept of a community can often seem nebulous to managers who favour more immediate solutions for their problems.

A further problem for management is that the cultural features of emergent communities often run counter to the established norms of the organization. Their implicit values tend to be based on collegiality, reciprocity and influence based on expertise. This may pose a challenge for organizations which have traditionally emphasized efficiency, contractual relationships and influence based on formal roles. A good example of the challenge posed by emergent communities comes from the Xerox case described above. It took some time for Xerox management to recognize the value of the community of practice amongst its customer service reps. Their original attitude, like that of many other management groups, was much more hostile. Informal gatherings of this kind run counter to management's desire to control activities and resources. The typical reaction of managers is to see them as a threat to efficiency. For these reasons, Xerox initially sought to eliminate the reps' informal meetings. This quickly had the apparently beneficial result of increasing the number of calls which reps made to customers. Unfortunately, because knowledge was no longer being shared amongst the reps, the number of repeat calls to deal with the same machine problem also increased. Greater productivity in terms of hours on the job was actually leading to greater inefficiency in terms of solving customer problems. Xerox quickly relented and allowed the informal gatherings to be reinstated.

Managed communities

With growing recognition of the advantages of emergent communities has come an increasing effort by organizations to exploit these advantages in a more systematic way. From the grudging acceptance offered by Xerox management, many companies have now moved towards a much more positive stance; not only accommodating or supporting emergent communities, but even attempting to develop new communities themselves. Some of these managed communities, as we will call them, overlap with emergent communities inasmuch as they are really formalizing and enhancing already existing identities and learning around shared practices. Where such overlaps exist, managed communities may find it easier to get the member engagement which – even with management support – is still required for success.

Research on managed communities is still at a relatively early stage. Initial studies have sometimes been sceptical about managers' ability to develop or sustain such communities. Thompson, for example, argues that communities are 'best left alone, free from interference by organisational managers and policy makers' (Thompson, 2005, p. 151). There have also been suggestions that such managed communities are a covert effort to overcome employee resistance to knowledge sharing (Contu and Willmott, 2003). These criticisms certainly reflect some aspects of the way in which the notion of community has been taken up by managers. One of the reasons for the success of the community of practice at Xerox, for example, was its democratic, non-hierarchical character. As the Xerox study showed, knowledge flows much more readily in horizontal peer-to-peer networks than in hierarchical structures, precisely because all the network's members see themselves as on the same side. Introducing managers into such networks only recreates the unequal power relations that make hierarchies such a poor medium for knowledge sharing.

These features help to explain why even writers who are more positive about managed communities believe that they can only be successful if managers find new ways of managing. Wenger (1998), for example, argues that managed communities can only succeed if managers limit their tendency towards controlling activities. Managed communities need to be *cultivated* rather than *controlled*. Such cultivation might involve a number of activities, including public events such as 'knowledge fairs' that bring the community together; multiple forms of leadership, including 'thought leaders', networkers and people who document practice; inter-community learning projects; and the creation and dissemination of artefacts such as documents, tools, stories, websites and so on.

Cultivation is not without cost. Not only does it require investment in new IT systems and event organization, but it may also involve the creation of new specialist roles. This was demonstrated in the Buckman Labs case described in the HRM chapter where the company developed what were in effect managed communities. These were based on underlying communities that emerged around the online problem-solving forums created by the K'Netix system.

As these informal networks of specialists evolved, and their value to the company became apparent, Buckman sought to cultivate them by providing additional resources, including specialist support roles. Thus the role of 'forum specialist' was created to maintain and update the community knowledge base. If a request to the community went unattended for a few hours, for example, the forum specialist would pick up the request, identify the potential experts and informally forward it to them for attention. Another, more formal, route involved bringing in 'section leaders' – that is, a group of experts who have volunteered to tackle some of the more stubborn problems in particular areas. These different specialists enabled the free flow of discussions on the company's problem-solving forums to be captured and recycled for future use. For example, when a particular topic was considered 'dead' or finally resolved, forum specialists and section leaders would process it further, validating and verifying it before it was uploaded into the knowledge base to be ready for distribution and reuse (Buckman, 1998).

CASE STUDY 8.1
KIN RESEARCH STUDY OF MANAGED COMMUNITIES

The impact of managed communities on organizational performance was investigated in a recent study carried out by the Knowledge and Innovation Network (KIN) at Warwick Business School. The study was carried out across 52 different communities with ten major firms that spanned a range of sectors (oil, consulting, aerospace) in both the United Kingdom and internationally. This study found that these communities were becoming increasingly formalized, with their own forms of governance, including community 'leaders' and business 'sponsors', as well as more explicit and organizationally focused goals. The study also identified a number of factors which were seen as increasing the impact of communities, including the provision of time and training support for leaders, and the holding of face-to-face events. These findings highlight the importance of active support and cultivation in ensuring that managed communities deliver benefits both to their individual members and to the wider organization.

A further important set of findings from this study highlighted the innovative approaches which some organizations were taking to communities. A few examples of these innovative approaches are outlined below:

Strategic communities: Following a merger between two oil companies, a new corporate KM support team was formed and with its new charter shifted its approach to developing the so-called 'strategic communities'. After two years, there were 54 of these in the company, ranging in size from 60 to 500 people, each of them with a clear business case that linked back to the improvement goals identified by the management improvement team. Community members were invited to join, based on their experience of the issue.

Organizational improvement: In one of the oil companies, communities reported into eight member management groups responsible for stewarding improvements in their area. There were four of these councils, one for each stage of exploration and development. The councils had challenging, measurable goals, such as reducing the number of unrecovered barrels of oil. Each community owned part of the overall improvement goal and tracked its progress towards achieving it.

Community as an agent of change: In one of the organizations studied – a government intelligence office – the managing director established a volunteer network of people aimed at increasing collaboration across its functional silos. The idea behind this community was to spread the experience of interacting differently so that there could be real change in the organization as a whole.

Ongoing coaching: In one of the oil companies studied, communities begin with a half day 'boot camp' in which the community leader and core members were introduced to the key elements of community, the goal-setting and assessment process, and the critical success factors for communities in that company.

The full report of this study is available in www.ki-network.org

>> ONLINE COMMUNITIES

Much of our discussion of social networks up to this point has been based on a traditional view of social relationships. They are normally seen as emerging from face-to-face interactions within a particular physical context. However, the advent of the Internet and other ICT systems has enabled new networks to develop amongst groups who are geographically dispersed and unable to communicate through face-to-face contacts. We now recognize that social relationships and even communities can equally well develop through online as well as face-to-face interactions. There are now many different types of online community. Some, such as the Ebay community, are very narrowly focused and transactional, simply helping their members buy and sell goods. Others are centred on shared life experience, such as communities of cancer sufferers, or people who have experienced divorce or infertility. Finally, another set, such as social networking groups or online gaming communities, are concerned with promoting social interaction.

Some of the earliest examples of online community, however, were focused on work and came from within large, geographically dispersed organizations who had both the infrastructure and shared work problems to make online interactions meaningful. Many of the managed communities highlighted above, for example, have been developed as online networks by large multinational companies which have employees dispersed across many sites around the world.

One such example comes from Xerox – the company which had originally proved so resistant to the emergent communities within its midst. The group of reps which Orr studied within Xerox included about a dozen people, but the total number of such reps within the company numbered around 25,000 worldwide. The lack of communication across this workforce meant that different groups were grappling with problems which had already been solved elsewhere. To overcome this problem and connect these different communities, Xerox initiated the 'Eureka' project to oversee knowledge dissemination. The aim was to create a database which would preserve useful ideas and learning points and make them available globally.

Clearly, there was a danger here, as noted in Chapter 7, of technology being viewed as a solution rather than a support to knowledge work. Many knowledge databases are underutilized by the people they are intended to serve. This is often because they are designed top-down with little reference to what users see as useful knowledge. In the case of the Eureka database, the development process was driven not by managers but by the customer service reps themselves. It was reps, not managers, who both supplied and vetted the tips. This ensured that the content of the database was relevant, reliable and up to date. With this kind of content, Xerox had no problems in ensuring that reps made use of the information available – these tips made the reps' work life easier, not harder, and in the process brought considerable savings to the company. Xerox estimated that Eureka saved the corporation around $100 million within a few years of its inception (Brown and Duguid, 2000a).

As yet, the factors which make some online communities successful while many others fail are still uncertain and complex. It is clear that the technology or Internet systems involved, though important pre-requisites, are far from being the primary drivers of success. Brown and Duguid (2000b), for example, highlight the importance of what they term 'cultural objects'. These can be texts, stories or problems as in the Xerox case. Where members of an online community share such objects, and are able to develop meaningful dialogue around them, the community is more likely to develop a distinctive meaning and value to its participants. In this respect, by facilitating conversations amongst groups and individuals, ICT systems can help to extend the experience of shared meanings and understandings beyond the realm of physical co-location into the virtual space of the company intranet or e-mail forum.

This insight underlines the different and often intangible benefits which online communities provide to their participants. For individuals they can be an important way of achieving status and identity within a particular group (McLure et al., 2005). They may also provide valuable sources of knowledge and information from other members. For the organization too, online communities can provide benefits by enabling the sharing of knowledge and collaboration across organizational boundaries. Such knowledge sharing is seen as important in transferring best practice, spreading innovations and improving processes (Wenger et al., 2002).

Clearly, these benefits are often linked to the connectivity which the community provides. By the same token, this is one reason why many communities fail. Communities which do not reach a critical mass – that is, having a sufficiently large and diverse membership – ultimately lose the interest and engagement of their participants. Where communities do achieve such critical mass, however, they can really take off, experiencing an upward spiral in membership growth. Such momentum can be maintained as long as the growth in participant numbers is matched by increases in the quality of the community dialogue and the forms of knowledge shared (McDermott, 2004).

>> CONCLUSIONS

This chapter has reviewed the major role which social networks play in knowledge work. Such networks are important because they represent one of the most effective means of sharing knowledge, and are often an important means of overcoming the limitations which functional silos and hierarchies place on knowledge sharing. As we have discussed, networks should not be seen as a panacea for the limitations of conventional organizational forms. For one, they tend to be local-ized and sometimes quite closed or exclusive – features underlining the impor-tance of boundary-spanning individuals who are able to move between different networks, and sometimes derive significant benefits from doing so.

As organizations have become more aware of the value of knowledge as a resource, they have become increasingly attracted to various forms of managed or online communities which seek to make knowledge flow across organiza-tional boundaries. Although these communities can be criticized for lacking some of the spontaneous and voluntary features of communities based on shared practices, they have become an increasingly widespread feature of organization structures. As such, they pose new challenges for management practice. These challenges – encapsulated by Wenger (1998) as cultivation not control – involve a move away from micro-managing community activities to creating the right environment in which self-confident and engaged communities can develop. As such, they underline once again our recurrent theme of identifying the most enabling contexts for knowledge work.

The following case returns to the question of the role played by social net-works, bringing our analysis of their positive and negative effects into a real world setting – the United Kingdom's National Health Service (NHS). The case shows the vital role which networks and boundary-spanning can play in developing change and innovation within an organization. At the same time, it also reveals some of the ways in which such networks can also limit the spread of even the most socially desirable innovations.

CASE STUDY 8.2
MIDLANDS HOSPITAL
(NHS TRUST)

Midlands NHS Trust Hospital is one of a large number of trusts that together make up the National Health Service of the United Kingdom. This case (reported in Newell, 2003) describes attempts to develop a new procedure for the treatment of cataracts (a disease of the eye) at the hospital.

The existing procedure involved cataract sufferers in a long and complicated process to receive treatment. For example, the patient would begin at the optometrist (the local high street optician) who would diagnose that the patient had cataracts that were significantly reducing vision, and then refer that patient to his or her general practitioner (GP) for further treatment. After a visit to the local GP, who not being an eye specialist would generally rely on the diagnosis of the optometrist, the patient was forwarded onto the hospital for further examination. At that time, the patient would meet briefly with the consultant and, in a separate appointment, meet with the hospital nurse for a physical examination. Only when all of these visits were complete would the patient get in the queue for obtaining a date for the cataract surgery. Post-surgery, another visit to the consultant was scheduled to check on the patient and then the patient was referred back to the optometrist for a new pair of glasses. Therefore, it took patients at least six visits and often well over a year to have a routine, 20-minute, outpatient, surgical procedure.

Streamlining this long and complicated process began with the formation of a project team which, unusually, brought together representatives from the whole range of groups involved in diagnosis and treatment. This included the head nurse in the eye unit, a hospital administrator, general practitioners, a set of optometrists from the local community, and a surgical consultant who was instrumental in championing the need for change and in leading the change process. Getting this team to work together effectively was not easy. There was a history of significant distrust amongst some of the professional groups involved. For example, eye surgeons were generally quite contemptuous of the expertise of optometrists.

Over a six-months period, however, and through working together, greater trust and social capital developed amongst the team members. This enabled the sharing of knowledge and an agreed analysis of the diagnosis and treatment problem. Based on this analysis, plus an increased awareness of the competencies and skills of the various groups involved, the team were now able to see alternatives to the traditional process. In doing this, each individual in the team drew upon his/her own experience and knowledge, but also used their personal networks to find out what was happening in other hospitals. For example, the project team went to look at treatments in a leading eye surgery clinic where they felt they might learn something useful to apply to their own context.

With the benefit of these insights the team developed a new procedure which radically streamlined the process. Non-essential visits to the general practitioner; the consultant and the nurse were eliminated. Instead, optometrists were empowered to decide if a patient needed cataract surgery. In doing so, they were required to fill out a detailed form that provided the consultant with specific information about the nature and severity of the cataract, and to call the hospital and book a time for the patient's surgery. Initially, there was some resistance from local optometrists who refused to get involved in the redesigned diagnosis process. This resistance was gradually overcome, however. For example, the transformation team member recounted the story of an optometrist with a large local practice, who refused to participate in the fast-track cataract process. As luck would have it, the transformation team member happened to need a new pair of glasses and so decided to visit the reluctant optometrist. She sang the praises of this new cataract procedure throughout her eye exam. By the time her glasses were ready, the optometrist had reconsidered his position and had decided to participate in the project.

The preliminary pre-operation physical was replaced with a self-diagnostic questionnaire that each patient was required to fill out and return to the hospital before surgery. Immediately before surgery, nurses were to telephone each patient to check the patient's details and answer any questions. Post-operation consultant appointments were also replaced with follow-up telephone calls. One indication of how much the process changed was the traditional post-operation meal. Under the traditional method, before discharge, each patient was treated to a plate of hospital food; under the new system, they were given a cup of tea and a biscuit and were then sent home.

The new cataract procedure resulted in a number of efficiency gains. Lead times were radically reduced from over 12 months down to six to eight weeks. In addition, theatre utilization rates improved due to the addition of an administrator whose sole responsibility lay in scheduling theatres. Finally, and most importantly, according to follow-up phone conversations with cataract project patients, patient satisfaction improved dramatically.

The redesigned cataract process was considered to be highly successful and the trust was even given a special award by UK Prime Minister Tony Blair. The team involved made a number of presentations to other groups within the NHS highlighting their re-designed process as a template which could be applied elsewhere. Despite its apparent benefits for both professionals and patients, however, there was little spread of the innovation from Midlands Hospital to other sites. This can be partly attributed to the problems of getting different groups to change their practices, and the related difficulties of translating the experience of the project team into approaches that would work in other contexts. There was also evidence, however, that the professional groups in other hospitals were reluctant to change the division of tasks between them. Information about the new process template was not enough, on its own, to overcome this resistance.

>> QUESTIONS

1. Identify different ways in which social networks and networking contributed positively to this innovation in cataract treatment.
2. How did the project team format support the development of new networks?
3. What role was played by boundary spanners in this case?
4. How do you explain the limited spread of this innovation to other hospitals? To what extent was this linked to the social networks operating within and across such hospitals?

Summary of key learning points

>> Social networks can be viewed as *channels* or *communities* – one emphasizing connectivity and the other shared identity.

>> Networks can have both positive and negative effects on knowledge flows, depending on how far they transgress or simply reinforce social and organizational boundaries.

>> Communities of practice link shared identities and norms to learning amongst community members.

>> Organizations sometimes fail to see the benefits of more emergent communities, but have been more enthusiastic about supporting managed communities which are focused on organizational goals.

>> Managed communities need to be cultivated, not controlled, and rely upon boundary spanners to maintain effective relations with other communities.

>> Online communities are effective where they create shared cultural objects which provide a focus for problem-solving, and where ICT is used to connect groups and individuals.

MANAGING KNOWLEDGE FOR INNOVATION

Chapter Outline

Learning Outcomes

At the end of this chapter you should be able to:

⇒ Explain the central challenges in managing knowledge work where the purpose is innovation.

⇒ Outline the characteristics of innovation as an episodic process that (i) relies centrally on knowledge sharing and integration and the development of new working practices; (ii) has uncertain outcomes, which are influenced by networks, power, technology and the context (organizational and institutional) in which the innovation process occurs.

⇒ Demonstrate a critical appreciation of different theoretical approaches (linear, process, practice) to managing knowledge for innovation.

⇒ Appreciate the challenges for managing knowledge work posed by the growth of service innovations, networked innovation and open innovation.

⇒ Identify appropriate techniques for managing knowledge in order to facilitate innovation.

⇒ Experience the difficulties of managing knowledge first-hand by engaging in a simulated innovation process (the Oakland Role-Play), involving a group of actors with different perceptions and interests, and suggest how these difficulties can be resolved.

>> INTRODUCTION

Throughout this book we have emphasized the idea that the processes used to manage knowledge work need to be customized for particular purposes in particular contexts. As we saw in Chapter 1, this is because managing knowledge only adds value when knowledge is applied to changes in practice (McDermott, 1999). This chapter focuses more closely on a major purpose of knowledge work – innovation. In this chapter we see how the changing nature of innovation itself is posing more and more challenges for managing knowledge work.

This chapter – and many of the case studies in previous chapters – show that innovation is more often than not a complex, uncertain, torturous and highly political activity, with numerous twists and turns along the way. It is difficult to know at the outset quite what will be achieved when knowledge is combined in new ways and getting people to 'buy into' the innovation process can be as much of a challenge as 'sourcing' the knowledge required. The outcomes of innovation are, therefore, not just unknown, but also unknowable in advance (Dougherty, 2007). Therefore, while it is easy to talk about managing knowledge to achieve innovation, it is less easy to do in practice. The major objective of this chapter, then, is to deepen understanding of what innovation entails and the implications this has for managing knowledge work.

Throughout this chapter, three critical features of innovation are highlighted:

1. Its dynamic, processual, practice-based nature.
2. Its implications for managing knowledge and practice.
3. Its relationship to context (social, organizational and national/institutional).

Students who have the opportunity to work in syndicate groups will also be able to engage in a role-play, designed to simulate a small part of an innovation process. This focuses on technological innovation – a task that typically involves changing peoples' practices as well as developing technical systems, and, therefore, one that poses major challenges for managing knowledge work (Clark, 2003), as seen in Chapter 3. A more forensic examination of the different dimensions of the innovation process and the ways in which knowledge might be managed more effectively is possible through the role-play. For students that cannot engage in the role-play, we present, in the first section, a case description – the case of Medico – that can be used to ground understanding of the topics in this chapter.

The scrutiny of innovation in this chapter reinforces the message that a single (in the universalistic sense) 'best practice' approach to managing knowledge work is highly problematic. Whilst writers have attempted to identify 'best' Knowledge Management practices for innovation – Coombs and Hull (1998), for example, provided a comprehensive list of some 80 'Knowledge Management Practices' for achieving innovation in R&D departments – these must be applied with extreme care as what is best for one organization may be worst for another (Hendriks, 2003). The chapter therefore provides a further challenge to the pursuit of 'best practice' in managing knowledge that remains a feature of much existing work. What is more useful to think about is the particular purpose that the practice of managing knowledge needs to serve over the varied and sometimes discontinuous life cycle of an innovation process (i.e. what are we trying to manage knowledge for?). We argue for a need to understand the relation between knowledge and innovation as both processual and deeply embedded in social practice – a theme running throughout this book.

>> THE IMPORTANCE OF MANAGING KNOWLEDGE WORK FOR INNOVATION

It has been recognized for a very long time that innovation is crucial for economic performance and governments worldwide have put major efforts into developing their innovative capabilities. However, it is also argued that innovation in the current era poses much greater challenges for managing knowledge work. This is because the knowledge economy is also a service economy. Hence we have seen massive growth in the service sector and major changes in the ways knowledge is applied to new service delivery. The pressures to develop, not just new products and technologies, but also new ways of dealing with shifting user needs and demands, often on a global scale, are, it is argued, significantly greater now than in years past (Dankbaar, 2003). In insurance and financial services, for example, forms of service delivery have changed drastically with the World Wide Web providing much greater information to consumers and online service providers. This means, more knowledgeable customers can 'shop around' much more easily.

It is also the case that the boundaries traditionally seen between services and products are blurring. Read carefully the case of Medico (Box 9.1) and you will see that this innovation involved, not just the development of a new product (a new suture containing radioactive seeds), but also a fundamental reorganization of the delivery of cancer treatment and of the professional roles and responsibilities that this incurred.

BOX 9.1   Case example – innovation in Medico

Medico was a large multinational biosciences company with a major part of its business devoted to the manufacture and delivery of imaging products for medical diagostics (e.g. radioactive isotopes for the diagnosis of cancer). Its European business comprised geographically dispersed divisions with high degrees of autonomy. The Prostate Cancer Therapy (PCT) project began as a small 'spin-off' to develop and market Healthco's 'brachytherapy' products. Put simply, brachytherapy involves the implantation of radioactive iodine seeds directly into a prostate (in this case) tumour to kill cancer cells from within. The PCT project was headed by a Vice President of Global Manufacturing.

Whilst the brachytherapy technique had been around for some time, Medico had recently developed a new technology that allowed much more accurate seed implantation (using a new product comprising a suture 'preloaded' with seeds that could be implanted under ultrasound visioning). This had significantly improved clinical effectiveness. Clinical trials data over a ten-year period were showing that long-term survival rates were as good with this new treatment as with prostatectomy, and that adverse side effects, often associated with the surgery for prostate cancer (incontinence and impotence) were greatly reduced, making brachytherapy a viable form of treatment for some kinds of patients. This was not just an innovation in technology, however. Brachytherapy also entailed significant innovation in the way in which treatment was to be delivered to patients. Traditionally prostate cancer had been treated with prostatectomy (surgery delivered by a consultant urologist) often followed later by radiotherapy. In contrast, delivering brachytherapy meant combining surgical skills (for implantation) with radiotherapy (for dosage). This represented a radical departure from established medical practice, requiring consultant urologists and radiologists, as well as nurses and physicians, to be involved in all stages of treatment decision and delivery.

A major challenge that Medico faced was to get different professional groups to work together and overcome resistance. As the Project Manager put it, 'Urologists deal with prostate cancer. Radiation oncologists deal with radioactive materials. One of the barriers has always been that the urologists can't offer brachytherapy by themselves, as compared with surgery, and so there is always going to need to be a team of physicians, radiation oncologists and urologist working together'. Yet the involvement and expertise of these professionals was essential, both to design the treatment and also to demonstrate and 'prove' it to the rest of the medical community. Consultant urologists, in particular, were very powerful and busy professionals, who often had little time for commercial ventures. As one Medico Sales Manager complained, 'Medical consultants don't even look up when you enter the room'. Significantly, because it relied so centrally on radiotherapy knowledge as well as knowledge of surgery, the new treatment threatened to shift primary authority for patient treatment decisions away from the consultant urologists (traditionally the most powerful group) towards radiation oncologists, which further increased resistance. The Scientific Marketing Manager commented wryly: 'there is quite a lot of resistance from urologists to the method because it is a method that directly competes with prostatectomy which is what they do... There is definitely a financial preference to them to do prostatectomies, although we are changing that. Also they are trained as surgeons and it is difficult for them to embrace a multidisciplinary approach when they have been used to being in charge of everything.

BOX 9.1   Continued

There is a feeling that they will lose control over the patients which makes them not very responsive at first'.

To make matters worse, medical therapeutics represented a major departure from Healthco's, long-established, diagnostics imaging business. As a result, the PCT project was not really recognized within the mainstream structure of Healthco – being described as an 'orphan project' and 'not really what we do'. This meant that the UK team had little formal authority over the divisional managers or sales staff that they needed to engage in the innovation process in order to communicate and sell the technology to potential users.

In this very difficult political and business context, the strategy of the UK team centred on raising awareness of the prostate cancer *disease*, and brachytherapy as a treatment, rather than on promoting their particular technology. An important aspect of this was to cultivate a 'community or care' around brachytherapy innovation. Thus, in the words of the project leader, the PCT project was about 'collaboration, creating communities, engagement and cooperation, enabling choice of treatments both by the doctors and the patients'. This discourse of 'collaboration' and 'community of care' was used quite deliberately by Medico to frame the team's activities in promoting brachytherapy amongst medical professionals and managers in the regional businesses, with metaphors such as 'creating a stage' and 'creating a shared sense of desire' being employed on a frequent basis by the Project Leader. The Medico team also appealed to personal aspirations of individuals to become involved with 'the first Medico product targeted at a cure' rather than just at diagnosis.

The PCT team's innovative activities were multi-fold. First, they assisted hospitals in establishing 'Centres of Excellence' where multidisciplinary teams could treat patients using brachytherapy techniques and where other professionals could be given 'hands-on' training. Second, most of the marketing budget actually went to developing training and education materials for medical professionals and Medico sales people. Third, specific events were organized to raise awareness amongst the medical communities about the brachytherapy innovation. Key opinion leaders (e.g. senior medical professionals) were identified and cultivated to address such events, and to speak on behalf of the therapy's success. One such event invited senior medical professionals across disciplines to a weekend meeting in a country hotel to discuss the advantages and disadvantages of brachytherapy. Significantly, an outcome of this was that this group established their own multidisciplinary professional network charged with identifying common standards for brachytherapy treatment across Europe. Finally, information flows were actively managed. For example, a website (under Medico's editorial discretion) provided educational material on brachytherapy treatments (including theirs) and a public relations firm was contracted to educate public opinion on the disease. One scientist-member of the team, who had previously worked as a medical doctor, was solely responsible for abstracting material from scientific articles to disseminate to the wider community of salespeople and professionals. To counter the dangers of the 'isolation' of the innovation project within Medico itself, informal, interpersonal networks were also used extensively by the team. These helped, for instance, to elicit knowledge from Medico's USA subsidiary on the development of the innovation there.

These activities were largely successful in overcoming overt resistance and a number of new Centres of Excellence were eventually established within hospitals across Europe. In fact the business was so promising that Medico set up a separate therapy division, eventually going into partnership with a cancer specialist firm to form a new company.

Indeed, some scholars even argue that 'material products (e.g. computers, mp3 players, mobile phones) are themselves only material embodiments of the services they deliver' (Dankbaar, 2003, p. 79). It can even be difficult to tell whether we are actually buying a service or a product – the iPhone is intrinsically linked to iTunes and 3 Mobile Media, for example.

The implications of the rise in services for managing knowledge work are extensive. With services innovation, relevant knowledge is nearly always distributed across a whole range of stakeholders including, on a much greater basis than before, the customer (Dodgson et al., 2005). Knowledge workers also need significant autonomy so that they can deal flexibly with more knowledgeable customers and actively match services to requirements. The deep frustration that many of us experience when we telephone service companies only to be met by inflexible, 'rote', responses is testament indeed to the need for worker autonomy. In short, in a service economy, innovation is fundamentally about managing knowledge and knowledge work (Coombs, 2003; Miles, 2003).

Scholars who write about managing knowledge also often cite innovation as a key objective. For example, Nonaka's work on 'the knowledge creating company' (discussed in Chapters 1 and 4) emphasized the need to use knowledge for innovation. The more recent literature on 'dynamic capabilities', similarly, highlights the importance of developing and managing knowledge processes – 'experience accumulation', 'knowledge codification' and 'knowledge articulation' – in order to generate and modify operating routines in the pursuit of organizational innovation and improved competitiveness (Bjorkman et al., 2004; Zollo and Winter, 2002). Indeed, the links between knowledge and innovation, and the virtue of Knowledge Management for improving innovation, are rarely questioned in the literature.

It is important, however, to retain a healthy scepticism about this rather straightforward, functionalist equation between (more) knowledge and (more) innovation (see debates in special issues of the *Journal of Management Studies*, 2001; *Journal of Information Technology*, 2001). For example, from the 'knowledge as possession' point of view (introduced in Chapter 1), there is no particular reason, *a priori*, why innovation should follow from increased quantities of knowledge – indeed, information overload might quite conceivably reduce innovative capability (Schultze and Vandenbosch, 1998). Equally, from a 'knowledge as practice' perspective, knowledge (or ways of knowing) required to develop and implement innovation is often widely distributed (amongst individuals, groups, organizations, even nations and cultures). As the Medico example shows, and as we saw in Chapter 4, the task of bringing this distributed knowledge together is time-consuming, difficult and mediated significantly by relationships of trust and power – innovation does not automatically result. These dynamics need to be considered carefully in understanding whether and how knowledge can be managed to achieve innovation.

>> WHAT IS INNOVATION?

Innovation is an extremely broad-ranging subject and we could not hope to do justice to the numerous studies of it here (for good reviews of theories and techniques, see Bessant et al., 2005; Conway and Steward, 2006; Hidalgo and Albor, 2008; van der Panne, 2003; Pittaway et al., 2004; Slappendel, 1996; Wolfe, 1994). Instead, we focus on outlining those theories and frameworks that help us to understand *the process* of innovation, as it is the dynamic, social and knowledge-intensive characteristics of innovation that pose the biggest challenges for managing knowledge work. Thus we focus on the process of innovation as 'the development and implementation of new ideas by people who over time engage in transactions with others in an institutional context' (Van de Ven, 1986, p. 591). This highlights the socially dynamic nature of innovation as well as its *context specificity*.

The first point to note is that the innovation process entails a lot more than just coming up with clever ideas (invention or creativity – covered in Chapter 4) it is also about putting them into practice (implementation) and about spreading them more widely (diffusion). Even well-known inventors – such as Thomas Edison (with over 1000 patents), Emeline Hart (who patented the first commercial oven in 1876) and Steve Wozniac (co-founder of Apple and infamous computer hacker) – had large groups of people helping to move their ideas into practice. Many inventions even spread and get used in ways quite unforeseen by the original inventors. For example, Sir Alec Jeffries, the scientist who invented DNA fingerprinting in 1984 warned recently how the huge expansion of the UK national database to contain details of over 2.5 million criminals could actually generate, rather than reduce, miscarriages of justice (Bennetto, 2004). Simply focusing on innovation as invention is therefore a very partial view. It helps, then, to unpack three core activities when we think about innovation.

- Invention – the generation of ideas
- Diffusion – the spread of ideas
- Implementation – the application of ideas in practice.

It is the interweaving of these activities that constitutes innovation, as we can see in the Medico example where the success of the invention relied on its uptake and further development by communities of medical professionals. You would not say that a new idea that never actually got used (implemented) was really an innovation (it may even be called 'a mistake'). For example, the Sinclair C5, despite being cheap (it sold for around £400), quickly became a commercial disaster and an object of ridicule, with only around 12,000 being sold. Moreover, these three activities interweave over time in often quite unpredictable, even bizarre, ways. As research on the spread of management fashions shows us, the efficiency of the invention or idea is often not what drives uptake (Abrahamson, 1996; Scarbrough and Swan, 2001). For example, the vitamin C cure for scurvy was known about decades before it was actually used. Another example is the now familiar Qwerty layout on the computer keyboard. This was originally invented when mechanical typewriters used letter 'hammers' that would get stuck together if the keys were arranged in a, more logical, alphabetical order. The diffusion of this type of keyboard resulted in it becoming deeply embedded into the practices of many social groups across the globe, including typists and manufacturers as well as teachers and educationalists. This means that, despite the fact that alternative designs might be a lot more efficient today and easier to learn, the Qwerty continues to be the design standard (Rogers, 1995).

The Medico case shows that innovation is, more often than not, highly political and 'the purpose' of innovation is actually several purposes in one (e.g. marketing/diffusing and at the same time co-creating the new brachytherapy product/service). In knowledge terms, innovation combines *both* purposes of *exploration* (i.e. inventing new knowledge) *and exploitation* (i.e. reusing existing knowledge in new contexts – March, 1991). Figure 9.1 shows schematically how the knowledge processes – creating, sharing and integrating, and codifying and connecting – considered throughout the earlier chapters in this book all, then, come to bear to a greater or lesser extent in the three core activities (Invention, Implementation and Diffusion) entailed when the purpose is innovation (as depicted by the dotted line).

Types of innovation

Traditionally, writers on innovation have made a distinction between 'product' and 'process' innovation (or 'technical' and 'administrative' innovation – Damanpour, 1987). Broadly speaking, product innovation involves the application of knowledge to the development of tangible new products or

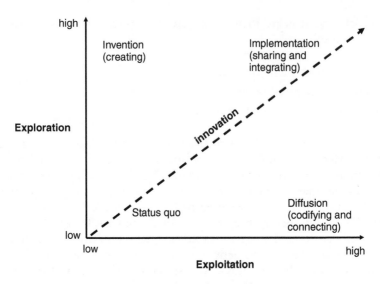

Figure 9.1 The purpose of innovation

services. For example, Grindley et al. (1989) described how the Richardson organization managed to buck the trend of the declining Sheffield cutlery industry in the 1970s by applying specialist knowledge of metallurgy to the development of a new type of knife blade – the 'Laser' range. This new blade, with its lifetime sharpness guarantee, was a result of continued commitment to product innovation that was said to have helped turn sales from £1 million in 1974 to £23 million in 1989.

Process innovation, in contrast, involves the development of new management, work or organizational practices. Innovations in service delivery, such as the one described in Medico, essentially entail process innovation. Medico's success resulted not only from the development of a new product but also from the development of core competencies in manufacturing, sales and marketing. Whilst much work in innovation has focused on the design and development of products, the growing importance of services has made process innovation as, if not more, important. Innovations in services seem to have distinctive characteristics that pose particular challenges for managing knowledge work – challenges that are summarized in the Table 9.1 (see also Miles, 2003; Vermeulen, 2003).

As seen in Medico, product and process innovations also often go hand in hand. For example, the major success of Apple's products such as the iPod is closely linked to online modes of product and service delivery in iTunes. That said, it is worth remembering that product and process innovations do pose potentially different problems for managing knowledge. Knowledge creation in product innovation, for example, tends to converge around the product itself. This means that the product – and associated physical artefacts such as blueprints and prototypes – can serve as a tangible 'boundary object' in bringing together relevant knowledge (Whyte et al., 2008).

Table 9.1   Service innovations and challenges for managing knowledge work

Characteristic	Description	Example (Medico)	Challenges for Managing Knowledge Work
Intangible	The value of the knowledge cannot easily be demonstrated in advance of the service actually being used.	Uncertainty in Europe about the 'effectiveness' of the brachytherapy treatment when it had not yet been used in this context.	• Protecting intellectual property, patenting against piracy. • Persuading people to use the service in advance of proof of effectiveness.
Interactive	New and more interactive modes of development and delivery require knowledge distributed across a wider range of stakeholders (including customers and end users). Production of knowledge simultaneous with consumption.	Development and delivery of brachytherapy required knowledge and involvement of surgical urologists, radiologists and Medico staff through Centres of Excellence model.	• Knowing what knowledge people have. • Getting relevant knowledge workers involved in the innovation process. • Can involve service provider innovating at the clients' premises (e.g. consultancy services).
Information intensive	Variety of information and modes of information delivery involved.	Professional training, educational materials and opinion leader reports coupled with marketing materials and scientific clinical effectiveness data.	• Using forms of information and modes of information delivery that are seen as accessible, of interest and legitimate by varied service users.
Heterogeneous	Different opinions as to the value of the information and what constitutes a good service.	Surgeon, radiologist and patient views of the 'effectiveness' of the treatment differ. Views temporarily 'reconciled' through active promotion of 'community of care'.	• Understanding and accommodating stakeholder interests and viewpoints. • Can generate tensions between standardization and customization.
Interdependent	Users of services (e.g. professionals) more powerful in relation to them because they are intangible and difficult to legitimate in advance.	Implementation slowed by resistance of more powerful consultant urologists overseen by regulation and professional standards.	• Enrolling powerful professional users and/or service regulators. • Developing professional standards and networks to legitimate new knowledge.

In contrast, knowledge produced through process innovation is largely intangible, tacit and context-dependent. It includes, for example, knowledge relating to changes in work practices, changes in roles and responsibilities, and changes in attitudes and cultural values. As seen in Chapter 5, this process knowledge is difficult to codify, at least in ways that could be easily understood when transferred to new contexts. Social and behavioural processes are therefore likely to be as, if not more, important to managing knowledge for process innovation than practices aimed at codification. For example, Hansen et al. (1999) found that 'personalization' strategies (the development of intensive personal relationships and social networks) were more effective than codification strategies where the knowledge to be transferred was largely tacit in nature. This broad difference between product and process innovation again highlights the need to be sensitive to the purpose of the innovation when devising strategies and approaches to managing knowledge.

>> TRADITIONAL VIEWS – INNOVATION AS A LINEAR PROCESS

There is a popularly held view that the innovation process corresponds to the kind of linear sequence depicted in Figure 9.2 (see, for example, Rogers, 1995).

Innovation is seen as a rational process whereby managers make decisions about the adoption of new forms of the so-called 'best practice' based on an objective assessment of their technical efficiency over existing techniques and practices. According to this perspective, once a new best practice has

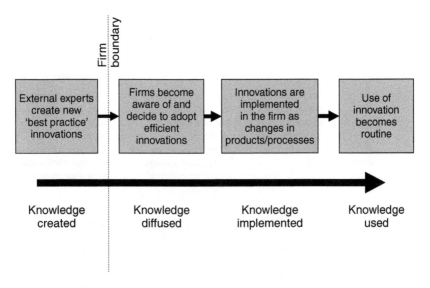

Figure 9.2   The linear view of the innovation process

been created, and rules for its implementation have been defined, the only problem is to make firms aware of it. Prescriptions about 'Six-Sigma' or 'Customer Relationship Management' or even 'Knowledge Management' as 'must have' 'best' practices are good examples. Research shows, however, that this is a misleading and potentially dangerous view (Ettlie and Bridges, 1987) that greatly downplays the problems of implementation and the knowledge requirements of innovation. Most innovation is simply not like that. Box 9.2 summarizes the key limitations of this traditional view. In Medico, for example, the creation of knowledge went hand in hand with its use in practice. Indeed the clinical data on the brachytherapy technique would not be available unless the technique had actually been applied by medical professionals. In short, knowledge was produced *through* use, not before it.

BOX 9.2   Limits of traditional views on innovation

- The innovation process is not linear – pivotal modifications in the innovation introduced during its implementation, for example, feed back into its design (Scarbrough, 2008a).

- The innovation process is not rational (in the traditional sense) – choices about innovation are based as much on claims made about their efficiency (e.g. by consultants, experts or different players within firms) as evidence of efficiency *per se* (Abrahamson, 1996).

- Innovation is not a 'thing' or entity with fixed and definable parameters that can be simply inserted into different organizational contexts. Implementation of technological innovation, for example, often involves significant reworking of the initial idea or technology so that it is blended and adapted together with features of the organization (Clark, 2003).

- Most innovation cannot, therefore, be introduced as a 'technical fix' with predictable outcomes.

- Innovation is not discrete but has an impact on many different areas of the organization and on many individuals and social groups within it. Effective implementation depends, then, on changes in knowledge, skills and organizational practices that lie outside the remit of the technical expert.

- The notion of a universally applicable 'best practice' is, in any case, misleading. Innovation is highly context-specific – what works in one context may not be applicable in another because of the different knowledge, skills and understandings of the social groups involved (Swan et al., 1999b).

Critics of the linear model argue, in fact, that linearity is little more than a feature of retrospective and rationalized descriptions of innovation and knowledge creation processes by those involved. For example, the Medico story, when retold, looks very much like a success resulting from the rational decisions of the Medico team. However, in practice, it was a very messy, highly ambiguous and context-dependent process, the outcomes of which could not have been foreseen. The country weekend meeting, for example, happened to result in a group of professionals getting together to set standards that then aided diffusion of the brachytherapy treatment. Although the Medico team made the event possible, this outcome was not planned by them. These kinds of 'accidental encounters' are actually typical of innovation processes, especially in the early stages (Kreiner and Schultz, 1993).

Linear descriptions, then, gloss over the discontinuities, iterations and political uncertainties that characterize all but the most simple innovation processes (Clark, 2003). For example, in the Medico case, political uncertainties amongst radiologists and urologists played a key role in driving, and also interrupting, the innovation process. That is not to say, however, that there are no 'stage gates' in the innovation process. In drug development, for example, regulatory approval mechanisms (e.g. for phased clinical trials) do play a role in shaping and concentrating innovation activities at particular points in time. For example, 'first-in-man' safety studies *must* be done prior to wider patient population trials. Yet, even here, there is considerable movement back and forth in terms of knowledge flows and processes, with the so-called 'preclinical' work often having to be revisited or redone *after* clinical results are known (Swan et al., 2007a). In other industries, where the regulations may be less disciplining, the stage gates are typically self-imposed in order to try and control the innovation process, as for example with the use of project management methodologies which include extensive planning protocols requiring scheduled milestone identification.

>> PROCESS VIEWS – INNOVATION AS AN INTERACTIVE PROCESS

In contrast to the linear model, process views depict innovation as a cumulative and iterative set of episodes, activities and fortunate (and unfortunate) coincidences, where multiple actors, multiple forms of knowledge and organizational tasks interact and serendipity has a major role to play (Clark, 2003). Key features of this view are summarized in Box 9.3. 'Managing' innovation, then, is more about creating a context that allows such new combinations of knowledge and practices to happen than about 'management' in the traditional control sense. Key aspects of this enabling context were described in Chapters 2 and 6. The use of the term 'episodes' (as opposed to 'stages') reflects the sporadic, iterative, recursive and sometimes discontinuous nature of innovation processes (Van de Ven, 1986). This view, in contrast with more broad-brushed prescriptive models, highlights the effective deployment and management of knowledge as critically contingent upon the different episodes of innovation as well as upon the social and organizational/political features of the context in which those episodes unfold.

BOX 9.3   Assumptions of process views on innovation

- Innovation is a dynamic design and decision process that is by nature both iterative and recursive and mediated by a range of cognitive, social and organizational factors (Swan and Clark, 1992).

- This process is influenced, not simply by judgements about technical efficiency, but also by the subjective beliefs, interpretations and knowledge of different social groups and actors both inside and outside the organization.

- Political interests, power and influence have a crucial impact on innovation (Swan and Scarbrough, 2005; Utterback, 1994). For example, firms may adopt innovations that are technically not the most efficient for political reasons, or professional groups will promote those new techniques and practices that enhance their own claims to knowledge, status and power (Avgerou and McGrath, 2007; Hislop et al., 2000).

- The innovation process is inherently uncertain and often sporadic (Dodgson et al., 2005; Dougherty, 2007). Unintended outcomes are common as different groups inside and outside the organization attempt to mobilize innovation in directions that suit their particular interests.

- Knowledge relevant to innovation may be widely distributed, both inside and outside the organization. Implementation of new organizational and technological solutions involves the gathering of both specialist expertise and tacit knowledge about existing practices from a wide range of sources, people and locations (Dhanaraj and Parkhe, 2006).

- The integration of relevant knowledge through the development of social processes and networks is crucial for innovation. Such networks are also important for encouraging the buy-in and commitment that helps innovative ideas to be actually implemented in practice (von Hippel, 2005).

- The ability to effectively integrate knowledge – and innovation – is often inhibited by structural, functional, occupational and status or hierarchical barriers (McLoughlin, 1999).

In sum, process views see innovation as a complex, iterative design and decision process involving the creation, diffusion, blending and implementation of new ideas in different contexts. Success depends on constructing a process that can draw upon widely distributed knowledge, is open to the views of the different groups involved and is capable of gaining their commitment, as seen in the Medico example. One such model, by Clark et al., 1992, is depicted

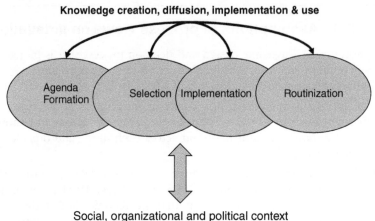

Figure 9.3 A processual view of innovation (e.g. after Clark et al., 1992)

schematically in Figure 9.3, describes the episodes of the process in a little more detail as:

- *Agenda formation* – the process of becoming aware of new ideas and of the problems that they may help to address.
- *Selection* – the further processing and promotion of ideas within the organization such that particular ideas are chosen to go forward for further development because they are seen as matching the problems the organization, or particular managers, are currently experiencing.
- *Implementation* – the process of actually introducing the selected ideas to the organization and applying them to the local context in the forms of new products, services, technologies or processes.
- *Routinization* – the situation where the understanding of the innovation has developed to a point at which its use has become 'normal' and it is now seen as a standard working practice to be adopted in other parts of the organization where relevant.

This emphasizes that, rather than occurring in a linear sequence, these different aspects of innovation are iterative, overlapping and conflated (Robertson et al., 1996) – hence the term 'episodes' as opposed to 'stages'. For example, lessons learned during implementation may refine definitions of problems or may influence the design and further diffusion of new ideas and technologies (Fleck, 1994; Leonard-Barton, 1988). Rather than seeing innovation as a fairly straightforward process of spreading and implementing a pre-fixed 'best practice' invention, the process view notes the inherently uncertain and open-ended nature of innovation. Unintended outcomes are common as different groups and individuals who get involved at different times attempt to own and influence the process in ways that suit their particular knowledge and interests. The role-play at the end of this chapter provides, albeit in a limited way, an experience of this socially mediated, and highly politicized, innovation process.

The process view is clearly a useful lens through which to see the issues encountered at Medico. It stresses, for example, the inherently uncertain, open-ended and politicized nature of knowledge and innovation and the recursive interactions among different sub-groups, agendas and forms of knowledge (e.g. consultant urologists, radiation oncologists and Medico staff). Process approaches assume a 'knowledge as practice' view and, in so doing, remind us of the subjective nature of knowledge and its deployment in such ways that privilege the interests of particular powerful social and professional groups. The ability of consultant urologists to effectively resist the new system, for example, was a reflection of their power compared to other professional groups. Attempts to manage knowledge by the Medico team needed, then, to be sensitive to the interests and interpretations of the different groups involved. For example, the use of key opinion leaders and Medico staff that had been medically trained to communicate the technology played an important role in persuading the medical community of its value. In contrast, the failure to transfer, the apparently successful, new treatments seen in the Cataracts case in Chapter 8 can be explained as a failure to take proper account of the culturally and politically mediated nature of organizational life (Newell et al., 2003). As Dougherty and Heller (1994) note, many innovations fail because they 'violate the existing systems of thought and action, or fall into a vacuum where no shared understandings exist to make them meaningful' (p. 201).

Process approaches also alert us to the need to tailor the management of knowledge to particular activities and episodes of innovation. Hendriks (2003) describes, for example, how, in order to innovate, particular knowledge processes (development, application, distribution, evaluation) need to be aligned with particular innovation activities (in his terms, creative/shared problem solving, market-technology linking, experimenting and prototyping, commitment and development, monitoring and evaluation) and, in turn, with knowledge-based measures and Knowledge Management practices. For example, 'creative problem solving' was found to be more dependent on 'knowledge creation and sharing' but less so on 'knowledge distribution'. In other words, different innovation activities invoke different knowledge processes and, therefore, pose different requirements for managing knowledge work. In the Medico case the summaries reporting scientific data on the use of their technology were effective in raising awareness of the innovation amongst the medical community but not in securing commitment to its use. The latter required, by contrast, that the Medico technology be framed as part of a wider discourse of 'care', legitimated by the development of professional standards and the active networking of key opinion leaders in the medical community.

Finally, the process view is, we suggest, a much more relevant model for understanding innovation in services (Miles, 2003). This is because service inno-vations fundamentally shift the locus of innovation from R&D departments and product designers to wider networks of producers, consumers and service users (Coombs, 2003; Powell et al., 1996). Knowledge-intensive business firms and intermediaries (e.g. consultants, or professional and trade associations) also play a crucial role in driving innovations in service delivery. This means managing knowledge flows, not simply from suppliers to users, but through the interacting networks of suppliers, users and intermediary groups. This view that the locus of innovation has fundamentally shifted underpins the growth of new, and more interactive, or networked, models of innovation, discussed next.

>> NETWORKED INNOVATION

Process views emphasize that innovation is fundamentally influenced by networks and social interactions including, for example, intra- and inter-firm networks, professional and occupational networks, educational networks, regional networks and so on. Networks of various kinds have been found to play an important role in communicating knowledge, as seen in Chapter 8, and also as trendsetters – legitimizing some new approaches over others (Pittaway et al., 2004). For example, the design and diffusion of advanced manufacturing technologies in the 1980s was heavily influenced by networks of professions (such as the American Production and Inventory Control Association) and consultants (such as IBM and the Oliver Wight consultancy in the USA). Through these networks knowledge about a particular technology (Manufacturing Resources Planning, or 'MRP2') was promoted as *the* new best practice despite the fact that other, arguably more efficient, technologies were available at the time (Swan and Newell, 1995). Similarly, networks of multiple users of mainframe computers, largely based in universities, were critical in the development of e-mail in the mid-1960s.

The nature of network interactions and their influence on innovation processes also depends quite crucially on the local organizational and institutional context in which they occur (Clark, 2000; Swan et al., 2007a). For example, in the biotechnology sector, networks connecting up-stream (e.g. academic research) and downstream (e.g. commercial firms and hospitals) producers of life science knowledge are generally denser in certain parts of the United States than those observed in Europe (Owen-Smith et al., 2002), making it easier for knowledge to flow across these domains. To some extent this gives the United States a natural head start in terms of being able to develop innovations that need knowledge to be combined across these different groups (Swan et al., 2007a). It also means that attempts to manage knowledge that involves bridging academic, clinical and commercial practice (e.g. knowledge-transfer networks) are likely to be more challenging in the United Kingdom than in some parts of the United States (e.g. Massachusetts or California).

These characteristics of networks, and national differences, are rarely taken sufficient account of by policy-makers when they set up network initiatives for innovation. One such initiative in the United Kingdom was the Genetics Knowledge Parks (GKPs), launched by the UK Department of Health and the Department of Trade and Industry to bring together academic genetics scientists, hospital clinicians, commercial forms, and legal and social scientists on a regional basis in order to better exploit genetics knowledge for improving medical practice (Robertson, 2007). This initiative was loosely modeled on a similar, highly successful, initiative in the United States (the Greenwood Genetic Centre). However, the competition for funding incurred by the GKP initiative had the perverse unintended consequence of actually disrupting many of the informal networks that already existed in the genetics community (and which were not organized on a regional basis). Moreover, while new collaborations did eventually start to produce some innovative projects, these took a long time to establish. Unimpressed by what they saw as lack of progress within the GKPs, the UK government announced that no further funding would be available after the initial five years of what had been expected to be a ten-year programme. This announcement was made in year three leading many of the knowledge workers involved to abandon the progamme for jobs elsewhere.

As this example illustrates, efforts to manage knowledge for innovation must pay attention to the networks (both formal and informal) through which knowledge in specific fields and contexts is produced and communicated, especially where innovation processes span knowledge domains. Different kinds and roles of networks were considered in more detail in Chapter 8. Here, the term '*networked innovation*' denotes a distinctive category, or type, of innovation process 'that occurs through relationships that are negotiated in an ongoing communicative process, and which rely on neither market nor hierarchical mechanisms of control' (cf. Hardy et al., 2003; Swan and Scarbrough, 2005). This definition makes a distinction between networked innovation and innovation processes that are driven primarily by hierarchical and/or market-based mechanisms (e.g. innovation in supply-chain relationships or top-down organizational change initiatives). It also includes intra- and inter-organizational relationships and competitive, as well as collaborative, relationships. Indeed the boundaries between inter- and intra-organizational relationships are often very blurred during innovation processes. Also competitive relations can be just as important in networked innovation as collaborative relations, for example in generating, or overcoming, resistance to change (Alter and Hage, 1993; Elg and Johansson, 1997).

The Medico case above is a good example of networked innovation. In this case the Medico team lacked hierarchical power over the professional groups that they needed to influence, and were generally viewed with suspicion for having purely commercial objectives. This meant that any attempts to directly market their product to clinicians would have failed. Faced with this very challenging networked innovation their strategy for managing knowledge rested on:

- Team building – creating a multidisciplinary project team whose membership actually reflected the different interests of the specialist groups that they needed to influence (it included, for example, people with scientific, medical and commercial backgrounds).

- Network formation – building and orchestrating both intra-organizational relationships (between the Medico team and sales staff needed to market their 'orphan' product) and also inter-organizational networks (between the Medico staff and different communities of medical practitioners).

- Brokering – for example, cultivating opinion leaders and gatekeepers in order to connect diverse interests and practices.
- Rhetorical devices – framing the brachytherapy innovation in the wider discourse of 'community of care' in order to mobilize commitment amongst diverse interest groups.
- Codification – using information tools and artefacts (such as scientific texts, clinical data, educational material, 'Centre of Excellence' templates) to foster communication across diverse groups.
- Representation – where the interests of different collaborators were reflected in the people and activities deployed (Hardy et al., 2003).

Many of these approaches (e.g. network formation) have been examined in depth in previous chapters. However, networked innovation has several defining features when it comes to managing knowledge work:

- processes of knowledge integration are central;
- understanding, forming, coordinating and realigning social networks is crucial;
- technology and other material artefacts can play important roles as 'boundary objects' linking different groups and interests;
- it is inherently politicized and relies on multiple sources of knowledge and power.

Taking each in turn:

Knowledge integration

Networked innovation is dependent on widely distributed and often very diverse kinds of knowledge and knowledge workers. Therefore integration is a central knowledge process. Views as to how this actually happens are varied, depending on the approach to knowledge being used. Writers adopting a 'knowledge as possession' view, then, see knowledge integration as the 'combination' of different bodies of explicit and tacit knowledge (Nonaka, 1994). In contrast those with a 'knowledge as practice' view place greater emphasis on the development of shared understandings and boundary spanning activities as a pre-requisite of integration (Boland and Tenkasi, 1995). Knowledge integration is discussed more fully in Chapter 4.

Social networks

Chapter 8 explored the important role of networks in knowledge work, either (or both) as channels for communicating information or as processes for building communities and sharing knowledge/practice. Social networks are often seen, then, as having a positive impact on the diffusion and implementation of innovation, in general, and networked innovation, in particular (Hansen, 1999). These include interpersonal networks connecting individuals (Grandori and Soda, 1995; Jones et al., 2001; Kreiner and Schultz, 1993); intra-organizational (connecting different groups within an organization, e.g. cross-functional teams); and inter-organizational (connecting different organizations, e.g. formal partnerships – Alter and Hage, 1993; Hardy et al., 2003; Oliver and Liebeskind, 1998). These different kinds of networks can be more or less formal, with formal relationships frequently being underpinned by more informal, interpersonal ones (Kreiner and Schutlz, 1993).

The view of networks as channels for knowledge transfer chimes with the 'knowledge as possession' view and features heavily in innovation research (Owen-Smith and Powell, 2004). This focuses on identifying important characteristics of networks (e.g. their strength, density, direction of information flow), relating these to the forms of knowledge which can be exchanged and to political effects on partners (Alter and Hage, 1993; Granovetter, 1973; Hansen, 1999). For example, strong inter-personal networks tend to provide the basis for the exchange of more informal and tacit forms of knowledge. In contrast, more formal networks typically involve the transfer of more explicit forms of knowledge and intellectual property (Oliver and Liebeskind, 1998).

In contrast, 'knowledge as practice' views (as seen in the discussion on communities of practice in Chapter 8) emphasize the role of networks in developing (and restricting) new ways of knowing by connecting (and disconnecting) diverse forms of practice. These highlight the ways in which partners in the innovation process learn, adapt and re-evaluate their roles and commitments, as a response to prior experiences of working together (Ring and van de Ven, 1994). They also highlight the importance of discursive practices through which relationships and ideas come to be communicated, negotiated and legitimated (Swan et al., 2003). For example, Hardy et al. (2003) studied collaborative networks in a small Palestinian NGO, and found that relationships based on partnerships (where people actually worked together) and representations (where people represented one another's interests to outside parties) were more effective for knowledge creation than transactional relationships (where resources were transferred but people did not actually work together).

The Medico example illustrates, further, that what is critical to achieving networked innovation is not the type or structure of the network *per se*, but the *co-ordination of networks* of different kinds (interpersonal, intra-organizational, inter-organizational) throughout innovation episodes. Networks in this case are not necessarily positive for innovation – take the difficulties of sharing knowledge across networks generated by professional occupations, for example. However, one set of network relationships can be used to trigger the development of another so providing momentum to innovation. For example, in Medico, discussions between medical professionals (helped by the weekend event), generated a new, cross-professional network to oversee the specification of new professional standards and fuelled the acceptance of the innovation by the medical community. In this way, 'the reach of coordinated action was progressively expanded, enabling more effective implementation of the innovation, despite potential resistance' (Swan and Scarbrough, 2005).

Technology and objects

Chapter 7 highlighted the pervasive role of technology, and particularly information technology (IT), in managing knowledge. McLoughlin et al. (2000) note further that technology, and, correspondingly, innovation involving technology, should be seen as 'part of a broad "socio-technical ensemble" or "network"' (p. 19). This role of technology is especially important in networked innovation processes where actors are distributed across knowledge/practice boundaries (e.g. different functional groups) and organizational contexts. Technology, and other physical artefacts, can play a critical role, both in communication and also in acting as 'boundary objects' around which conversations, negotiations, decision practices and sense-making can converge. Indeed it is hard to imagine any kind of networked innovation process that does not involve, at least to some extent, technology.

The development of the so-called smart product, 'Persona', described in Box 9.4 (Fleck, 2003), provides a stark example of the mediating role of technology in networked innovation. This prototype hand-held contraceptive device provided a material object around which producers (Unliver, Boots-the-Chemist), users (women seeking contraception) and wider social groups (the World Health Organization and Religious Groups) could interact and negotiate. The Persona device – as well as its component elements (the plastic case, the test sticks, the digital display, the Persona label and so forth) – acted as a 'boundary object' of the kind discussed in Chapter 4. As Carlile (2002) found, in the case of highly novel or innovative projects, such objects play a critical role in overcoming boundaries created by differences in language (syntactic boundaries), meanings (semantic boundaries) and practices (pragmatic boundaries).

BOX 9.4   The case of Persona (after Fleck, 2003)

'Persona' is a hand-held 'smart device' that, using regular urinary tests, tells a woman when in their monthly cycle they can have sex without getting pregnant. Essentially, it acts as a much more reliable (claiming to be 95 per cent reliable) version of the 'rhythm method' and, as such, has become popular with groups of women that, for medical or religious reasons, cannot use other forms of contraception. Persona, for example, received official endorsement from the Roman Catholic Church. The design of Persona involved a number of key groups with rather different interests, including users. In the 1970s the World Health Organization, interested in lowering high birth rates in developing countries, was working on research investigating hormonal indicators of fertility. Following this, in 1984, the Unilever company launched a subsidiary firm (Unipath) to develop their business on monoclonal human antibodies – antibodies that could be used to identify hormone metabolites. Unilever had also developed the 'Clear Blue' pregnancy test (based on monitoring urinary hormones), pioneered the first 'one step test' stick for pregnancy in 1988, and conducted research on hormonal profiles of fertility cycles.

In the 1990s these pieces of the jigsaw fell into place and the path for Persona was set. Unipath, in addition, conducted research into women's attitudes to contraception and how the information provided by Persona should be presented (e.g. 'red days' and 'green days'). Aesthetics (the device is portable and unobstrusive) was another input into Persona's design but 'perhaps the most interesting and challenging of all the knowledge inputs required was understanding the nature of the interaction between persona and its users' (Fleck, p. 244). This relied on user education and involvement and was an intrinsic part of the design process.

Persona proved extremely successful in the United Kingdom, with over £100,000 worth of sales. But, the innovation process was not without problems. For example, it was not approved in the United States and Unipath's exclusive deal with Boots-the-Chemist to sell the Persona device (and more importantly the urinary test sticks) had negative ramifications, with other pharmacists refusing to stock Unipath products.

However, the fact that an object can mitigate boundaries does not mean that actors need to understand it in exactly the same ways. As Boland and Tenkasi (1995) noted, boundary objects 'do not convey unambiguous meaning, but have instead a kind of symbolic adequacy that enables conversation without enforcing commonly shared meanings' (p. 362). For example, religious groups and producers saw the Persona object in very different ways – the former as a vehicle for avoiding unwanted conception, thereby upholding Catholic values, and the latter as a product providing an alternative, non-invasive, and therefore safer, means of contraception. Once it was on the market, it also became clear that some women were interpreting its use in rather different ways to those intended by the manufacturers. As well as indicating which days a woman was unlikely to become pregnant (as a 'green day') on the display, the device also indicates ovulation (as a small 'o'). As a result, some women began to use it to plan, rather than avoid, pregnancy, leading eventually to the development of a new product with similar technology – 'Clear Plan' (Fleck, 2003).

This is a good illustration of the different interpretation and meanings that occur amongst actors at boundaries created by divisions in knowledge/practice (Carlile, 2002). The Persona object served to mobilize interests and changes in practice but people came to change their practices for different reasons. Indeed, it is this very 'interpretive flexibility' that makes some objects more powerful than others in overcoming boundaries (Bijker et al., 1987). Objects that have the ability to both reveal different perspectives and be seen as 'desirable' across groups with very different political interests may play a more powerful role in generating commitment to a shared course of action.

In practical terms, then, objects such as design drawings, flowcharts and work plans – objects that both reveal differences between people and specify interdependencies (Garrety and Badham, 2000) – may be more useful in encouraging knowledge integration than 'fixed' objects such as PowerPoint presentations. However, in using objects for managing knowledge for networked innovation, we also need to be aware that such objects can also become sites for significant conflict. The 'revolt' against Unipath by pharmacies left out of the exclusive Unipath/Boots-the-Chemist network (see above) is a useful reminder of how the 'creating and reshaping boundary objects is an exercise of power that can be collaborative or unilateral' (Boland and Tenkasi, 1995, p. 362).

Power and politics

The literature on power in management and organization studies is far too extensive to be given adequate treatment here. However, in studies of innovation, there has been a tendency to view power in narrow, and often quite negative, terms as the ability of one party to coerce another by controlling resources that the latter needs (e.g. finance, information, staff). This is probably because many such studies have focused on innovation *within* firms where those higher in the hierarchy often (though not always) have more control over required resources. However, when we look at networked innovation, required resources (including knowledge and information) are distributed across organizations and the ability to exercise such hierarchical power is often very limited. In developing their brachytherapy product, for example, the Medico team needed clinicians to help them to design and test the product but they had very limited hierarchical power. Nor were they likely to be persuasive through direct marketing techniques since their commercial objectives were viewed with, at best, suspicion by medical professionals.

Rather than thinking of power like the classic 'Sword of Damocles', a more useful approach is to see it in more neutral terms simply as a way of getting things done. Power, then, is defined as 'a force that effects outcomes, while politics is power in action' (Hardy, 1996, p. S3). This wider view of power opens our eyes to alternative kinds of power that can be brought to bear in managing knowledge for innovation. Hardy (drawing from earlier work by Lukes, 1974) provides a useful summary of three kinds of power that can be used strategically to mobilize change across, as well as within, organizations. They are the following:

- resource power – the power to bring about desired behaviours through the deployment of key resources on which others depend.

- process power – the power derived from organizational decision-making processes, procedures and political routines that enable or prevent certain groups from participating in decision-making.
- meaning power – the power that operates through the semantic and symbolic aspects of organizational life (such as cultural norms and expectations) and that legitimizes (or de-legitimizes) particular activities.

Linking these wider sources of power to the dynamics of networked innovation has important implications. It tells us that building social networks can shape the distribution of not just resources, but also of process power and meaning power by creating new patterns of interdependencies between groups (Hardy et al., 2003). Process power, then, results in part from an actor's particular position in the network and their ability to act as 'obligatory passage points' in the decision process (Callon, 1980). For example, while the Medico team could not have directly controlled decisions amongst medical staff over treatment standards, they did acquire process power by abstracting and editing critical scientific and educational materials (including the public website) and by moulding the informal channels through which different groups had access to information. The careful selection of Medico Team members and opinion leaders (i.e. people who could link the Medico project to the interests of different stakeholders) further enhanced their process power.

However, the major strategy of Medico managers was to use meaning power to legitimate new forms of collaboration and knowledge integration. The innovation was framed, then, not in terms of Healthco's own product, but in terms of the importance of curing the prostate cancer disease by developing brachytherapy as a treatment. The discourses of 'community of care' and 'Centres of Excellence' appealed to multiple professional interests and were crucial in reframing, what were at one level blatant commercial goals, as medical goals. This both lowered potential resistance and encouraged new networks to form across groups, so further encouraging knowledge integration through the formation of a new 'community of practice' around this particular form of cancer treatment.

Paying attention to the different kinds of power, then, suggests that the ability to mobilize networked innovation depends on managing – in a 'middle-out', rather than 'top down', sense – the generative relationship between power, network formation and knowledge integration. This relationship, as played out in the Medico case, is outlined in Figure 9.4. Hence we can see how Medico's cultivation of networks and the exercise of alternative sources of power (process and meaning power) facilitated both knowledge integration and the further generation of new networks, and contributed to successful innovation outcomes. As Dougherty and Hardy (1996) put it, for organizations to become innovative they must 'reconfigure the power embedded in the organizational system – in its resources, processes and meanings'. Of course, this relationship between network building, power and knowledge integration is by no means smooth or

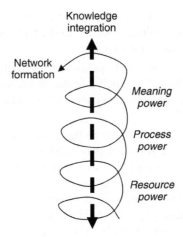

Figure 9.4 Dynamics of networked innovation (after Swan and Scarbrough, 2005)

uninterrupted (as indicated by the dotted line). Sometimes this spiral may even be vicious rather than virtuous (hence the two-way arrow) – as, for example, where different forms of power are applied to resist, rather than promote, innovation and knowledge sharing (compare with, for example, the Research Team case in Chapter 4).

>> OPEN INNOVATION

The phenomenon of networked innovation moves our understanding of the innovation process far away from the kind of closed sets of actors and contexts, predefined objectives and sequence of knowledge flows seen in the linear model. Conversely, as innovation processes become more complex and knowledge-intensive, and networks enable the much more rapid flow of knowledge across all kinds of organizations, innovation has itself become much more open-ended. As we have seen in the case of smart products (e.g. automatic collision avoidance, smart phones, personal health monitoring devices) and many types of service innovation (e.g. online services, Ebay, iTunes) it can be difficult to tell where design (or invention) ends and use (or implementation) begins. The growth of the open-source software 'movement' – Linux being a good example – highlights this conflation of design and use and the power of an open-ended innovation approach.

In the recent period, a number of organizations have begun to embrace the idea of 'open innovation' more formally. The term was coined by Henry Chesbrough to describe a 'paradigm shift' in the way companies go about commercializing knowledge (Chesbrough, 2003a, b). The old paradigm – referred to as 'closed innovation' – is the linear mode in which companies are self-reliant in terms of creating knowledge and introducing it in the form of new products to the markets. Chesbrough argues that, in the current era, a number of factors have undermined the logic of Closed Innovation. These include the following:

- dispersion of scientific and technological knowledge due to the mobility of highly skilled workers;
- the growing presence of venture capital;
- the increasing role of user groups in the innovation process;
- the shortening of technology lifecycles.

Chesbrough suggests, along with others, that the current context of shorter product life cycles and rapid advances in technology makes it harder for firms to justify expending money on innovation. Open innovation can meet the requirements for innovation whilst keeping costs down by leveraging external R&D resources, while at the same time securing revenue through various kinds of partnering arrangements. Chesbrough defines open innovation as 'a paradigm that assumes that firms can and should use external ideas as well as internal ideas, and internal and external paths to market, as the firms look to advance their technology' (Chesbrough, 2006, p. 1). This, he argues, requires a new business model and redesign of organizational innovation processes. In the open innovation model, then, projects can be launched internally or externally and taken to market via a variety of different mechanisms, including traditional sales channels, and also partnerships, spin-off ventures, outlicensing and so forth (Chesbrough, 2003a, b; Fredberg et al., 2008).

In moving towards this open model, firms are placing greater emphasis on the acquisition of external knowledge, the greater role of users in co-producing knowledge, and a more collaborative approach to the management of intellectual property (von Hippel and von Krogh, 2003, 2006). The development of partnerships, where partners are treated as peers in the co-production process, not as 'suppliers' or 'consumers', is what makes open innovation different to traditional outsourcing and market arrangements (Chiaromonte, 2006). The key to managing knowledge for open innovation hinges, then, on developing or enhancing networks capable of supporting new forms of collaboration and knowledge flow. It also means exploiting the different and complementary skills/roles of partner organizations (summarized in Figure 9.5) rather than trying to do it all yourself, whilst securing a share of the final profits.

An example of open innovation can be seen in Proctor and Gamble's 'Connect and Develop' system. The goal of this was to achieve 50 per cent of innovations being sourced externally by 2008 (from 20 per cent in 2000) using a range of mechanisms including turning 80 R&D staff into technology 'scouts', using electronic R&D networks (such as yet2.com), generating consumer-driven innovation (through programmes such as 'CoCreate') and using retirees as a source of innovation. As Sakkab Nabil, the VP of R&D put it: 'The future of

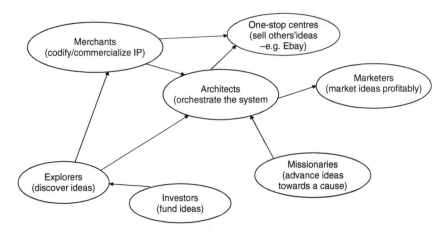

Figure 9.5   An opening innovation system

R&D is Connect and Develop – collaborative networks that are in touch with 99% of the research that we don't do ourselves.'

Managing knowledge to achieve open innovation rests on many of the knowledge processes and features of enabling contexts discussed in this book (team work, network building, communication technology, supportive organizational design and leadership, supportive HRM practices). We must be very careful, however, about depicting the open innovation model as a new panacea for innovation. The jury is out, for example, on whether the model is equally applicable across contexts, on how far the model is applicable to innovation in services as compared to products and on how far many organizations actually have the human or organizational capabilities required to support an open innovation model (Fredberg et al., 2008). As Witzeman et al. (2006) observe, open innovation implies a major cultural shift: 'Harnessing external technology for innovation requires a fundamental change in employee thinking. The "Not Invented Here" syndrome is replaced with the "Invented Anywhere" approach' (p. 27).

>> PRACTICE PERSPECTIVES ON INNOVATION

Practice perspectives have featured less centrally to date in studies of innovation. Communities of practice (Chapter 8) have been studied in relation to their positive effects on learning and incremental change but even here their role in relation to more radical forms of innovation and change is open to question. As Fox (2000) observes, 'communities of practice theory tells us nothing about how, in concrete practice, members of a community change their practice or innovate' (p. 860). Practice perspectives were introduced in Chapter 1. Like process accounts they highlight the situated nature of knowledge and the very provisional, improvisational and iterative ways that things get done in innovation.

They also highlight four additional features, introduced in Chapter 1, that we should consider when managing knowledge for innovation – the nested nature of practices; the stickiness of knowledge; the materiality of innovation and investment of practices.

Nested practices

As noted in Chapter 1, core to practice-based thinking is the idea that practices (including innovation practices) unfold within a broader 'field' of interconnected practices (Schatzki et al., 2001). Importantly, micro-level practices (e.g. work practices) help create this broader field of practices (e.g. professional practices) and, at the same time, are influenced by them. This is what we mean when we say that practices of innovation are 'nested' – change at one level of practice is both a medium for and an outcome of change at another level of practice.

Take, as in the Medico case, the practice of an individual consultant urologist deciding on surgery as the treatment for a prostate cancer patient. In practice terms, this decision (if repeated often) can be understood, both as helping to form, or create, the professional practices of urologists (i.e. surgery becomes an integral part of what these professionals do) and also as being influenced by professional practices (i.e. their professional practices and standards reinforce surgery as the most legitimate decision to take when treating prostate cancer). The practice of doing surgery, therefore, occurs within, but also creates, the broader field of consultant urology.

This view allows us to see why it is that the introduction of what seemed to be a much better treatment for many patients was so contentious. In particular, the new brachytherapy treatment moved the practice of deciding treatment for patients away from consultant urologists and towards radiotherapists. Hence it threatened to violate a whole system of well-established and collectively agreed upon practices around medical roles and responsibilities. It was not until the 'field of practice' shifted a little – when new professional standards were triggered by individual practices in attending a weekend event – that the new brachytherapy treatment could gather momentum. This helps us to explain a central puzzle in innovation, noted at the start of this chapter, which is why some apparently successful innovations fail to be used while others continue to be used, despite their success being highly questionable. Consider this explanation, also, in relation to the failure to diffuse the new cataracts treatment in the Midlands Hospital case (Chapter 8).

Stickiness of knowledge

By zooming in on actual practices 'on the ground', so to speak, practice perspectives also shed light on the *micro-challenges* of managing knowledge for innovation (Nicolini, 2008). These arise from the 'stickiness' of knowledge to practice. As you will be able to see, if you have a chance to do the role-play at the end of this chapter, organizations exist precisely so that the work practices (and effort) can be distributed across individuals and groups. This means, quite naturally, that people assume different work roles (e.g. managing director, consultant, operations, technical specialist) linked very often to different types of knowledge and expertise (e.g. operations, sales, finance, design, IT) and to different political agendas and interests. These divisions of practice result in knowledge boundaries, making it especially difficult to design and implement innovations (e.g. ERP Systems) that cross these boundaries (as seen in Chapter 3). Someone in Sales, for example, may want to promise 'the world' to customers and may simply not appreciate the burden this places on in the practices of someone else in production.

Practice perspectives remind us, then, that the problem of innovation is less to do with the amount of knowledge and information available and more to do with the way knowledge sticks to (divided) practices. More practically, it suggests that we need to identify where divisions of practice lie (which may or may not coincide with the formal structures of the organization) and work on connecting up practices for knowledge to be transformed into innovation. For example, Dougherty (2003) studied to the ability of firms to exploit 'practice-based knowledge' for innovation. Practice-based knowledge involves 'connecting scientific or technical principles to details of the specific context, piecing together an understanding of the problem from the situation itself, and generating possible solutions through action' (Dougherty, 2003, p. 267) and is built through ongoing interactions among practitioners and clients. She investigated innovation in eight service companies, focusing on the way they exploited different types of practice-based knowledge (in particular around making sense of users needs, identifying problems and trends and designing services/using technology). She found, on the whole, that service firms were very bad at exploiting practice-based knowledge and attributed this to two main problems:

(i) The organization of work into discrete parts and the divisions of knowledge/practice this creates make it very difficult for people to develop shared understandings about what they are doing. This prevents knowledge processes (i.e. developing, sharing, integrating) from actually happening or, as Dougherty (2003) put it, 'everyday interactions were organized so that they systematically dispersed or dismembered practice-based knowledge about technologies or user needs' (p. 283).

(ii) People quite naturally focus attention on their local, day-to-day practices. This means that the overall complexity of the wider organization of work practices they are part of is shifted into the background. The complexity of organizational practices are reduced, then, into abstract, highly simplified, norms and 'rules of thumb' (e.g. about 'the way we treat patients') that are often rigid, inflexible and non-negotiable, and, yet, govern what happens on the ground. This, Dougherty argues, is problematic for innovation. For example, in Medico the 'interpretive scheme' of Medico staff when faced with the product innovation was initially to dismiss it as 'a medical device and we are not a medical device company'.

Faced with these challenges, Dougherty argues that a way forward is to articulate work practices and knowledge flows in a more holistic way that pulls the whole flow of actual practices into the foreground and makes actual practices 'concrete, observable and doable, not just abstract concepts' (Dougherty, p. 279). This, she argues, can be done by developing straightforward, concrete images of the flow and value of interconnected knowledge and work activities – for example, through prototypes and demonstrations – which helps pull together the design of technologies and services with the needs of users. Such articulations allow people to 'collectively invoke a shared representation of their joint work...to select elements of practice from their established repertoire and fit them to a situation, and to develop new elements of practice in new settings, thus enlarging and recreating practice-based knowledge' (p. 275). For example, in Medico, the Centres of Excellence played the dual role, both in illustrating the technology and its usefulness for certain types of patient and in making the interconnected practices of medical staff visible and concrete to previously dispersed groups.

Materiality of innovation

We saw above how using technologies and objects that have 'interpretive flexibility' can help span boundaries within organizations. Practice perspectives take this further by focusing explicitly on the material properties of everyday life as central to the mediation of practice. This includes, not just 'boundary objects' but also physical spaces, layouts, equipment (e.g. computer equipment, telephones, white boards). For example, the pressing of a 'mute' button in a telephone conversation, the ability of some actors to start or stop a conference call or the physical layout of a room can change the flows of knowledge between actors acting, as Orlikowski (2006) puts it as 'scaffolds' for human interaction (see also Chapter 3).

In relation to innovation, physical and visual representations provide particularly useful 'platforms' for the interrelationship between designers and users, becoming 'a ground, so to speak, in which people come together and interact over their work even as the practice *per se* emerges' (Dougherty, 2003, p. 280). Practice-based studies deepen our understanding of the particular features that such material artefacts need to have in order to encourage innovation. In her research on groups of designers (e.g. in the construction industry), Whyte and her team found that visual representations (e.g. design drawings) played a crucial role, both in encouraging learning, knowledge-sharing processes and coordination across the different professional and occupational groups involved, and also in legitimating ideas (Whyte et al., 2008). As well as having 'interpretive flexibility', their detailed analysis of practice found that representations that were more 'successful' in this regard were those that had the following features (encapsulated in Figure 9.6):

Figure 9.6 Example boundary object

- they could 'move' between being fluid and being frozen. For example, design sketches in pencil could easily be 'frozen' as design plans but could also be changed (the pencil could be erased).
- they were 'parsimonious' – in other words, not so complex that they defied any interpretation.
- they were always partially incomplete, so that they permitted different interpretations to come to light.

Investment in practice

We saw above how power and politics comes to bear on managing knowledge for innovation. As we saw in Chapter 1, practices (like diagnostic practices) also become institutionalized – different groups, including managers, professionals, scientists and technicians develop distinctive perspectives, or worldviews, which become *invested* over time in their practices and shape their interactions with other groups (Carlile, 2002). The notion of 'field of practice' reminds us that wider systems of power reinforce separations of practice (e.g. the power of surgeons who have authority). Innovators, therefore, need to work with these structures (e.g. the development of professional standards) not against them.

This helps to explain why innovation, in particular, can be so challenging. Innovation, by definition, requires departures from, or breaks with, previously invested practices. This means that actors (some would include here non-human actors) will seek to sustain power and control within their own knowledge domains and over their own work practices (Carlile, 2002). Medical consultants, for example, in part derive their professional power by retaining control over the diagnosis of patients, and so may be resistant to any change that threatens to undermine this power. It also helps to explain why apparently successful innovations so often fail to travel into new contexts (see, e.g. the Midland Hospital case in Chapter 8). In short, changing practice, and the wider systems practices in which they are embedded, is difficult even where the advantages of doing so are clear.

>> INNOVATING ACROSS INSTITUTIONAL CONTEXTS

Practice perspectives, and the notion of invested practices, also tells us that, over time, certain practices gradually become institutionalized – that is, generally accepted and deeply entrenched in the societies in which we live, and reinforced by the institutional machinery that supports them. This poses particular challenges in terms of managing knowledge for innovation, as it means that certain practices within their own societal contexts are simply not questioned and, therefore, not easily amenable to, or prepared for, change. For example, early ideas about Just-in-Time technologies – which were very successfully embraced in Japanese manufacturing – were initially rejected by managers in the United States because they simply did not fit with the predominant accepted management knowledge/ practice at the time (Clark, 1987). Indeed there are many examples of innovations that fail to travel across national borders for this reason, or of innovations that are changed significantly when they do travel, in order to fit the new institutional context (the British game of rugby which changed into American Football when it travelled to the United States, for example – Clark, 1987).

We do not have space to deal with these issues in depth here (though, see Clark, 2000; Nelson, 1992; Owen-Smith et al., 2002; Scott and Meyer, 1994; Swan et al., 1999a). However, it is important to be aware that the institutional context is a critical aspect of the enabling (or disabling) context for innovation. It plays an important role in shaping both innovations and also possible approaches to knowledge creation and to the management of knowledge work. In relation to the former, institutional differences in the ways in which knowledge is created and legitimated by different professional groups have been found to have an important influence on knowledge creation. For example, in our earlier research comparing knowledge creation processes in different professional settings, we found that consultants working in the legal profession deployed more heavily codified forms of knowledge when compared with consultant scientists, who relied more strongly on experimentation and 'learning by doing' (Robertson et al., 2003). In relation to the latter, research in the biomedical industry has found broad macro-level differences between the United States, the United Kingdom and other parts of Europe in terms of how easy it is for knowledge to move across academic, business and clinical organizations (relational capabilities) and between up-stream and down-stream science (integrative capabilities – Owen-Smith et al., 2002). These differences seem to derive from highly institutionalized practices surrounding, for example career mobility, perceptions and values, and can have a significant influence on innovation processes within organizations at the micro-level (Swan et al., 2007a). This suggests that approaches to managing knowledge work may not be equally possible or applicable across national contexts.

These institutional influences remind us of a further important dimension of power – named 'the power of the system' (Hardy, 1996). This is the power that derives from deeply embedded, and historically taken-for-granted, ways of working within particular organizational, institutional and historical contexts (e.g. from the organization of professions, work occupations, educational and regulatory systems). Whilst system power is not so amenable to direct forms of management (except, perhaps, by changing policy or regulatory contexts), it is important to recognize that it can pose significant constraints on the ability of individuals to deploy other forms of power in order to produce, or resist, change (Foucault, 1980). Medico managers' deployment of power, for example, was limited by the power of the system imbued upon medical professionals and reinforced by professional standards. It is crucial to remember that the past poses a major constraint on the ability for organizations to learn in the present, so that the 'zone of manoeuvre' open to an organization at any point in time is limited (Clark, 2000).

>> CONCLUSIONS

The examination of knowledge and innovation presented in this chapter emphasizes the message conveyed throughout this book that a single 'best practice' approach to managing knowledge work is deeply problematic. Approaches to managing knowledge need to be linked to particular purposes (in this case innovation activities and episodes), knowledge processes (e.g. sharing and integrating), and enabling (and disabling) contexts (organizational, political, institutional). The tendency to neglect these linkages reflects a still quite deeply entrenched assumption that there is a relatively straightforward and positive relationship between knowledge, innovation and performance outcomes. It is highly questionable, however, how far this is generally the case. The nature of the alignment between purposes, processes and contexts will be summarized in the final concluding chapter, next.

This chapter has also highlighted the need to see innovation as a highly iterative, politically contested and context-dependent, process of knowing – one that involves not only developing new ideas, products, processes and technologies, but also changing existing and future practices. Such a view sees networks and power as crucial drivers of innovation. Indeed, we have argued that, as knowledge becomes more widely distributed, and innovation processes become more knowledge intensive (e.g. with the growth of service innovation), networked forms of innovation become yet more central. The practice perspective outlined in this chapter, and earlier in this book, highlights, further, the stickiness of knowledge to divisions of practice and the practical role of material artefacts (including new products) as tools to encourage knowledge integration across boundaries.

This knowledge-centred approach moves us well away from more narrow structural views of innovation as products, or entities, to be transferred from inventors to users. As Hendriks observes, however, 'managing innovation as knowledge work is only an improvement to knowledge-lean approaches to innovation management if efforts are made to develop a rich, activity-based conception of the knowledge sides to innovation' (Hendriks, 2003). The work outlined in this chapter has begun to develop this conception but it is also clear that much work remains to be done.

Summary of key learning points

>> Knowledge should not be seen as valuable in itself but as adding value when created and applied for specific tasks and purposes.

>> A major purpose of knowledge work is innovation. This entails both exploration and exploitation, where knowledge, skills, values *and changes in practice* are central.

>> Innovation is an episodic process that: (i) relies centrally *on knowledge sharing* and integration and the development of new working practices; (ii) has uncertain outcomes, which are influenced by networks, power, technology and the context (organizational and institutional) in which the innovation process occurs.

>> Knowledge relevant for innovation is typically *distributed* across a wide range of sources, people, roles and locations, both inside and outside the organization. Processes of *sharing and integrating* of knowledge are therefore crucial.

>> With increasingly distributed knowledge and the growth of services, innovation in many industries has become more knowledge intensive and more reliant on different kinds of networks and open innovation models.

>> Episodes of the innovation process (e.g. agenda formation, selection, implementation and routinization) are not linear and sequential but are overlapping, iterative and recursive, with uncertain outcomes. They may also have different requirements with respect to the deployment of knowledge.

>> Regardless of what approach is taken to managing knowledge for innovation, outcomes are mediated by: (i) *social networks*; (ii) *different forms of power*; (iii) *technology and material artefacts*; (iv) *organizational and institutional contexts*. Recognizing these factors is a major step towards the more effective and successful management of knowledge for innovation.

>> Knowledge is sticky and invested in practice, which makes innovation challenging.

>> Understanding the politics of innovation processes, and deploying different forms of power, is central so that stakeholders are willing to engage and share what knowledge they have, and so that conflict can be used to mobilize rather than resist change.

GROUP EXERCISE: INNOVATION AT OAKLAND FURNITURE – A ROLE-PLAY*

This role-play simulates the early episodes (agenda formation and selection) of an innovation process. These episodes involve a consideration of the problems facing Oakland, a furniture manufacturing company, and a decision about whether or not to select a particular new technology – an Enterprise Resources Planning (ERP) system (earlier versions of this technology were referred to as Manufacturing Resources Planning systems – MRP2). Nine different players are involved – eight work within Oakland with different functional role responsibilities, the ninth is an external consultant and an expert in ERP technology. Managing knowledge is therefore critical to this decision.

>> THE COMPANY

Oakland Furniture Ltd is located on a single site near a town in England called High Wycombe, where many other furniture companies, some very small, are also based. Oakland is quite large in furniture industry terms and employs 300 people. There are 210 employees on the shop floor, of whom 144 are skilled (65 machine operators and 79 cabinet-makers and finishers). The remaining 66 are semi-skilled or unskilled, and work on general handling jobs, packing and unpacking and so on. There are 90 other staff: 25 production people including foremen and women, supervisors and managers; 25 sales field staff and managers; and about 40 clerical staff. Most shop-floor workers and some staff are members of the furniture industry trade union, the FTAT (Furniture, Timber and Allied Trades).

Oakland specializes in high-quality 'English' furniture, using oak, beech and yew solid timber stock and veneers. Their present product range is quite restricted. It is focused on the dining and occasional furniture (i.e. living room cabinets, coffee tables and so on) sectors of the market. It grew very rapidly some 25 years ago, largely due to one particular dining-room range, the 'Oakland', which gave the company its

* This role-play is an abridged version of the original produced by James Fleck (now Dean and Professor of Innovation Dynamics at the Open University Business School) with two of the authors (Jacky Swan and Harry Scarbrough). The original was part of an initiative funded by the Economic and Social Research Council (ESRC) to develop training materials in innovation. The full original version provides much more detailed role information and is intended to run over a longer session (approximately three hours). This can be found at http://omni.bus.ed.ac.uk/opsman/oakland/oak1.htm. The case of Oakland is a fictional one but the information about the company is based upon a number of real research cases.

name. This sold very well in high street retailers up and down the country. Oakland Furniture now produces five coordinated ranges and a few 'specials' – such things as one-off tables and matching sets of chairs for town halls, university council chambers and company boardrooms. Oakland's major competitors are firms such as Stag, Parker Knoll, Bradley Furniture and Neville Johnson.

The company was purchased more than ten years ago at the peak of its earnings by a major conglomerate. But it languished, declining into losses four years in a row. This opened the door for a management buyout two years ago, organized by the present Managing Director, Alex Rheingold, in close association with Rowan Gregory, the Chief Designer.

>> TECHNOLOGICAL CHANGE AT OAKLAND

In the enthusiasm unleashed by the buyout, and the injection of cash made available, various opportunities for improving Oakland's operations were implemented and others were being closely examined. Several numerically controlled machine tools were bought second-hand. A major new machine, designed with expert contribution from Rowan Gregory and produced by a German manufacturer, was obtained on special terms. Various marketing initiatives were also launched. These certainly improved the situation, and the company was breaking even, despite having to cover the heavy burden of interest on the loans used to finance the buy-out.

However, though fundamentally sound in market position, product range and quality, it was clear that the company desperately required improved means of stock control and production planning. It was in this general context that Alex Rheingold was impressed by a presentation on the benefits of ERP by a consultant, Sandy Corbett, at a furniture industry conference. ERP is sold as an integrated computer-aided system for materials handling and production scheduling. The latest version of such systems links production planning to other functional areas of the firm and more broadly to manufacturing strategy on a company-wide level. As a result of the consultant's presentation, Alex suggested that Oakland should look into the pros and cons of introducing ERP technology (including software to support it).

>> THE MEETING

Alex has convened a meeting (to last around one hour) of a working group to discuss the pros and cons of introducing ERP technology, and to decide on a way forward for the company in terms of technological innovation. The aim of the meeting is to decide whether or not to pursue the development of an ERP system in Oakland. Because of the company-wide potential for ERP a group of eight key Oakland employees has been called together. In addition, Sandy Corbett, the external consultant, has also been invited to advise the company and is ready to answer any questions that members of the working group might have. Those invited to join the meeting include the following:

1. Alex Rheingold: Managing Director. Chairs the meeting. Knows about the furniture industry. The driving force behind the recent management buyout. Impressed by a

recent conference presentation by the ERP consultant, Sandy Corbett. Initiated the present event.

2. Chris Duncan: Financial Director. Knows about the turnover and profitability of the firm. Tough on the payback of proposals. Suspicious of any control system not under the Financial Director's direct control.

3. Jan Pettigrew: Operations Director. Worked entirely within the furniture industry, and believes it to be unique and distinct. Took a course about ERP but unsure whether it would work in Oaklands.

4. Rowan Gregory: Chief Designer. Ambitious to promote a quality 'Oakland's style'. Technologically progressive but concerned that ERP might restrict the design scope and force excessive standardization.

5. Sam Newton: Sales and Distribution Manager. Responsible for sales and customer care, and worried about the company's present bad image over delivery times.

6. Jo Armstrong: Purchasing Manager. Responsible for maintaining adequate stocks of quality timbers. Also knows something about just-in-time.

7. Robin Johnston: Production Scheduler. Time-served, with excellent intuitive judgement but sceptical about computer-based systems. Are they going to make the scheduler's special skills redundant?

8. Jean Lamont: Systems Administrator. Knows about the existing computer systems and about data-handling practicalities. Very enthusiastic about ERP but might leave a 'time bomb' if not respected.

9. Sandy Corbett: Outside Consultant. Knowledgeable about the ERP approach. Does not directly sell software but can recommend a supplier. Knows little about the furniture industry but believes that any manufacturing environment would benefit from ERP software and its philosophy for production planning.

To perform the role-play in syndicate groups you should go now to pp. 219 to see your tutor-allocated role brief in full (note: you only need to read and prepare your own role brief for the role-play).

>> QUESTIONS

Having performed the role-play, syndicate groups can discuss the following question:

1. *What were the main barriers to knowledge sharing and integration and what specific approaches to managing knowledge could be introduced to overcome these?*

2. *Did everyone agree on the decision that was taken? If not why not?*

3. *Which view of innovation in this chapter (linear, process, practice) helped you best understand the decision?*

APPENDIX 9.1
INNOVATION AT OAKLAND FURNITURE – THE ROLE PLAYERS

>> ALEX RHEINGOLD: MANAGING DIRECTOR

In a few minutes, you will be chairing a meeting of a working group you have established to discuss the possible adoption of ERP in Oakland. During this meeting – which you will ensure keeps to time as is your usual practice – the group will be addressed by a consultant, Sandy Corbett, on the benefits of ERP. You saw Sandy (of Corbett Consulting) giving an impressive talk at a recent industry conference on this topic – hence the invitation. You want to give people in Oakland an opportunity for discussion before the final decision has to be made. Knowing Oakland's propensity for inertia you are keen that some decision is made to take the company forward. ERP seems to have great potential for Oakland. You have a keen personal interest in this since you were the driving force behind the recent management buyout, which at one point involved taking out a second mortgage on your family home. Although this brought you close to your Chief Designer, Rowan Gregory, some other members of the management team have criticized you in the past for not really trusting them. They have suggested that you sometimes go in and do things to suit you that are properly their responsibility.

You are highly knowledgeable about the furniture industry and about Oakland's place in it. You appreciate the variety of products in the industry (including upholstery, bedding, and bedroom, kitchen, dining, occasional and office furniture) and are aware of trends in the industry. These include the increased importance of fitted kitchens and other fitted furniture over the last decade or so; the 'furniturization' of many industrial and consumer products (such as TV cabinets, DVD/CD/video storage, gas and electric fires, refrigerators and dishwashers); the emergence of 'minimalist Scandinavianstyle' kitchen and bedroom furniture; the growth of a bespoke sector; and increased competition from firms across Europe. You are also aware that different products necessitate quite different design parameters. Even where ergonomically similar, furniture is manufactured to different severity grades as specified by FIRA (the Furniture Industry Research Association). Oakland has focused on dining and occasional furniture, both of which have been slower growing. It has suffered somewhat as a result, leading the firm into losses after its initial very successful early growth. Nevertheless, since the buyout two years ago and the minor restructuring which took place then, the basic quality of Oakland's products has enabled it to break even on annual sales of around £15–20 million. This represents about 10 per cent of the relevant UK market. Moreover, there are indications that if lead times could be improved and stock levels reduced, the firm could move to healthy profits and be well-set for growth, especially with the introduction of new ranges.

>> CHRIS DUNCAN: FINANCIAL DIRECTOR

In a few minutes, you will be attending a meeting of a working group chaired by Alex Rheingold (your MD) to discuss the possible adoption of an ERP system in Oakland. The meeting will include a consultant's presentation. You joined Oakland Furniture not long after the management buyout had established the company's independence. Not being part of the original buyout team means that you sometimes feel left out in the cold in decision-making. However, as a fully qualified accountant, you are the company's expert on the turnover (currently around $15–20 million) and profitability of the firm and the capital investment in the machinery. Oakland has just returned to an operating profit since the buyout. Normally, one would expect profits in the industry to be running at some 6 per cent of sales. Prior to the management buyout, funding had been a mixture of inter-company loans from the holding company and bank borrowings. When Oakland was purchased by its management from the parent group that had owned it, the financial structure of the company was altered with the introduction of outside finance. The existing management purchased the ordinary shares in the company assisted by a specialist finance institution. This institution also provided dividend preference shares and arranged both new overdraft facilities and a term loan. Fortunately interest rates are currently favourable. However, the strength of UK sterling is further squeezing Oakland's exports and profit margins.

You are always interested in anything that can improve the present situation, characterized, as you see it, by an endemic lack of control, but not at any price. You have to be very tough on the payback of proposals, especially given the recent disappointing performance of the company. At present, despite improving their performance since the buyout, the company has no scope for funding investments and is scarcely breaking even. They have major cash-flow worries. Long and uncertain lead times presently result in delays of nearly a year in many cases between paying for the raw materials and the receipts for the final goods. You are consequently rather suspicious of any significant new control system unless it is going to be under your own personal control. Currently, you have established a control target of $60,000 worth of production every day to keep the company on an even keel financially. You believe that simple payback within two years is a perfectly adequate criterion. If an investment proposal requires any fancy number-juggling, then clearly it cannot be that good. In particular you are rather concerned about a recent deal that Rowan Gregory, the Chief Designer, managed to swing. This involved the purchase of a very sophisticated machining centre. This was partly because of the initial buyout conditions (Gregory was one of the principals), and partly because of special payment terms. These were in recompense for Gregory's design contribution to the new machine's development. You are not entirely satisfied that that investment was properly scrutinized. Worse still, you have yet to be satisfied that it was in reality a good deal for the company, since it does not seem to be producing the savings promised. You will need some persuading that further costly expenditure on production systems can really help the firm.

>> JAN PETTIGREW: OPERATIONS DIRECTOR

In a few minutes, you will be attending a meeting of a working group chaired by Alex Rheingold (your MD) to discuss the possible adoption of an ERP system in Oakland. The meeting will include a consultant's presentation. Since you started way back as a shop-floor lathe operator, you have always worked in the furniture industry. It is unique and distinct, partly because of the heterogeneity and special character of wood (the major material) and partly because of the design/fashion element and the resulting intensity of craft skill. Wood is a natural material so one piece is never quite the same as the next. It is also hydroscopic (absorbs and retains moisture), causing it to swell and shrink with obvious implications for production. This offers certain problems for mass production. Fewer problems are offered by the manufactured items such as blockboard and chipboard. These are also used extensively, faced with veneer and finished with suitable edgings, to make surfaces and panels.

The manufacturing process follows a fairly logical path. First a range of furniture is designed, and drawings, dimensions and the appropriate fabrication processes specified. Prototypes are made up in the craft area with visits to the appropriate machine lines, to 'prove' the design. This information is then passed on in standard paper forms to the machine shop and assembly processes when the production schedule requires. You have been on an IOM (Institute of Operations Management) course on ERP, but would it really work in Oakland? However, the improved production planning and control claimed for these systems is certainly very attractive and you know at present you do have problems with inventory levels, quality control and scrap. This is in part because you are fighting a running (but friendly) battle with the Chief Designer, Rowan Gregory. Rowan keeps fiddling about with the product specifications for no good reason. These changes necessitate slightly different machining operations and mean that the shop floor has to be continually given new instructions. It also means that a plethora of different piece parts exist, ostensibly for the same bit of furniture. This is a monitoring and control nightmare, and has caused some horror stories: once a batch of tables was assembled with the wrong legs! You also know that Sam Newton, the Sales and Distribution Manager, puts in inflated sales forecasts to try to speed up the assembly process and hence delivery times to customers. This unfortunately causes huge inventory holding costs, and so you do not take Sam's sales too seriously. It is better to keep the shop floor busy and working on reasonable-sized batches. The present company monitoring systems do not help either. They run in purely monetary terms, with a target of $60,000 value of production a day (in terms of ultimate sales prices). You are concerned that the present production control system depends too much on Robin Johnston, the Production Scheduler. Robin quite clearly enjoys the influence afforded by special knowledge of the finished goods inventory and makes the most of it. But what would happen if he fell under a bus? Or took a dislike to one of your policies? You shudder to think.

>> ROWAN GREGORY: CHIEF DESIGNER

In a few minutes, you will be attending a meeting of a working group chaired by Alex Rheingold (your MD) to discuss the possible adoption of an ERP system in Oakland. The meeting will include a consultant's presentation. As an ambitious designer, you are keen to make a name for yourself in the industry. You would like to challenge the quality image of Scandinavian design with a distinctive English 'Oakland style'. Oakland presently produces five major ranges: the York, the Winchester, the Westminster, the Salisbury and the Coventry. These are distinguished by their overall style, by the wood used (variation in wood is part of its natural beauty), by hardware and by the elements available within the range. This leads to many possible permutations. You want to continue to create successful, established ranges, with new and imaginative product introductions within these ranges. This contrasts with the current policy of continual turnover of established ranges and a more or less standard range of products within each range. You are also very keen on bespoke opportunities. Indeed the company has established quite a reputation in this respect, mainly thanks to your creative efforts. You think new technology is a great thing in general – the computer-aided design system in the Design shop is brilliant. But will a standardized ERP software platform restrict your scope for refining designs? Will it force the company even more down a standards route?

You became involved in the management buyout to increase creative scope, not diminish it. You were the main driver and ideas person behind the recent investment in a new computer-controlled panel machining centre and were able to get special terms from the German machine tool firm which developed the machine. This automated machine greatly facilitates the production of high-quality, complex (and ornate) designs of panels, surfaces and doors. It allows complicated cuts to be made in panels, enabling the automatic replication of, for example, surface carving. Your contribution was to help devise a 'clever' adaptive randomization program. This enables variation in replication to be achieved. It is also able to cater (up to a point at least) for variations in the natural characteristics of the wood being machined. Together, these features enable the machine to provide a convincing emulation of the unique variation found with hand carving. It is also very flexible: once the complicated programs had been developed, machine set-up time was quite fast. The acquisition of this machine is an essential part of your longer-term plans for CAD/CAM (computer-aided design and manufacturing). Unfortunately these benefits have not yet shown up clearly, as they could only come to the fore with smaller jobs than Oakland is currently running. This has led to a difference of opinion with the Financial Director, Chris Duncan. Duncan has no imagination and makes no secret of his opinion that you are indulging yourself with expensive and useless toys.

>> SAM NEWTON: SALES AND DISTRIBUTION MANAGER

In a few minutes, you will be attending a meeting of a working group chaired by Alex Rheingold (your MD) to discuss the possible adoption of an ERP system in Oakland. The meeting will include a consultant's presentation. You are responsible for sales lead times and customer care. You are very worried about the image the company gives to customers. There is total confusion over delivery times at present, partly because Oakland's products are in demand. There are often 1000 telephone calls a day enquiring when orders are going to be delivered. This absorbs a lot of unproductive time just chasing things up. When an irate customer phones to enquire about their order, one of the sales clerks has to go down to the assembly shop floor and literally *look* for the items of furniture, going round all the work benches asking the people there if they had completed that order. Sometimes it is a matter of checking even further back, to see if the piece parts required are available. Meanwhile the customers hanging on the phone are not always too impressed.

Oakland is currently quoting 20 weeks' lead time (an improvement on our previous 25 weeks), but it often seems more a matter of luck than planning if they are able to achieve that. This leads to constant interruptions of fabrication work, and ties up a team of ten people who do little else other than progress-chase and expedite crucial orders. However, Oakland is highly regarded for quality, and all of the ranges sell well. Indeed you could probably sell much more if lead times were reduced to a level similar to those of our competitors, some of whom are quoting ten weeks. In this connection, Oakland's bespoke and 'specials' service is a nice sideline (very much Gregory's baby) and certainly gives you market prominence, contributing significantly to the firm's reputation for high quality. You are also well-aware of increasing demand for such products. But it does add to the confusion on the shop floor, sometimes interrupts other standard batched jobs (fitted bedroom and kitchen furniture is a big seller), and tends to take raw material unpredictably, thus leading to shortages. Other competitors have similar problems, although some have reduced their lead times to ten weeks, while others try to offer a guarantee on the lead time they quote. As a result of the lead times problem, you tend to inflate sales order forecasts, so that more piece parts stock is held. Then the final assembly stages can be more quickly carried out. In this context, ERP is an intriguing proposition. From talking to sales colleagues in companies that have introduced some form of ERP system, it has both positive and negative possibilities. Speaking positively, the ERP system is driven to some extent by 'demand management' where forecasts of future sales are important. This may gave you more strategic influence within the company.

On the other hand, it becomes more difficult to massage sales forecasts as these feed the system. This limits your room for manoeuvre and the ability to play the role of 'cheerleader' in the management team.

>> JO ARMSTRONG: PURCHASING MANAGER

In a few minutes, you will be attending a meeting of a working group chaired by Alex Rheingold (your MD) to discuss the possible adoption of an ERP system in Oakland. The meeting will include a consultant's presentation. You are responsible for controlling the raw materials stock levels. The maintenance of adequate stocks of quality timbers is a particular concern. You are interested in what you see as Japanese-style management technologies and ideas such as just-in-time (JIT), although you do not know how to go about introducing them. You are not sure how relevant JIT is to your timber stocks; timber requires conditioning before it can be processed. But, you feel that a simple JIT system might be more appropriate for Oakland than ERP. You think this is because JIT is based on a 'pull system' – pulling production through based on orders received at the shop floor. In contrast, ERP seems to be no more than an elaborate name for the conventional Western approach or push system that people used to call MRP2 (Manufacturing Resources Planning) – pushing through production to meet anticipated sales controlled by a centralized production plan. OK, so ERP is broader, but what is the real difference? Currently Oakland tries to operate a simple reorder point system for raw materials. This is certainly possible with the manufactured items such as hardware and chipboard. As far as possible, you negotiate bulk discounts through competitive tendering. This can lead to substantial cuts in purchase prices, but it does mean that you have to carry very large stocks of certain items. However, Oakland's manufacturing suppliers (who provide chipboard, block board and the like) will only deliver in certain minimum batches, for example, 10 tonnes of ply – 10,000 square metres or so. The purchase of solid timber is particularly problematic.

You know a lot about timber, especially in choosing high-quality stock. Here it is very rare for large purchases to be made. The variation in wood as a natural material and the selection necessary means that unpredictable and varying amounts will be purchased as and when timber stock of the appropriate quality and type becomes available. Moreover, because of the natural characteristics of wood, timber stocks have to be held under controlled conditions sufficiently long for the material to stabilize. In some cases the company takes an option on wood still standing. In these cases, of course, the final yield is difficult to estimate. There are also occasional opportunities to purchase excellent specimen timber stocks in small quantities, for instance following gales or storms which inevitably bring some trees crashing to the ground unexpectedly. You are always on the lookout for such opportunities. In such cases, you keep close contact with Rowan Gregory, the designer, who will come up with 'specials' which incorporate the specimen timber as a feature.

>> ROBIN JOHNSTON: PRODUCTION SCHEDULER

In a few minutes, you will be attending a meeting of a working group chaired by Alex Rheingold (your MD) to discuss the possible adoption of an ERP system in Oakland. The meeting will include a consultant's presentation and then there will be a further meeting to take a decision. You are a time-served craft worker, and everyone knows you have excellent intuitive judgement about scheduling and keeping things running smoothly in the factory. They all depend on you. You know all there is to know about wood (a naturally variable material) and its production. Your main task is to ensure that enough of the correct furniture parts are available so that complete assemblies can always be made up from the machined parts store. The assembly kits are made up to meet firm customer orders first, subject to a minimum batch of 25. If the order is for less than 25, the balance goes into the finished goods store. You have what seems to outsiders an uncanny memory for everything that is in the finished goods store and are rarely wrong. This provides a considerable measure of influence in running operations and you know that your boss, Jan Pettigrew (the Operations Director), very much relies on your skills in this regard. The task of remembering exactly what is in the machined parts store is, however, altogether more formidable: the company produces some 400 products requiring more than 20,000 separate parts. Many of these are left- or right-hand versions of the same piece, which often (but not always) go together in pairs (e.g. table legs). To further complicate matters, due to the particular difficulties of machining and matching wood, there is usually quite a high rate of rejects. This means that although you might have started out making 100 left- and right-hand pairs you could easily end up with 96 of one and 91 of the other. Ensuring that enough of the appropriate parts are available for the assembly kits is a major problem. To make life even more difficult, Jan Pettigrew always attempts to meet the Financial Director's control target of $60,000 worth of production per day. To achieve this, the bigger batches are progressed ahead of the smaller ones. These then sit on your shop floor somewhere until eventually someone comes down from Sales chasing up an irate customer's late order. By this time, it is more than likely that the assembly kit has been raided for some piece to replace a damaged part for another assembly, hence leading to further delays.

OK, so you know there are a few problems but nothing you can not handle. And what is this new IT system going to do to your job? You know that Jan Pettigrew is a little bit unhappy over the undoubted influence you enjoy because of your special skills and central role. Is this a ploy to undermine your position? Even if it is not, it is certainly going to change what you do. The computer system will issue the order releases and make your judgement redundant. What will there be left for you to do?

>> JEAN LAMONT: SYSTEMS ADMINISTRATOR

In a few minutes, you will be attending a meeting of a working group chaired by Alex Rheingold (your MD) to discuss the possible adoption of an ERP system in Oakland. The meeting will include a consultant's presentation and then there will be a further meeting to take a decision. Currently Oakland has a number of unconnected software systems (for payroll, accounts and sales and a CAD package). You know all about them and thoroughly enjoy keeping them working in good order. There are three staff working for you in this area. The payroll and accounts systems are standard packages with 'bits added in here and there'. The CAD package has evolved way beyond the original version, largely on account of Rowan Gregory's enthusiasm and predilection for experiment – aided and abetted by you. However, this is now getting very creaky and unwieldy – far more effective packages can be bought on the market. The sales system is a customized one with few problems. This is good for generating the appropriate paperwork for vendors and for linking up with the accounts but it is useless for tracking materials or for stock control within the company. There is no systematic parts numbering system – the present plethora of piece parts (some 22,000 and growing) is described in a vast array of drawings and process specifications that reside in an untidy set of filing chests in the design office. There are good systems available but Robin Johnston, Rowan Gregory and Jan Pettigrew between them hold the information necessary for linking the final products to the raw materials, essentially in their heads!

You are interested in the ERP idea but also understand the practicalities of implementing associated software, like how long it takes to read in data and set up new systems and parameters. This always takes far longer than people expect and they never give you enough resources to do the job properly. Computers and web-based communication technologies are obviously the way forward, the life-blood of any organization, yet they never get taken seriously enough. You are often treated like some sort of semi-skilled mechanic – no one appreciates how good you are really are. Sometimes, when you feel that you are underappreciated, you remind yourself that there are many good opportunities elsewhere. In particular, Alex Rheingold seems insufficiently appreciative of your special skills. Alex is apt to think that buying in new systems or some form of facilities management arrangement would eliminate entirely the need for the systems group. You are always stressing how your group forms the essential link between the systems and actual business processes. Is the consideration of ERP an opportunity for demonstrating the true value of your systems expertise? Or is it just an attempt by Alex to eventually outsource systems development entirely. Well, if so they'd better watch out. There might be a few surprises if they try to get rid of you! It might just be rather difficult for anyone else to take over.

>> SANDY CORBETT: CONSULTANT

You are a consultant with access to the latest technology, the ability to work closely with senior management and a track record of success. In your previous job as a production engineer and manager in an aerospace company, you were directly involved in the implementation of MRP2 – a precursor of ERP. You are very much an enthusiast for this approach to production control. This technology allows the integration of business functions and achieves and sustains tight discipline in shop-floor operations. You know what it can do in terms of: increasing financial control of operations; banishing paperwork from the supply chain; drastically reducing lead times; reducing waste and scrap; providing continuous improvement of supplier performance. All of this, as you tell your clients, leads to enhanced profits and competitiveness. You understand the philosophy of the technology and try to get this over to your clients. ERP is essentially based on the 'push philosophy' of the original MRP2 system that matches the purchasing and scheduling of raw materials and parts to centralized production plans based on sales forecasts so that materials are available when they are needed for production without holding unnecessarily high levels of inventory. ERP though also considers how planning, scheduling and control can be aligned to broader business (enterprise) objectives in particular markets.

Operationally, the planning systems and software needed to achieve ERP break activities into a front end, an engine and a back end. The front end produces the master production schedule (MPS). The MPS plans the production of the goods offered to customers over a given planning horizon based on sales forecasts. The back end handles factory scheduling and manages materials from suppliers. Material requirements planning (MRP) is the *core* of the engine. It takes a period-by-period set of MPS requirements and generates a related set of component parts and raw materials requirements. These MRP data make it possible to generate a *time-phased requirement record* for any part number. This can also drive the *detailed capacity planning* modules – a massive computational task. MRP is therefore the natural starting point for many companies to begin to computerize their overall production control where they are starting more or less from scratch. Then the systems can be developed into a more sophisticated version that provides continual updates of the various components and materials requirements to match changing circumstances.

This enables better priority-setting and fine-tuning of shop-floor operations. As well as managing material flows, these enhanced systems can allocate resources (such as machinery and personnel) more efficiently. They can also include financial modules. Simulation techniques allow the examination of various 'what if' scenarios. Such enhanced systems are clearly more company-wide, being less narrowly focused on production control. Indeed, their scope is so much wider than the original concepts of MRP, that the guru Oliver Wight coined the new term – MRP2 – 'Manufacturing Resource Planning'. Later versions are known even more grandly as ERP.

ERP is much more exciting because it allows you to work with clients, aligning their production planning with financial accounting and much broader strategic objectives. It also usually means a much longer-term (and more costly!) relationship with clients. You read a recent study some years ago reporting a large survey of 2000 ERP users that described the benefits and costs of ERP systems. This showed substantial benefits. For example, performance on delivery promises increased from 61 per cent to 88 per cent and lead times reduced from 71 to 44 days (almost 50 per cent). Typically paybacks begin within some six to nine months of 'going live' with the software. It also found that average costs of systems installation were substantial, ranging from as little as $113,000 in small companies to $2,876,000 in the largest companies (you do not usually broadcast the upper end of these costs when asked by potential clients). Interestingly, it did not cost more to achieve high ERP benefits – the degree of computerization, management support and the implementation approach used were more important in predicting benefits than the amount of money spent on the IT system.

You are also aware that a lot of companies have run into problems introducing ERP software but then they did not have the benefit of your expertise.

You are fairly cynical about how good some other consultants in this area are – some say sweet things but do not seem to have much of a clue when it comes to actually implementing systems. Although you know little about the furniture industry, basically all manufacturing businesses are the same. They take in bits, process them, combine them, and then sell them according a broad strategic plan. And in between, the actual flows of all the bits have to be monitored and accounted for. For this, essentially identical systems can be used. The nature of the bits does not really matter. You have special links with one software supplier, but of course you do your best to offer impartial advice. It would not serve your interests to recommend a system that will eventually cause problems. Once a company has bought into MRP/MRP2, they will probably continue to invest and upgrade over a number of years before achieving a full ERP system. And you will continue to help them. In making your presentation to the working group at Oakland Furniture, you are very aware of the political dynamics of the situation. Not everyone there is likely to welcome ERP. You only have limited access to key decision-makers (e.g. Alex Rheingold) and you need to make the most of it.

10

CONCLUSIONS: UNDERSTANDING THE RELATIONSHIPS BETWEEN KNOWLEDGE PURPOSES, KNOWLEDGE PROCESSES AND ENABLING CONTEXT

Chapter Outline

Learning Outcomes

At the end of this chapter you should be able to:

⇒ Draw together the lessons from other chapters.

⇒ Understand the inter-relationship between knowledge purposes, processes and enabling context.

⇒ Apply the framework to a complex organizational setting.

>> INTRODUCTION

We have seen in previous chapters that the attempt to 'manage knowledge' within organizations is not new. Indeed, if we go back to traditional craft industries, young people entering an industry learnt their trade by serving an apprenticeship. This was effectively a system of managing knowledge that involved watching and learning from a skilled craftsperson. While the apprenticeship system left the knowledge and skill with the individual craftspeople, Taylor's Scientific Management was a break from tradition in that it attempted to separate decision-making from practice. As we saw in Chapter 1, Taylor wanted managers to have the knowledge about how, why and when to carry out the various production activities in order to maximize productivity – to be the 'brains'. Workers were to be simply the 'hands'. To some extent this approach is still prevalent today in jobs and industries based on a mass production and mass consumption philosophy. So a worker in a fast-food restaurant is following a set of clearly defined procedures in making a hamburger, and a person working in a call centre is following a script in responding to a customer enquiry. In both cases, where a customer requires a service that falls outside the defined procedures the worker, in principal at least, is not equipped to deal with this situation. Indeed, if they did attempt to service the customer by ignoring standard procedures they would likely be reprimanded.

Such an approach to managing work may well still be appropriate in some jobs and in some industries. However, as we saw in Chapter 7 and the case of BankCo, divorcing knowledge from concrete tasks and actions (i.e. the brain from the hands) risks major problems. While Scientific Management spread rapidly from the car industry into other mass-production industries before and after the Second World War, the years since the 1970s have seen managers in many industries – including the car industry itself – realize the limitations of this approach. This realization was stimulated by the success of Japanese forms of work organization such as quality circles, 'just-in-time' and 'lean' production which made much greater use of the tacit knowledge of the shop-floor workforce – knowledge which even the most rigorous kinds of Scientific Management had been unable to eliminate.

Moreover, as we saw in early chapters, the environment in which the majority of industry sectors operate is increasingly dynamic, knowledge-intensive and globalized. Organizations need to respond rapidly to such environments, using knowledge to develop new and innovative products, services and organizational processes to suit changing circumstances. To seek to concentrate decision-making power and authority in the managerial technostructure, while the major part of the organization simply obeys its commands, is slow and cumbersome. Worse, it ignores the extent to which much of the most valuable knowledge within the organizational domain simply cannot be concentrated at the centre. Very often, the employees who are closest to the rapidly changing business environment are not the managers, but the rank-and-file sales people, production operatives and so on. It is their experience built up over time with the organization and tacit understandings of the way outcomes are achieved which are most relevant to making decisions. It follows therefore that in this kind of environment, power and authority need to be decentralized – indeed they will almost inevitably be so to some extent – so that empowered workers can use their knowledge and experience to develop solutions to problems and opportunities that confront them on a day-to-day basis.

>> STRATEGIC KNOWLEDGE PURPOSES

This trend is apparent across a range of industries, jobs and tasks. It is most advanced, however, in the jobs, tasks and industries that we have characterized as knowledge-intensive. Here, we see a very different approach to managing knowledge work, one that recognizes the strategic significance of knowledge for sustained competitive advantage. In these contexts management strive to implement and promote the use of specific *knowledge processes* and actively foster an *enabling context* to achieve their overall strategic aims around managing knowledge, that is their strategic knowledge purpose. Throughout this book we have focused on the core aspects of knowledge work in these knowledge-intensive settings. The aim has been to highlight that depending on the overarching strategic knowledge purpose (e.g. knowledge exploitation, knowledge exploration or a combination of both), then particular knowledge processes need to become embedded at individual, team, project, organization and/or inter-organization levels in order to achieve the overarching purpose. Policies and techniques also need to be established in order to create the necessary enabling context to support and promote the practice of these knowledge processes.

Figure 10.1 depicts the relationship between the overarching purposes that lie behind a strategic approach to managing knowledge and the knowledge practices and processes that can help achieve them.

Broadly speaking, organizations that adopt a strategic approach to managing knowledge have one of two main purposes in mind – knowledge exploration or

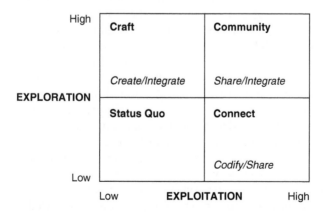

Figure 10.1 Purposes and process involved in managing knowledge

knowledge exploitation – or aim for a combination of both (but typically with more emphasis on one than the other). In Chapter 2 we saw that many knowledge-intensive firms compete primarily on the basis of innovation, developing new products processes and services for clients. Work practices in these contexts can be thought of as largely *craft-based* and closely resemble the work of traditional artisans, relying largely on the *creation and integration* of scarce expert knowledge that workers have developed over time. The major difference between these knowledge-intensive firms and traditional artisan firms is that that the products are often intangible and knowledge-based. For example, ScienceCo often develops new products or services for clients in the form of intellectual property. Advertising and public relations campaigns are other examples of knowledge-based products developed for clients. The design of knowledge-intensive work in these settings is, therefore, very different from that advocated by Taylor. We can characterize this as a change from simplified, clearly defined and individualized job design to complex, problem-oriented, loosely defined and team-/project-based job design. Management and the knowledge workers employed focus predominantly on knowledge exploration – creating new knowledge. These firms are often quite small and entrepreneurially driven.

In this kind of craft-based context, firms place far less strategic emphasis on knowledge exploitation – re-using existing knowledge – as knowledge is created in practice and integrated within the context of self-forming and self-managed project teams. The discussion around the types of innovation and innovation diffusion in Chapter 9 emphasized, however, that knowledge exploration in, and of itself, is not particularly valuable. Innovations have to diffuse, be adopted and be implemented by users (clients) for knowledge exploration to generate competitive advantage for these firms. The work conducted in ScienceCo, for example, only generates profit for the firm if clients are satisfied with the outcomes produced. In order for clients to make use of the products, processes and services developed by ScienceCo, the innovation needs to be implemented within the client organization.

Chapter 3 discussed the emergence of new, more fluid and modular or project-based (inter) organizational forms which have been enabled by developments in ICT. In these contexts much of the work is geographically dispersed across individuals, projects and organizations and is largely conducted and co-ordinated through ICTs. Chapter 6 also discussed a recent trend in outsourcing and offshoring some forms of knowledge work which firms do not consider part of their core competencies, specifically knowledge work that is highly reliant on codified knowledge such as IT-based services. Typically these *connected* firms are large and well-established in their sectors, offering recognized products and services on a global basis. Management's overarching aim in these types of organization is to operate and respond to competitive demands in a dynamic manner. Often this means perpetually looking to make efficiency savings and identify new markets and new product/service offerings. In these types of firm, innovation of core products and services is typically incremental rather than radical. The main strategic aim is therefore to exploit the organizational knowledge that already exists across individuals, teams and projects around the world, such that this knowledge is made widely available as a shared organizational resource. Work practices are therefore concerned largely with connecting individuals, projects and organizations and significant emphasis is placed on *codifying and sharing* knowledge across teams and projects, often through the medium of ICTs. These processes are particularly important in large knowledge-intensive organizations where standardized processes are used across the organization in order to sustain high levels of efficiency, for example in the pharmaceutical sector, or where there is a significant amount of repeat business and relatively standardized solutions are developed for clients and customers, for example in global consulting firms. The BankCo case in Chapter 7 and the discussion across Chapters 4, 5 and 8 have all highlighted, however, that codified knowledge is to all intents and purposes inert and meaningless divorced from context. Investments in KMS that operate purely as repositories for knowledge are therefore unwise. If organizations adopt this limited view of what managing knowledge is, then the KMS will be quickly viewed as a poor investment and fail.

Nowadays with the advent of Web 2.0 technologies, active collaboration via codified, visual and oral means across continents has been massively enhanced and many large organizations are now exploiting these technologies to encourage (virtual) networking and the sharing of knowledge more broadly in order to radically innovate. Effective team- and project-based working in these *community* contexts relies on work practices centred on community building and social networking within and across dispersed business units and organizations. These practices are vital in order for a shared identity, shared perspectives and trust to develop which will promote the effective *sharing and integration* of knowledge which promotes innovation – particularly radical innovation. In these organizational contexts then both knowledge exploration and exploitation are afforded equal strategic significance.

Finally there are organizations, both large and small, which are yet to realize the strategic significance of knowledge for competitive advantage, and in those organizations that choose not to actively manage knowledge, the status quo prevails.

>> KNOWLEDGE PROCESSES AND ENABLING CONTEXT

In the following section the most pertinent aspects of each of the four major knowledge processes are discussed with reference to previous chapters and cases. The emphasis throughout this book has been on the process and practice perspectives of managing knowledge work. Both these perspectives highlight the importance of the intra- and inter-organizational context which acts to either enable knowledge work or, conversely, obstruct knowledge work processes. Organizational culture, time, diversity, autonomy, shared identity, shared perspectives, trust, social networking, boundary spanning, boundary objects and so on are all crucial enablers of knowledge work. In totality these all constitute the 'ideal' enabling context for knowledge work. However, in practice, different aspects of the enabling context play a greater or lesser role in facilitating particular knowledge processes. On this basis issues such as trust, boundary spanning and so on are discussed in relation to particular knowledge processes where they specifically play a major enabling role. The section concludes by summarizing the most important aspects of the enabling context which support particular knowledge work processes.

Creating knowledge

Creating knowledge requires the application of tacit and explicit knowledge via experimentation, discussion and so on in teams and projects in order to generate new knowledge. It is in this way that completely new and novel products, processes and services are invented. The discussion in Chapter 9 around the Medico case highlighted that some innovations will be perceived as radical and highly disruptive (to existing practice) by potential users and it may be difficult for the innovating firm to diffuse their new product or service. The emphasis here is on perceptions of what the new product or service has to offer to potential users. Once particular products and services have become embedded over time, it can be difficult for new innovations to diffuse, as users become resistant to change. This highlights just how uncertain the innovation process can be. Nevertheless creating knowledge is a fundamental starting point in the innovation process.

It was highlighted in Chapter 2 that different types of knowledge workers, for example scientists, engineers, lawyers, advertising creatives, rely on tacit and explicit knowledge to varying degrees in their work and thus place more or less reliance on codified knowledge and codification during the process of knowledge creation. Regardless of the emphasis placed on codified knowledge, knowledge creation is primarily reliant on the application of workers skills, intellectual ability and expertise in team and projects settings. Therefore developing and supporting workers engaged in the kind of complex knowledge-intensive work requires a particular management approach and form of control. Chapter 2 emphasized this point and explained that knowledge workers operate most effectively when they are given the opportunity to largely self-organize and self-manage their work as individual's or in teams. Management therefore have to find approaches to organizing that they believe will deal with the tension that exists between the autonomy demanded by knowledge workers and organizational efficiency in order to satisfy themselves that they have provided a context in which knowledge workers will be motivated to work hard in the interests of the firm.

Significant managerial effort needs to be placed therefore on developing an enabling context for this particular type of highly knowledge-intensive work, one that will promote (in relative terms) efficiency (often when outcomes are highly uncertain) and simultaneously provide a significant degree of autonomy or knowledge worker discretion. The importance of a culture that promotes a strongly shared sense of identity grounded in elitism was highlighted as a key enabler, in combination with cultural conditions that recognize and celebrate diversity. A number of ways that this can be achieved are highlighted in Alvesson and Robertson's (2006) work which considered the way in which four very different types of consulting firm managed to create a shared identity grounded in elitism. As was highlighted in Chapters 2 and 6, the characteristic 'carrot-and-stick' command-and-control approach of Scientific Management is not appropriate and challenges can arise in terms of developing appropriate HRM policies that will deal with the inherent tension between autonomy and control. Close attention needs to be paid to the development of human resource practices that engender commitment and engagement from knowledge workers. Money is rarely a motivator in these contexts. Rather, in these contexts, we have stressed the importance of combining recruitment and selection practices, training and development opportunities and sophisticated reward systems in synergistic and mutually reinforcing ways. For example, the performance management system at ScienceCo emphasized revenue targets which encouraged consultant's to actively seek a variety of project work to engage in, fostering collaborative working. In addition, however, contribution to client sales and contribution to strengthening the organizational culture were also assessed as part of the annual appraisal and reward system which encouraged workers to consider all of these in their daily work activities.

Chapter 6 emphasized that the policies underlying these HRM practices have important long-term effects symbolically and practically on the development of the psychological contract between knowledge workers and management. The psychological contract influences individual worker's motivation and commitment and the extent and quality of knowledge sharing within teams. It was also highlighted in Chapter 2 how easy it is for management, sometimes unwittingly, to disrupt the context – introducing aspects of bureaucracy – and how damaging this is when knowledge creation is a core work process. Given the importance of developing a shared understanding for knowledge creation around what the problem is and how it can be solved, it is important that individuals are given the time to share ideas and information with others as well as the tools to facilitate this, as discussed in Chapter 4. This may be time to codify experiences for others to read, time to read about the experiences and ideas of others, and/or time to engage in debate and dialogue in order to further understanding. This issue of time provision can be related to Cyert and March's (1963) notion of 'organizational slack'. In this respect ScienceCo and LiftCo certainly made more resources available for the projects compared to the resources made available at BankCo or Research Team. For example, in the Research Team case, given the diversity of backgrounds, not enough time was spent interacting and sharing information and ideas whereas in the LiftCo case 'spaces' for social interaction were built into the project plan. Adequate resources – particularly time – are therefore a fundamental aspect of the enabling context for knowledge creation.

Integrating knowledge

Knowledge creation is rarely an individual act. In particular, in organizational and inter-organizational contexts invention and innovation – particularly networked innovation – occurs through knowledge integration in a team- or project-based environment. The cases in Chapters 4, 5 and 9 were all team or project based. As diversity is widely recognized as promoting innovation, teams and projects should ideally be set up with a mixed skills set and expertise. However, this in itself can, and often does, create problems as inevitably, at least at the outset, knowledge boundaries will exist across the team or project. Chapter 4 discussed the need to overcome syntactic, semantic and pragmatic boundaries in order to create a shared perspective on what needs to happen, which promotes knowledge integration. Individuals' often fail to effectively integrate knowledge, not because they are particularly resistant, but merely because they operate in different 'life worlds' with different understandings, priorities or 'logics of action' (Cyert and March, 1963). Chapter 4 highlighted that clearly defined aims and objectives and detailed project planning can support collaborative working in team- and project-based environments. Project plans can be thought of as boundary objects in these contexts as in some cases they do help to overcome some of the pragmatic knowledge boundaries that exist in a team which facilitates knowledge integration. Boundary spanners also have an important role to play in knowledge integration, particularly when knowledge needs to be integrated across projects. The consultant in the Midlands Hospital case in Chapter 8 was recognized as a boundary spanner because he had the necessary hierarchical status to be able to span the boundaries of the different medical and non-medical groups involved in the redesign of the cataract process. Firms can identify boundary spanners by conducting relatively simple social network analyses across particular groups or business units. Many software packages are now available that help identify those individuals who have significant interaction and are therefore connected to a variety of different groups. In principal then these individuals are potentially useful boundary spanners.

It is unlikely that a team or project operates in isolation. The discussion in Chapters 4, 8 and 9 highlighted the importance of networking by team or project members in the wider context and the role of social capital (Nahapiet and Ghoshal, 1998) in promoting knowledge integration. Each team or project member has a network of interpersonal relationships which they can choose to draw upon in their work. In some instances, particular groups put considerable effort into developing networks and promoting networking both internally and externally to foster knowledge integration as highlighted in the Medico case in Chapter 9. The configuration and quality of these networks help to influence the kinds of knowledge which the individual or group is able to draw on. Strong network ties are important for the sharing of tacit knowledge (cf. Hansen, 1999). At the same time, the value of personal networks also has to be balanced against the possible limiting effect of strong or redundant ties on information flows. So in the Research Team case in Chapter 4, the selection of one of the research officers (ROs) was based on an existing strong tie but this had a negative impact on the project, culminating in the exit of this RO from the project team.

Chapter 4 also emphasized many of the other problems associated with team and project work more generally which can lead to sub-optimal and poor outcomes such as conformity, Groupthink, group polarization, diffusion of responsibility, satisficing rather than optimizing decision-making and peer surveillance which can all hinder processes of knowledge integration. Management need to be cognizant of these when overseeing teams and project-based working and recognize that some of the most successful teams and projects in the past may not continue to be so in the future if any of these group dynamics emerge. Regular brief reviews with team or project members (other than the team leader) can often identify when problems are emerging that might hinder knowledge integration as can 360-degree appraisal feedback systems.

As with knowledge creation, knowledge integration takes time, as inevitably at the outset there will be different perspectives on the nature of the problem and the route to solve the problem. In order for a shared perspective to emerge the team or project needs the time and opportunity to interact either face-to-face or virtually. The Midlands Hospital case in Chapter 8 highlighted that it took around six months for the team working together to develop the necessary trust and social capital to agree on a way forward in re-designing the cataract procedure. Despite its success in Midlands Hospital, the innovative new procedure did not diffuse to other hospital trusts. This was in part because teams in other hospitals had not developed the same shared perspective on the problem and how it could be solved.

Sharing knowledge

Chapter 4 highlighted the important role that trust also plays in knowledge sharing. The development of trust in teams and projects is recognized as one of the most important aspects of an enabling context for collaborative work although companion trust may also militate effective team-working as the Research Team case highlighted. Trust takes different forms and it was highlighted that each form – companion, competence and commitment – has particular strengths and weaknesses. For example, competence trust can be extremely useful in terms of sharing knowledge but is relatively more fragile than either companion or commitment trust and may quickly dissipate if competence is not manifest in practice. Trust clearly emerges organically in teams and projects and the development of trust clearly cannot be 'managed'. Nevertheless it does serve as a major integrating mechanism that helps to overcome knowledge boundaries and so on.

The development of trust, and a shared identity and common agreed perspectives on the nature of the problem are most apparent in communities. Sharing knowledge within these contexts is less problematic from the outset, compared to formally appointed teams and projects. Chapter 8 highlighted that emergent communities are generated by shared social practices and the socialization of newcomers. In principal knowledge boundaries are minimal in these contexts as community members have typically developed a set of shared meanings deriving from common experiences. Unlike teams and projects they are informal and individuals self-select which communities they participate in. Communities have long been recognized as important sights of innovation. Low knowledge boundaries and the ease by which knowledge is shared clearly promotes innovation.

More recently organizations have attempted to exploit the benefits of communities by cultivating 'managed' communities but there has been little research that has demonstrated the performance benefits or whether these are substantively different to teams and projects. The KIN study in Chapter 8 highlighted that many of these managed communities had developed elaborate governance structures and formal positions which made them appear to be indistinguishable from project teams. However, there was some evidence of performance benefits when the communities were given sufficient time to interact on a face-to-face basis (particularly at the outset) and when training was provided for the leaders. Since they tend to emerge out of informal interaction, communities cannot be managed in conventional ways – they require assiduous cultivation, not heavy-handed control. All this is not to say that promoting 'communities of practice' are a panacea for the management of knowledge work. The community approach is also more appropriate in situations where the goal of the joint activity is relatively intangible and context-dependent. This applies particularly to interdisciplinary projects that focus on both technical and organizational change, such as the process innovation projects described in the Medico, LiftCo and BankCo cases. In these situations, knowledge is much more tacit and difficult to capture in explicit forms. Nevertheless it is important to remember that communities can also represent sites of conservatism, inertia, entrenchment and resistance – for example, their social boundaries and restricted codes may actually retard innovation projects that cut across different communities.

Chapter 5 highlighted that sharing knowledge and learning across projects is very difficult. The major problems centre on three main issues. First, often projects operate highly mechanistically and project team members work inter-dependently but individually such that collective knowledge about the project does not emerge. The influence of payment and promotion systems cannot be overlooked here. The 1990s saw a major shift in HRM policies towards individual performance as the basis for pay, this was happening at the same time as a shift towards project and team-working which demands greater knowledge sharing amongst team members which is somewhat contradictory. As many organizations quickly realized, focusing too narrowly on individually based reward places collaboration and knowledge sharing within teams in great jeopardy – and with it the collective willingness to exchange ideas and experience which is critical. ScienceCo's reward system based on individual revenue targets and divisional revenue targets appeared to effectively manage this tension between individual and group-based rewards.

Secondly, project teams often fail to actively seek out knowledge beyond the confines of the project that may be helpful unless they have explored all avenues internally within the project. Finally attempts that are made to 'capture' the knowledge and lessons learned are typically codified and do not capture the 'softer' lessons – the process including the trials and tribulations experienced in actually doing the work – consequently the information is not perceived as particularly helpful by other projects. Programme managers were highlighted in Chapter 5 as playing an important role in aiding knowledge sharing across projects. These intermediaries or boundary spanners often oversee several projects and can then potentially identify how knowledge that has been created on one project could be exploited and used by another and should therefore be shared. Intermediaries are often in a position to do this as they are able to translate the experience of particular individuals and groups into the language understood by other individuals and groups.

Projects spanning different functions and organizations which are characterized by complex project ecologies and high interactivity which were discussed in Chapter 5 have the greatest need to share knowledge across the sub-projects which are separated by both time and space. In these particular contexts the knowledge that is produced across projects needs to be mutually constituted through a more continuous form of collaboration which is far more elaborate than simply knowledge sharing. The Theragnostic and Skin cases in Chapter 5 highlighted the problems and outcomes associated with problems around poor knowledge sharing in complex project ecologies.

Enabling knowledge sharing was an important motivation for the development of KMS – the recycling of knowledge being highly cost-efficient – but it is often difficult to achieve in practice via KMS. As we noted in Chapter 7, the use of ICTs is often most effective when used dialectically, helping to connect, engage and develop communities rather than to try and share knowledge. Moreover, where knowledge sharing does happen, it often takes place accidentally or through the sharing of embodied knowledge that accompanies movements of personnel between project teams and between assignments, as illustrated in the ScienceCo and LiftCo cases. This suggests that staff rotation and career development systems may be key in facilitating knowledge sharing. Yet these elements often remain unrecognized in initiatives to manage knowledge work, maybe because they appear unexciting or mundane compared to new KMS. However, such staff movements crucially impact on personal networks, widening the range of contacts of an individual, and thus increasing his or her social capital (Nahapiet and Ghoshal, 1998). These personal networks influence knowledge share in at least two ways. First, personal networks can be important in identifying and accessing the knowledge needed for a given activity. Second, personal networks can enhance the informal sharing of learning by helping to develop the relationships and trust that underpin it, as discussed in Chapter 4.

Knowledge sharing can also take place, of course, via the sharing of documentation and through electronic means (intranet and e-mail). However, we have already discussed how such codified knowledge sharing is only effective in situations where there is some common understanding and a sufficiently well-defined task. Given this, ICTs may link geographically diverse teams but may inhibit knowledge sharing if it becomes a substitute for face-to-face interaction, as demonstrated in the BankCo and Research Team cases.

Aside from these questions of the mode of knowledge sharing, the organizational imperatives and political environment will also crucially influence the efforts individual's place on knowledge sharing. For example, at the organizational level, the time horizons of management objectives and political agendas exert a strong influence on the willingness of individuals and groups to capture learning and share knowledge across internal boundaries. This was seen in relation to BankCo, where individual departments were not willing to engage in global knowledge sharing because in the short term this would distract from the goals and objectives against which they, as a department, would be judged. Similarly a common outcome in the Oakland Furniture role-play is that individuals representing different departments fail to share relevant knowledge, or even conceal knowledge, because it is in their particular interests, and/or in the political interests of their department, to do so. On the other hand, in Buckman Labs, global knowledge sharing occurred because this was promoted from the top by a powerful CEO and managers were rewarded for this activity, rather than simply for improving the profitability of their own particular unit.

Codifying knowledge

Having highlighted many of the problems associated with codified knowledge, there are contexts where codification is a very useful process and an efficient way to exploit individual and organizational knowledge. So, for example, a group of software engineers who have already developed a common language for software development may well be able to rely entirely on e-mail to jointly develop a new software program. They may have little requirement for any face-to-face contact in this process. Many large, global consulting firms have successfully introduced KMS where codified knowledge around projects and clients is stored and continually updated and maintained. It is important to recognize however that these KMS require significant support in order to ensure that the knowledge is up-to-date and relevant. Thus most of these firms employ a specialist group who are solely tasked with this activity. Global consulting firms largely compete on the basis of the solutions they develop for clients and knowledge about clients. Whilst they clearly do not rely solely on codified knowledge, it is strategically critical that project and client knowledge is codified *to some extent* and they typically invest significantly in developing and maintaining KMS. Firms in other sectors, however, may not have the resources necessary to maintain up-to-date KMS or be able to so clearly identify exactly what knowledge needs to be codified.

Similarly documentation strategies in LiftCo were quite useful at the point where the innovation had become sufficiently well-routinized and a common set of languages and understandings had developed around the innovation. This meant that the documentation could be interpreted. This can be contrasted to the Midlands Hospital case where there was a significant need to meet face-to-face to overcome knowledge boundaries in developing the process innovation. In this case then codification was de-emphasized and when the re-designed process was codified in order to be shared with other Trusts, the necessary shared perspective on the issue did not exist and there was therefore very little value placed on the codified knowledge made available to other hospital trusts. It was also highlighted in Chapter 2 that different groups of knowledge workers rely more or less on codified knowledge in their work. Lawyers were highlighted as relying almost entirely on codified knowledge and their professional working practices ensure that what is codified is as unambiguous as possible. In so doing the law generates vast quantities of codified knowledge that takes the form of legislation and judgements which are subsequently applied and revised over time.

Codified knowledge may also be more applicable where the objective of knowledge sharing is the creation of a tangible entity (e.g. in product innovation projects – see Chapter 9). For example, in the Buckman Labs case (Chapter 6), the sharing of knowledge about pitch-control strategies was possible because the knowledge effectively became codified and embodied in the technology itself. This knowledge was then able to be shared across the global organization, at least among people with a basic understanding of the technology. Similarly, and using an example closer to many people's experience, knowledge about how to use Windows software applications (e.g. the ability to open, save, edit and drag files) is effectively codified and communicated in the form of technology itself. This embodies strict rules over what actions are permissable, or advisable, and we are reminded of these in very explicit ways – for example, with error messages, beeps and 'helpful' paperclips and dogs. In other words knowledge on how to use the technology (or product) is effectively codified into the design of the technology (or product). This means that, once users learn the basic codes for operating in a Windows environment, they can learn new Windows applications relatively quickly.

Figure 10.2 below summarizes the discussion in the previous four sections.

Important aspects of the enabling context	Knowledge process			
	K Create	**K Integrate**	**K Share**	**K Codify**
Self-formed and managed teams	*			
Time	*	*	*	*
Diversity	*	*		
Strong psychological contract	*			
Shared identity	*	*	*	
Trust	*	*	*	
Networking	*	*	*	
Boundary objects	*	*		
Boundary spanners	*	*		
Social capital		*	*	
Shared perspective	*	*	*	
Common language			*	*
Tangible output				*

Figure 10.2   The most important aspects of the enabling context supporting the four major knowledge processes

>> THE IMPORTANCE OF THE WIDER SOCIAL CONTEXT FOR MANAGING KNOWLEDGE WORK

The very different outcomes of attempts to manage knowledge work that we see in all our cases have been explained for the most part in terms of management practices and approaches. However, it is also clear from reviewing these cases that there are significant societal influences at work here too. Consider, for instance, the strong HRM orientation that we see in developments at LiftCo – a company with a strong Swedish base – or the problems of decentralization in the highly multinational BankCo organization. The classic account of knowledge creation is based on a Japanese firm, where, as described by Nonaka (1994), a knowledge spiral translates tacit knowledge into innovative products. What is often forgotten in descriptions of the knowledge spiral is how far it depends on the sheer dedication and collective team spirit which were characteristic features of large Japanese firms around that time – and which depend (or, arguably, depended) on the wider cultural norms, institutions and systems of control in Japan.

There is also a large body of research that demonstrates the ways in which wider institutional arrangements, such as the organization of professions, educational systems and social and science policy, both structure and channel the production and consumption of knowledge (Clark, 2000; Nowotny et al., 2001). This research lies mainly outside the scope of this book, but it is important to be aware of it because it underlines the influence of the societal and institutional context on the management of knowledge work. Although this influence is often diffuse and difficult to specify, its importance is not to be underestimated. The recent shift we have seen towards organization's adopting an open innovation model (Chapter 9) is a good example of fundamental change in the way organizations interact with consumers and how the boundaries between the two are becoming increasingly blurred. This serves as a useful example of the way in which approaches to managing knowledge work themselves need to be constantly revised in the light of different stakeholders and new modes of organizing.

The summative case in this final chapter: BioTech aims to explore both the internal organizational knowledge practices, processes and context in combination with some consideration of specific sectoral and institutional challenges that influence knowledge work in the biomedical sector. As in previous chapters, following the Conclusions, the case is described. This is followed by a set of questions for analysis.

>> CONCLUSIONS

The points in this chapter, along with the case analyses and discussions in previous chapters, all reinforce the value of adopting process and practice perspectives on knowledge work. These perspectives recognize, given differences in contexts and practices, that alternative interpretations, meanings and understandings are inevitable, even when people are presented with the same information (as you will have found for yourselves if you have been involved in the role-play provided in Chapter 9). Not only are they inevitable, but alternative interpretations are also desirable, being a great source of innovation and change – provided, that is, that tensions and conflict can be used constructively rather than destructively.

We have stressed how it is important to recognize that the value of knowledge depends on the context of its application; this leads to a much more nuanced approach to managing knowledge work. In particular, it leads us to recognize that, while examples of 'good practice' may be identified in one part of an organization, it may be highly problematic to codify and share knowledge about these practices across other parts of the organization or across organizations. While 'best practice' is a seductive idea in theory, not least because it avoids reinventing the wheel, it often founders on the context-dependent nature of what is 'good' at any point in time. Simply put, what works in one department or one organization may not work in another, not simply because the context is different, but also because typically what is shared cannot capture all of the knowledge involved in actually making it effective. Thus, templates and knowledge about a so-called 'best' practice will be interpreted differently in each context of application. Indeed, in many cases, what is considered to be a 'good practice' in one context may be deemed unworkable in another, because the sense-making in these other social contexts remains bounded by traditions and assumptions that are anchored in professional practices that have developed over time. As Dervin (1998) observes, reading about a best practice makes little sense without an understanding of the struggle and gaps it was designed to overcome.

This concluding point is well-illustrated in the BioTech case study that follows. This case provides examples of numerous attempts to introduce good practices around knowledge sharing and knowledge integration in order to streamline and improve the drug development process. However, inevitably in such a complex inter-organizational context, problems are encountered which throw into sharp relief the way in which different professional practices and particular features of the biomedical sector can constrain knowledge sharing and knowledge integration. This final case draws together major themes of this book, and highlights the importance for managing knowledge work in context, not just of sharing knowledge about facts and things, but also of creating a shared context for knowing. This does not mean that the role of management is to create an environment where everyone thinks the same. Rather it means adopting a more *pluralist and pragmatic* approach to managing knowledge work. This involves recognizing the importance of diverse cultures, understandings and 'logics of action' that in all likelihood are quite sector specific. It also involves recognizing the importance of developing a social context where diverse individuals and groups can both coexist *and* learn from one another. The key issues in creating a shared context for knowing have been a major theme in this book. Such an approach helps to redress the reification of knowledge and makes its successful application to knowledge purposes, practices and processes more promising.

CASE STUDY 10.1
BIOTECH – THE DEVELOPMENT OF A RADICAL NEW THERAPEUTIC FOR AN ACUTE INFLAMMATORY DISEASE

>> BACKGROUND

BIOTECH is a biopharmaceutical company which mainly develops human *monoclonal antibody* therapeutics. BIOTECH seeks to develop products both independently and in collaboration with partners, using its capabilities and technologies in the discovery and development of medicines in selected therapeutic areas. BIOTECH also seeks to license its technologies to enable others to develop new medicines. BIOTECH is a publicly listed company, with 600 employees based on the west coast of the United States. It has net cash and liquid resources in excess of $500 million. BIOTECH's most significant (and growing revenue) is from the royalties it receives from a drug it developed and subsequently licensed to a large pharmaceutical firm who took it on during later stage Phase II trials and though to commercialization (see Figure 10.3 for a description of the entire drug development process). BIOTECH has ten further licensed product candidates in clinical development, funded by BIOTECH's licensees. BIOTECH also has two proprietary product candidates which it is currently developing. BIOTECH's expertise predominantly lies in early stage/preclinical development. Its financial strategy is that all its R&D activities, excluding later stage product development, are to be funded from revenues. This is to ensure that the business itself is effectively self-financing up until the demonstration of efficacy (see 'Glossary of terms') in clinical trials. The strategy is aimed at enabling BIOTECH to continue to pursue its own, carefully targeted, proprietary discovery programmes in-house. Decisions regarding the funding of any later stage clinical development activity are taken on a case-by-case basis. To date BIOTECH has taken only four development programmes into clinical trials itself from a total of 11 in trials development.

>> THE FOCAL INNOVATION PROJECT – BIOTECH-123

BIOTECH-123 is a therapeutic aimed at tackling an acute respiratory disease which affects significant proportions of Western populations and which continues to increase in prevalence. As such then the drug has the potential to become a

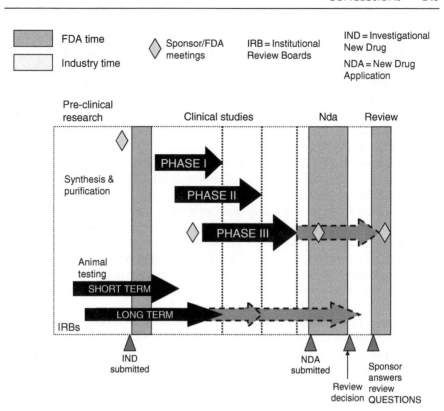

Figure 10.3   The new drug development process: Steps from test tube to new drug application review (Adapted from Centre for Drug Evaluation and Research (CDER) Handbook)

'blockbuster' if it succeeds in development. Industry pundits suggest that blockbuster drugs generate $1 million each day in revenues, therefore each day saved in development, in principal, is worth a $1 million. However, BIOTECH-123 is a radical new treatment for the disease and will change the approach and practices that clinicians' use in the treatment of this disease. The profile of the BIOTECH-123 project was raised considerably internally following Phase II/III clinical trials failure of another drug in development six months previously. BIOTECH has tried to learn considerably from the failure of this drug and is attempting to avoid making the same mistakes by adopting a formal project management approach and developing a more 'professional' approach to the design of clinical trials which it has had little experience of conducting and managing. The project comprises basic research as well as Phase I and II clinical studies. Basic research is being carried out to further understand the biological mechanism in action (note: drugs can enter clinical trials based on satisfactory testing in animals and without the biological mechanism in humans ever being established). This basic research is being carried out in collaboration a number of universities across the United States with scientists who specialize in this scientific area.

In September 2006, BIOTECH announced that following recent approval from the FDA (the US regulatory agency) it would start a Phase I clinical trial coded BIOTECH-123. This Phase I, placebo-controlled, single dose, dose escalating, trial in 34 patients was initiated at a Drug Development Clinical Research Centre located close to BIOTECH. Results reported nine months later demonstrated that BIOTECH-123 was well tolerated at all doses and no safety concerns were identified. BIOTECH's Chief Medical Officer commented, 'We are very optimistic about BIOTECH-123 as a potential treatment for this respiratory disease'.

At this point in time BIOTECH took the strategic decision to actively attempt to out license (see 'Glossary of terms') and announced it was looking for a partner for BIOTECH-123. The team also decided to attempt a second Phase I trial which would involve inducing a severe respiratory reaction in patients who had a mild form of the disease and then treating with BIOTECH-123. The clinical team believed that if this trial was successful then this would make partnering arrangement far more attractive, potentially increasing future revenues. Setting up this trial however proved problematic as it was very difficult to recruit sufficient patients so in practice the trial did not go ahead. This time-consuming mistake was seen as something that needed to be avoided in the future.

Subsequent discussion on another proposed trial centred on where it would most likely get regulatory approval. Canada was seen as 'less restrictive in requirements for reproductive toxicity but more restrictive in other ways' (Regulatory Manager) and she was asked to talk to a regulator she knew personally to 'sound out' the feasibility of the proposed study. As the clinical team suggested (jokingly), it was important to find ways of 'getting around regulators by fair means or foul'. The likely reactions of regulators were frequently being 'anticipated' in project meetings and drove several of the discussions around clinical trials (more so, it seemed, that the science itself). BIOTECH had also experienced 'miscommunication' with the regulatory agency – the FDA – in the past and wanted to avoid this in all future projects.

Around this time BIOTECH had also already received regulatory approval to commence a repeat-dose (multiple dose) safety study of BIOTECH-123 in patients with mild/moderate forms of the disease. This was to be another safety study to assess tolerability and pharmacokinetics (see 'Glossary of terms'). This trial was planned to run in the first quarter of 2007 with three dose groups (1, 5, 10 mg/kg, max dose three per month), containing 12 patients per group and a placebo group with a further 12 patients (total 48). This trial was named BIOTECH 123–3. Given BIOTECH's limited experience in trials they were taking advice from a clinical research organization who could provide specialist advice on clinical trials development and regulation. In addition BIOTECH had also contracted a local specialist unit in a hospital to recruit patients and run trials. Results were expected no later than six months time at a cost of $1.6 million. However, at a project meeting late in 2006, BIOTECH was still debating whether 48 patients were necessary. The trial itself could be done with fewer (24) and it was unclear from the future trial plans (see section on 'Partnering process') that had been proposed by potential partners, whether a larger sample was needed. However if, as the project team leader believed the main purpose was to have a large enough sample to be able to go on to conduct Phase III large-scale trials in patients with severe disease then, 'the magic number for subjects to be exposed needs to be around 50'. On soliciting a final group view from the whole project team on numbers of patients, the project manager commented, 'you might as well stick your finger in the air as to how many patients you need'. This doubt over on patient numbers possibly reflected BIOTECH's lack of experience in Phase II clinical trials. However, equally it was felt that potential partners may not have the experience either 'it's our guess against their guess, so let's stick with 48 – it's the answer to everything isn't it?'

A decision was taken in January 2007 as to who the partner pharmaceutical firm was to be to take development forward on BIOTECH 123. The partner was referred to by a code name 'Stallion' in order to maintain the strictest confidentiality both internally and externally until the deal was finalized. The project team decided that the 123–3 study should go ahead with BIOTECH taking the lead. So although it was expected at this time that BIOTECH would have signed the deal with the partner before the trial was finished BIOTECH was still responsible for the study and the costs associated with it. It was initially thought that this study would be complete by mid 2007. However, this trial experienced significant problems.

In order to conduct a multiple dose safety study the therapeutic needed to be suspended in a solution, then bagged and labelled for each patient, to be administered to the patient intravenously. Further through the development process, the therapeutic would actually be administered in much smaller, concentrated doses and the suspension and bagging process would not occur. However, suspending in a solution was a requirement in this early trial. A clinical unit in a hospital 100 miles from BIOTECH was going to run the trial. The suspension was going to be bagged by BIOTECH and then delivered to the hospital where patient labels would be added. This constituted an amendment to the manufacturing process for which approval needed to be given by the FDA. It also came to light that whilst the majority of prescribing/trials units in hospitals are exempt from the need to have a license to carry out labelling processes, this particular hospital – because of its charitable status – was not exempt and it did not have a license! This was discovered quite late in the day and the clinical trials manager felt that manufacturing should have made them aware of this requirement much sooner. BIOTECH therefore needed to find a licensed facility that could add the labels to the bags in transit to the hospital where the trial was to be conducted. This was not easy as many manufacturing firms were not keen to be involved in such a minor process.

A firm was eventually found 50 miles away to carry this out. Unfortunately however when the labelled bags were returned to BIOTECH for inspection, particles were discovered in the suspension. No one had any idea why this had occurred. Clearly however, the solution could not be intravenously administered to patients containing particles as it could well cause death! It seemed to be more prevalent in the higher concentrations of 123. BIOTECH's chemists, who are usually involved primarily in basic research, were called in to try and discover why this was occurring. This was a major problem affecting the start of the new trial but it was also recognized that the FDA had also not yet given approval for the change in protocol (labelling external to BIOTECH) and this was also a delaying factor. By February 2007 the chemists could still not agree on what might be causing the formation of particles. The clinical trials team were very keen to establish this as soon as possible as they kept repeating that every day 'saved' in development was potentially worth $1 million but the same sense of urgency was not manifest in the chemists. Suggestions were made to delve further into the published literature, ask others (possibly academics) to become involved but this was going to take a lot of time. Eventually two of the three chemists that were present at the project team meeting decided on a way forward, counter to what had been proposed by another chemist, and went away 'to solve the problem quickly and internally'. At the time the study ended at BIOTECH, the 123–3 trial was way behind schedule and reluctantly a decision had been made to inform the partner. There was uncertainty regarding how Stallion would react to this news.

>> PARTNERING PROCESS

BIOTECH has started to assess interest in 2006 from a limited number of potential licensees (all large pharmaceutical firms), with a final decision on the choice of partner scheduled for early 2008. Those who expressed an interest were given an information pack developed by the project team specifically about the project. The project team had significant involvement in supporting partnering negotiations but knew nothing of the financial details surrounding the negotiations. A shortlist of four potential partners had been identified and future clinical trials development plans had been soliticited from each by the BIOTECH Business Development team. These plans were discussed around three key areas: (i) whether the plans indicated that the partner had appropriate expertise to take the product to market efficiently; (ii) whether the plans gave any clues to BIOTECH about whether or not to start particular clinical trials in advance of partnering being agreed; (iii) what questions the BIOTECH Business Development team should seek potential partners to answer helping them decide on the final partnering agreement. In this way BIOTECH was conducting a form of due diligence (see 'Glossary of terms') on potential partners.

Clinical team recommendations for future trials were also presented to the Development Project Team (DPT – see section on 'Knowledge share and project management') in November 2006. There was significant debate around which proposed trials to fund on the basis of future partnering. The major problem facing the project at this point in the development process then was managing the tensions that arise in clinical trial design whilst simultaneously identifying a partner. Even after the partner had been identified in early 2007, negotiations regarding the precise terms of the agreement could continue for another 9–12 months. The clinical team spent a significant amount of their time 'guessing' what potential partners might require when attempting to decide on whether or not to go ahead with proposed future trials. This was made more difficult by the fact that there was no clear consensus amongst the partners about what kind of studies should be done. The DPT had explicitly instructed the clinical team to suggest what would be crucial to the partnering deal but 'with our knowledge of partners we can't say hand on heart what will be critical' (Clinical Trials Manager). Moreover the knowledge of partners also appeared to be limited – 'partners don't necessarily know what trials they need' and 'any partner is going to stop most things that are going on'. BIOTECH had previously had a bad experience with a partner who took almost a year to get things going (and 'then screwed it up'). The uncertainty created by future partnering for clinical decisions was summarized neatly by the clinical trials manager, 'In the absence of knowledge about what's happening with partnering we have to assume that we will have partnered by September (2007) and base our decisions on that assumption.'

When the clinical team reported options on trials to the DPT, the trials plans for each partner were also considered to see whether they 'gave any clues' as to what trials were likely to be wanted and/or needed by the partner. The problem here was that each plan proposed by the four potential partners was completely different, with varied combinations of studies. Moreover, some of the partners plans were 'not very well developed' and some seemed to be at odds with what BIOTECH themselves would suggest or what they thought would be acceptable from a regulatory standpoint. The major issue then appeared to be estimating what risk to take on (in terms of committing financial resources to a particular trial when outcomes may not be favorable) for an expected return from the partnering arrangements that are finally agreed. The more robust the evidence for the efficacy of BIOTECH 123, the better the financial deal would be with a partner. However, there was a risk that the results of further trials may not be ideal. At worst, that they may jeopardize the partnering agreement by putting the partner off completely, or by the partner wanting to await trial results before proceeding to complete the agreement. Given partners were also likely to stop progress on trials it was also important only to commit to those that could do something worthwhile in the timeframe. BIOTECH would also have accrued significant costs as trials typically cost anywhere between $1–2 million each to conduct.

Some of the team were concerned that particular firms were not serious about taking the project further given what the team considered to be the poor quality of the trial designs that were being suggested (see above). All of the partner's plans for further clinical trials were presented and they were all very different insofar as the patient numbers they presented were much larger and varied wildly as did the recommended dosages they would use which some people on the team considered not feasible from a regulatory perspective.

Finally a shortlist of two firms was decided upon and these firms had to go through another round of capability presentations with the team where all of the detail about how the development process would progress was discussed. From a business perspective, BIOTECH would receive payments at particular stages of the development process and royalties if and when the product went to market. Eventually the decision was taken to go with Stallion. The only commitment BIOTECH had – other than a very large knowledge share issue – was to conduct the 123–3 trials which had recently stalled.

>> KNOWLEDGE SHARING AND PROJECT MANAGEMENT

Knowledge sharing was going to be major issue at this stage in the project. A KM system – TARGET – had been introduced in the firm and a document management structure had been agreed for all projects ongoing in BIOTECH and 123 had adopted this system. The only problem that had been found was inputting information from clinical research organizations who were involved in the trials as they did not provide their data in a way that was compatible with the system. On completion of the deal all of the documentation pertaining to 123 held on this system and elsewhere would be owned and shared by the partner. In addition, as soon as agreement had been reached BIOTECH people were meeting their equivalents in the partner firm. As far as possible the business development manager who had led the negotiations was to be present at face-to-face meetings to ensure consistency in terms of what was said at these meetings.

In terms of project management in September/October 2005 senior management had introduced a more co-ordinated project team structure to handle decisions on all product development. In this, the (satellite) clinical team, for example, report to a strategy team referred to as the Development Project Team (DPT) – on recommendations for trials, who in turn seek final approval from the Product Steering Committee (PSC), who oversee all BIOTECH development projects. It was mentioned that in the past decisions regarding clinical trials had been taken on a rather ad-hoc basis but with the failure of an earlier project in Phase III trials this more formalized process was introduced.

An external consultant had been brought in on a part-time basis to manage the BIOTECH 123 project. October 2007 she introduced a new co-ordinated project matrix structure. This structure was to replace the large unwieldy weekly meetings that had been occurring. These previous meetings were characterized by people attending who did not contribute and many operational matters being discussed that were not particularly relevant to the project process. In this new structure the DPT – which she chairs – receives recommendations and issues to be addressed from operational project sub-teams (called 'satellite teams') for clinical, preclinical, manufacturing and business development. The DPT comprises representatives from these satellite teams and the agenda is constructed around reports back and issues raised in each satellite team area. This way the satellite teams get a better understanding of the whole BIOTECH product development process and the work can be coordinated. The DPT reports to the BIOTECH Product Strategy Committee (PSC) who make the final go/no go decisions.

The project manager also introduced formal project management techniques and a high level strategy and time line to take the 123 project to a successful partnership. For example, in the same way that 'due diligence' is performed for products, the new DPT/satellite team structure completed its own 'due diligence' on potential partners (discussed above) from which key decisions were made about the new team process. These included a process for satellite teams to capture key learnings so that other teams could benefit from their experience. A decision to produce a template for each satellite area to complete which would 'highlight both the positives and issues raised during the due diligence process, together with recommendations for new projects' was developed that other subsequent projects could use and a decision to have 'meeting processes' (i.e. feedback on how satellite teams were working) as a standard DPT agenda item was also introduced as good practice. The project and business development manager also took all of the lessons learned from the due diligence process on BIOTECH-123 and prepared a report that was going to be made available to other projects explaining what had worked well and what had caused problems. This was being circulated across BIOTECH so that future projects could hopefully avoid making the same mistakes.

This is the first time that the firm has adopted such techniques and ways of working. In the past line managers were perceived as taking too much responsibility for 'their babies' (i.e. projects) and insufficient delegation occurred. Those involved in the satellite teams were now empowered to make decisions. That said, there were hints in the DPT meetings of lack of agreement and differences of interpretation despite outward consensus. For example, in discussing a clinical study update a figure of 10 per cent false negatives was described by some as 'nice data that works really well' even though there was clearly some disagreement across the whole about whether this data was in fact good or bad. Another potential impact of the new project team structure was increased pressure on the satellite teams to meet very tight deadlines. This was because the clinical team now had to report back to the DPT who in turn reported to the PSC. For example, because the clinical team now had to report back in time to the DPT who in turn reported to the PSC, members were reporting to very tight timescale. If one person was on holiday (or training), for example, these deadlines were almost impossible to meet. Interestingly the language used in meetings – particularly around trials – was imbued with imperatives to meet timescales and report deadlines, for example 'close outs', being 'on track for a hard lock by', 'dropdead lock'. In this context 'scheduling well ahead' for the clinical team meant in practice giving people only two weeks' notice to complete particular tasks as 'every day counts'.

>> TO CONCLUDE

At the time the study ended, the problems with the granules had been solved but by then Stallion had been made aware of the issue. Stallion had decided they needed time to consider their position so negotiations had been temporarily suspended. BIOTECH however had to continue with the trial and hope for favourable results regardless of whether Stallion or some other large pharmaceutical finally licensed the therapeutic.

>> GLOSSARY OF TERMS

Efficacy – in terms of new drugs this means demonstrating the effectiveness of the development drug compared to other therapeutics that are already on the market.

Out license – 'sell-on' the developmental drug to a larger firm who would take it through Phase II/III trials and hopefully to commercialization for which the originating firm receives royalties.

Pharmokinetics – establishing optimum drug dosages for different populations.

Due diligence – the due diligence process varies for different types of companies. In this instance it is about establishing the financial, legal, labour, tax, environment and market/commercial situation of BIOTECH by partner firms and in this case vice versa (i.e. BIOTECH establishing as far as possible that a potential partner has the capabilities and the will to proceed with development.)

>> QUESTIONS

1. Strategically what was BIOTECH's main knowledge purpose?
2. What knowledge processes existed in BIOTECH and how well embedded were they?
3. Critically evaluate whether overall the context enabled or disabled knowledge processes in BIOTECH.
4. What other factors external to the organization may have influenced BIOTECH's ability to manage knowledge?

Summary of key learning points

>> Attempts to manage knowledge are not new, but the classical approach of separating 'the brains' from 'the hands' (decisions and actions) is no longer appropriate as organization need to respond to dynamic, global and highly competitive environments.

>> It is important that firms identify for what major purpose they aim to manage knowledge in order that they can then establish what major knowledge processes need to be embedded across the firm.

>> It is management's responsibility to attempt to foster appropriate enabling contexts to support particular knowledge processes.

>> Different institutional and sectoral contexts will influence the management of knowledge work.

References

Abbott, A. (1988). *The System of Professions*. London: University of Chicago Press.

Abrahamson, E. (1996). Management fashion. *Academy of Management Review*, 21, 254–285.

Ackoff, R. L. (1989). From data to wisdom. *Journal of Applied Systems Analysis*, 16(1), 3–9.

Alavi, M. (2000). Managing knowledge. In R. Zmud (Ed.) *Framing the Domain of IT Management*. Cincinnati, Ohio: Pinnoflex Educational Resources Ltd. Chapter 2, pp. 15–28.

Alavi, M. and Leidner, D. (1999). Knowledge management systems: Issues, challenges and benefits. *Communications of the AIS*, 1(5), 1–35.

Alavi, M. and Tiwana, A. (2003). Knowledge management: The information technology dimension. In M. Easterby-Smith and M. Lyles (Eds) *Handbook of Organizational Learning and Knowledge Management*. Oxford: Blackwell. Chapter 6, pp. 104–121.

Allen, T. J. (1977). *Managing the Flow of Technology*. Cambridge, MA: MIT Press.

Alter, C. and Hage, J. (1993). *Organizations Working Together: Coordination in Interorganizational Networks*. Newbury Park, CA: Sage.

Alvesson, M. (1993). Organizations as rhetoric: Knowledge-intensive firms and the struggle with ambiguity. *Journal of Management Studies*, 30(6), 997–1015.

Alvesson, M. (1995). *Management of Knowledge-Intensive Companies*. Berlin/New York: De Gruyter.

Alvesson, M. (2001). Knowledge work: Ambiguity, image and identity. *Human Relations*, 54(7), 863–886.

Alvesson, M. (2004). *Knowledge Work and Knowledge-Intensive Firms*. Oxford: Oxford University Press.

Alvesson, M. and Karreman, D. (2007). Unravelling HRM: Identity, ceremony and control in a management consulting firm. *Organization Science*, 18(4), 711–723.

Alvesson, M. and Robertson, M. (2006). Going public: The emergence and effects of soft bureaucracy within a knowledge-intensive firm. *Organization*, 11(1), 123–148.

Amabile, T. M., Conti, R., Coon, H., Lazenby, J. and Herron, M. (1996). Assessing the work environment for creativity. *Academy of Management Journal*, 39, 1154–1184.

Amabile, T. M., Elizabeth, A. S., Giovanni, B. M. and Steven J. K. (2004). Leader behaviors and the work environment for creativity: Perceived leader support. *Leadership Quarterly*, 15(1), 5–32.

Amabile, T. M., Sigal, G. B., Jennifer, S. M. and Barry, M. S. (2005). Affect and creativity at work. *Administrative Science Quarterly*, 50(3), 367–403.

Amidon, D. M. (1998). The evolving community of knowledge practice: The Ken awakening. *International Journal of Technology Management*, 16, 45–63.

Attewell, P. (1990). What is skill. *Work and Occupations*, 17, 422–448.

Australian Government. (2008). The incidence of teleworking in the Australian population. Department of Communications, Information Technology and the Arts.

Avgerou, C. and McGrath, K. (2007). Power, rationality, and the art of living through socio-technical change. *MIS Quarterly*, 31(2), 293–315.

Bailey, D. and Kurland, N. (2002). A review of telework research: Finding, directions and lessons for the study of modern work. *Journal of Organizational Behaviour*, 23(4), 383–400.

Bailyn, L. (1988). Autonomy in the industrial R&D lab. In R. Katz (Ed.) *Managing Professionals in Innovative Organizations*. New York: Ballinger, pp. 223–236.

Banker, R., Bardhan, I. and Asdemir, O. (2006). Understanding the impact of collaboration software on product design and development. *Information Systems Research*, 17(4), 352–373.

Barker, J. (1993). Tightening the iron cage: Concertive control in self-managing teams. *Administrative Science Quarterly*, 38(3), 408–433.

Barley, S. (1990). The alignment of technology and structure through roles and networks. *Administrative Science Quarterly*, 35(1), 61–104.

Barley, S. R. (1986). Technology as an occasion for structuring: Evidence from observation of CT scanners and the social order of radiology departments. *Administrative Science Quarterly*, 31, 78–108.

Barley, S. and Tolbert, P. S. (1997). Institutionalization and structuration: Studying the links between action and institution. *Organisation Studies*, 18(1), 93–117.

Barnes, B. (2001). Practice as collective action. In T. Schatzki, K. Knorr-Cetina, and E. von Savigny (Eds) *The Practice Turn in Contemporary Theory*. London: Routledge, pp. 17–28.

Barney, J. (1991). Firm resources and sustained competitive advantage. *Journal of Management*, 17, 99.

Baron, J., Hannan, M. and Burton, D. (2001). Labor pains: Change in organizational models and employee turnover in young, high-tech firms. *American Journal of Sociology*, 106(4), 960–1012.

Beath, C. and Orlikowski, W. J. (1994). The contradictory structure of systems development methodologies: Deconstructing the IS-user relationships in information engineering. *Information Systems Research*, 5(4), 350–377.

Becker, G. S. (1975). *Human Capital: A Theoretical and Empirical Analysis*. New York: National Bureau of Economic Research.

Bell, D. (1973). *The Coming of Post-Industrial Society*. New York: Basic Books.

Bennetto, J. (2004). Inventor of DNA fingerprint testing warns flaw could lead to miscarriages of justice, Crime Correspondent, Thursday, 9 September.

Bernstein, B. (1975). *Class, Codes and Control: Towards a Theory of Educational Transmissions*. London: Routledge & Kegan Paul.

Bessant, J., Pavitt, K. and Tidd, J. (2005). *Managing Innovation: Integrating Technological, Market and Organizational Change*. London: Wiley.

Beth, A. B. (2003). Sharing meaning across occupational communities: The transformation of understanding on a production floor. *Organization Science*, 14(3), 312.

Bijker, W. E., Hughes, T. P. and Pinch, T. J. (1987). *The Social Construction of Technological Systems*. Cambridge, MA: MIT Press.

Bjorkman, I., Barner-Rasmussen, W. and Li, L. (2004). Managing knowledge transfer in MNCs: The impact of headquarters control mechanisms. *Journal of International Business Studies*, 35, 443–455.

Black, L. J., Carlile, P. R. and Repenning, N. P. (2004). A dynamic theory of expertise and occupational boundaries in new technology implementation: Building on Barley's study of CT scanning. *Administrative Science Quarterly*, 49(4), 572–607.

Blackler, F. (1995). Knowledge, knowledge work and organizations: An overview and interpretation. *Organization Studies*, 16(6), 1021–1046.

Blair, D. (2002). Knowledge management: Hype, hope or help. *Journal of the American Society for Information Science and Technology*, 53(12), 1019–1028.

Boisot, M. (1995). *Information Space: A Framework for Learning in Organizations, Institutions and Culture*. London: Blackwell.

Boland, R. J. and Tenkasi, R. V. (1995). Perspective making and perspective taking in communities of knowing. *Organization Science*, 6(4), 350–372.

Bourdieu, P. (1990). *The Logic of Practice*. Cambridge: Polity.

Braverman, H. (1974). *Labor and Monopoly Capital*. New York: Monthy Review Press.

Brown, J. S. and Duguid, P. (1991). Organizational learning and Communities-of-practice: Towards a unified view of working, learning and innovation. *Organization Science*, 2, 40–57.

Brown, J. S. and Duguid, P. (1998). Organizing knowledge. *California Management Review*, 40(3), 90–109.

Brown, J. S. and Duguid, P. (2000a), Balancing act: How to capture knowledge without killing it. *Harvard Business Review*, 78, 73–77.

Brown, J. S. and Duguid, P. (2000b). *The Social Life of Information*. Boston, Mass.: Harvard Business School Press.

Brown, J. S. and Duguid, P. (2001). Knowledge and organization: A social-practice perspective. *Organization Science*, 12(2), 198–213.

Buckman, R. (1998). Knowledge sharing at Buckman Laboratories. *Journal of Business Strategy*. January/February, 19, 11–15.

Burns, T. and Stalker, G. M. (1961). *The Management of Innovation*. London: Tavistock.

Burrell, G. and Morgan, G. (1979). *Sociological Paradigms and Organizational Analysis*. London: Heinemann.

Burt, R. S. (1992). *Structural Holes: The Social Structure of Competition*. Cambridge, MA: Harvard University Press.

Cabrera, E. F. and Cabrera, A. (2005). Fostering knowledge sharing through people management practices. *International Journal of Human Resource Management*, 16, 720–735.

Callon, M. (1980). The state and technical innovation: A case study of the electrical vehicle in France. *Research Policy*, 9, 358–376.

Carlile, P. (2004). Transferring, translating and transforming: An integrative framework from managing knowledge across boundaries. *Organization Science*, 15(5), 555–568.

Carlile, P. R. (2002). A pragmatic view of knowledge and boundaries: Boundary objects in new product development. *Organization Science*, 13(4), 442–455.

Castells, M. (1996). *The Rise of the Network Society*. Oxford and Malden, MA: Blackwell.

Castells, M. (2000). *The Information Age: Economy, Society and Culture, the Rise of the Network Society*. Oxford: Blackwell.

Chesbrough, H. (2003a). *Open Innovation: The New Imperative for Creating and Profiting from Technology*. Cambridge, MA: Harvard Business School Press.

Chesbrough, H. (2003b). The logic of open innovation: Managing intellectual property. *California Management Review*, 45(3), 33.

Chesbrough, H. (2004). Managing open innovation. *Research Technology Management*, 47(1), 23–26.

Chesbrough, H. (2006). *Open Business Models: How to Thrive in the New Innovation Landscape*. Cambridge, MA: Harvard Business School Press.

Chiaromonte, F. (2006). Open innovation through alliances and partnership: Theory and practice. *International Journal of Technology Management*, 33(2–3), 111–114.

Child, J. (1972). Organizational structure, environment and performance: The role of strategic choice. *Sociology*, 6, 1–22.

Christensen, C., Bohmer, R. and Kenagy, J. (2000). Will disruptive innovations cure health care? *Harvard Business Review*, September/October, 78, 102–112.

Ciborra, C. (1998). Crises and foundations: An inquiry into the nature and limits of models and methods in the information systems discipline. *Journal of Strategic Information Systems*, 7, 5–16.

Clark, P. (2000). *Organizations in Action: Competition Between Contexts*. London: Routledge.

Clark, P. (2003). *Organizational Innovations*. London: Sage.

Clark, P. (1987). *Anglo-American Innovation*. Berlin: deGruyter.

Clark, P. and Staunton, N. (1989). *Innovation in Technology and Organization*. London: Routledge.

Clark, P., Newell, S., Burcher, P., Bennett, B., Sharifi, S. and Swan, J. (1992). The decision-episode framework and computer aided production management (CAPM). *International Studies of Management and Organization*, 22, 69–80.

Cohen, W. M. and Levinthal, D. A. (1990). Absorptive-capacity – a new perspective on learning and innovation. *Administrative Science Quarterly*, 35(1), 128–152.

Collins, H. (1985). *Changing Order; Replication and Induction in Scientific Practice*. London: Sage.

Contu, A. and Willmott, H. (2003). Re-embedding situatedness: The importance of power relations in learning theory. *Organization Science: A Journal of the Institute of Management Sciences*, 14, 283.

Conway, S. (1995). Informal boundary-spanning communication in the innovation process – an empirical-study. *Technology Analysis & Strategic Management*, 7(3), 327–342.

Conway, S. and Steward, F. (2006). *Managing Innovation*. Oxford: OUP.

Cook, S. D. N. and Brown, J. S. (1999). Bridging epistemologies: The generative dance between organizational knowledge and organizational knowing. *Organization Science*, 10, 381–400.

Coombs, R. (2003). The changing character of 'service innovation' and the emergence of 'knowledge intensive business services'. In B. Dankbarr (Ed.) *Innovation Management in the Knowledge Economy*. London: Imperial College Press, pp. 83–96.

Coombs, R. and Hull, R. (1998). Knowledge management practices and path dependency in innovation. *Research Policy*, 27, 237–253.

Cooper, D., Hinings, R. and Greenwood, R. (1996). Sedimentation and transformation in organizational change: The case of Canadian law firms. *Organization Studies*, 17(4), 623–647.

Courpasson, D. (2000). Managerial strategies of domination: Power in soft bureaucracies. *Organization Studies*, 21(1), 141–162.

Cross, R. and Sproull, L. (2004). More than an answer: Information relationships for actionable knowledge. *Organization Science*, 15(4), 446–462.

Cross, R., Davenport, T. and Cantrell, S. (2003). The social side of performance. *MIT Sloan Management Review*, 45, 20.

Crozier, M. (1964). *The Bureaucratic Phenomenon*. Chicago: University of Chicago Press.

Cyert, R. M. and March, J. G. (1963). *A Behavioral Theory of the Firm*. Englewood Cliffs, NJ: Prentice-Hall.

Damanpour, F. (1987). The adoption of technological, administrative and ancillary innovations: Impact of organizational factors. *Journal of Management*, 13, 675–688.

Dankbaar, B. (2003). *Innovation Management in the Knowledge Economy*. London: Imperial College Press.

Davenport, T. (2000). *Mission Critical: Realizing the Promise of Enterprise Systems*. Cambridge, MA: Harvard Business Press.

Davenport, T. (2005). *Thinking for a Living*. Boston: Harvard Business School press.

Davenport, T. and Prusak, L. (1997). *Information Ecology: Mastering the Information Knowledge Environment*. New York: Open University Press.

Davenport, T., Jarvenpaa, S. L. and Beers, M. C. (1996). Improving knowledge work processes. *Sloan Management Review*, Summer, 37, 53–65.

David, G., Chand, D., Newell, S. and Resende-Santos, J. (2008). Integrated collaboration across distributed sites: The perils of process and the promise of practice. *Journal of Information Technology*, 23(1), 44–54.

Deal, T. and Kennedy, A. (1982). *Corporate Cultures: The Rites and Rituals of Corporate Life*. Reading, Mass.: Addison-Wesley.

Dervin, B. (1998). Sense-making theory and practice: An overview of user interests in knowledge seeking and use. *Journal of Knowledge Management*, 2(2), 36–45.

Desouza, K. and Evaristo, J. R. (2004). Managing knowledge in distributed projects. *Communications of the ACM*, 47(4), 87–91.

Dhanaraj, C. and Parkhe, A. (2006). Orchestrating innovation networks. *Academy of Management Review*, 3(3), 659–669.

DiMaggio, P. J. and Powell, W. W. (1983). The iron cage revisited: Institutional isomorphism and collective rationality in organizational fields. *American Sociological Review*, 48, 147–160.

Dodgson, M. (1993). Learning, trust and technological collaboration. *Human Relations*, 46(1), 77–95.

Dodgson, M. (1994). Technological collaboration and innovation. In M. Dodgson and R. Rothwell (Eds) *The Handbook of Industrial Innovation*. Aldershot, UK: Edward Elgar.

Dodgson, M., Gann, D. and Salter, A. (2005). *Think, Play, Do: Technology, Innovation and Organization*. Oxford: OUP.

Donnelly, R. (2006). How 'free' is the free worker? An investigation into the working arrangements available to knowledge workers. *Personnel Review*, 35(1), 78–97.

Dougherty, D. and Hardy, C. (1996). Sustained product innovation in large, mature organizations: Overcoming innovation-to-organization problems. *Academy of Management Journal*, 39(5), 1120–1153.

Dougherty, D. (1992). Interpretive barriers to successful product innovation in large firms. *Organization Science*, 3, 179–202.

Dougherty, D. (2003). Organizing practice-based knowledge for innovation in service organizations. In B. Dankbaar (Ed.) *Innovation Management in the Knowledge Economy*. London: Imperial College Press, pp. 267–288.

Dougherty, D. (2007). Trapped in the 21st century: Why models of organizational knowledge, learning and capabilities do not fit with bio-pharmaceuticals and what to do about that. *Management Learning*, 38, 265–271.

Dougherty, D. and Heller, T. (1994). The illegitimacy of successful product innovation in established firms. *Organization Science*, 5(2), 200–218.

Drexler, K. E. (1989). *Engines of Creation*. New York: Doubleday.

Dreyfuss, H. (1991). *Being-in-the-World: A Commentary on Heidegger's Being and Time, Division One*. Cambridge, MA: MIT Press.

Drucker, P. (1969). *The Age of Discontinuity: Guidelines to our Changing Society*. London: Heinemann.

Drucker, P. (1988). The coming of the new organization. *Harvard Business Review*, Summer, 66, 53–65.

Earl, M. J. and Fenny, D. F. (1996). Information systems in global business: Evidence from European multinationals. In M. Earl (Ed.) *Information Management: The Organisational Dimension*. Oxford: Oxford University Press.

Edelman, L. F., Bresnen, M., Newell, S., Scarbrough, H. and Swan, J. (2004). The benefits and pitfalls of social capital: Empirical evidence from two organizations in the United Kingdom. *British Journal of Management*, 15, S59–S69.

Elias, J. and Scarbrough, H. (2004). Evaluating human capital: An exploratory study of management practice. *Human Resource Management Journal*, 14, 21–40.

Elg, U. and Johansson, U. (1997). Decision making in inter-firm networks as a political process. *Organization Studies*, 18(3), 361–380.

Engwall, M. (2003). No project is an island: Linking projects to history and context. *Research Policy*, 32(5), 789–808.

Ettlie, J. E. and Bridges, W. P. (1987). Technology policy and innovation in organizations. In J. M. Pennings and A. Buitendam (Eds) *New Technology as Organizational Innovation*. Cambridge, MA: Ballinger, pp. 117–137.

Evaristo, R. and van Fenema, P. C. (1999). A typology of project management: Emergence and evolution of new forms. *International Journal of Project Management*, 17(5), 275–281.

Faems, D., Janssens, M. and van Looy, B. (2007). The initiation and evolution of inter-firm knowledge transfer in R&D relationships. *Organization Studies*, 28(1), 1699–1728.

Fleck, J. (1994). Learning by trying: The implementation of configurational technology. *Research Policy*, 23, 637–652.

Fleck, J. (2003). Managing knowledge in the design of smart products: Persona – the electronic contraceptive, In B. Dankbarr (Ed.) *Innovation Management in the Knowledge Economy*. London: Imperial College Press, pp. 235–259.

Flood, P. C., Turner, T., Ramamoorthy, N. and Pearson, J. (2001). Causes and consequences of psychological contracts among knowledge workers in the high technology and financial services industries. *International Journal of Human Resource Management*, 12, 1152–1165.

Fombrun, C., Tichy, N. M. and Devanna, M. A. (1984). *Strategic Human Resource Management*. Chichester: Wiley.

Foucault, M. (1980). *Power/Knowledge: Selected Interviews and Other Writings 1972–1977*. New York: Pantheon.

Fox, S. (2000). Communities of practice, Foucault and actor-network theory. *Journal of Management Studies*, 37(6), 853–867.

Fredberg, T., Elmquist, M. and Ollila, S. (2008). Managing open innovation – Present findings and future directions., VINNOVA Verket för innovations system/Swedish Governmental Agency for innovation systems, Report VR 2008:02.

Frenkel, S., Korczynski, M., Donoghue, L. and Shire, K. (1995). Re-constituting work: Trends towards knowledge work and info-normative control. *Work, Employment and Society*, 9(4), 773–796.

Friedman, A. (1977). *Industry and Labour*. London: Macmillan – now Palgrave.

Fuller, M., Hardin, A. and Davison, R. (2006). Efficacy in technology-mediated distributed teams. *Journal of Management Information Systems*, 23(3), 209–235.

Gajendran, R. and Harrison, D. (2007). The good, the bad, and the unknown about telecommuting: Meta-analysis of psychological mediators and individual consequences. *Journal of Applied Psychology*, 92(6), 1524–1541.

Galliers, R. (2006). In Agile information systems, K. DeSouza (editor) pp. 163–177.

Galliers, R. and Newell, S. (2003). Back to the future: From knowledge management to data management. *Information Systems and E-Business Management*, 1(1), 5–14.

Garfinkel, H. (1967). *Studies in Ethnomethodology*. Englewood Cliffs, NJ: Prentice Hall.

Garrety, K. and Badham, R. (2000). The politics of socio-technical intervention: An interactionist view. *Technology Analysis & Strategic Management*, 12(1), 103–118.

Gattiker, T. F. and Goodhue, D. L. (2005). What happens after ERP implementation: Understanding the impact of inter-dependence and differentiation on plant-level outcomes. *MIS Quarterly*, 29(3), 559–585.

Gherardi, S. (2001). From organizational learning to practice-based knowing. *Human Relations*, 54(1), 131–139.

Gibbons, M., Limoges, C., Nowotny, H., Schwartzman, S., Scott, P. and Trow, M. (1994). *The New Production of Knowledge: The Dynamics of Science and Research in Contemporary Societies*. London: Sage.

Giddens, A. (1984). *The Constitution of Society*. California: University of California Press.

Gourlay, S. (2006). Conceptualizing knowledge creation: A critique of Nonaka's theory. *Journal of Management Studies*, 43(7), 1415–1436.

Grandori, A. and Soda, G. (1995). Inter-firm networks: Antecedents, mechanisms and forms. *Organization Studies*, 16, 184–214.

Granovetter, M. S. (1973). The strength of weak ties. *American Journal of Sociology*, 78, 1360–80.

Grant, R. (1996). Prospering in dynamically competitive environments: Organizational capability as knowledge integration. *Organization Science*, 7(4), 375–387.

Grant, R. (2000). Prospering in dynamically-competitive environments: Organizational capability as knowledge integration. *Organization Science*, 7(4), 375–387.

Gratton, L. and Ghoshal, S. (2005). Beyond best practices. *MIT Sloan Management Review*, 46(3), 49–57.

Greenberg, J. and Baron, R. (2000). *Behavior in Organizations*, 7th edn. Englewood Cliffs, NJ: Prentice-Hall.

Greenwood, R., Hinings, C. R. and Brown, J. (1990). 'P2-Form' strategic management: Corporate practices in professional partnerships. *Academy of Management Journal*, 33(4), 725–755.

Grindley, P., McBryde, R. and Roper, M. (1989). *Technology and the Competitive Edge: The Case of Richardson Sheffield*. London: London Business School.

Guest, D. E. (1990). Human resource management and the American dream. *Journal of Management Studies*, 27(4), 377–397.

Hackman, R. (1990). *Groups That Work (and Those That Don't): Conditions for Effective Teamwork*. San Francisco: Jossey-Bass.

Halliday, T. (1985). Knowledge mandates: Collective influence by scientific, normative and syncretic professions. *The British Journal of Sociology*, 36(3), 421–439.

Hansen, M. (1999). The search share problem: The role of weak ties in sharing knowledge across organizational sub-units. *Administrative Science Quarterly*, 44, 82–111.

Hansen, M., Nohria, N. and Tierney, T. (1999). What's your strategy for managing knowledge? *Harvard Business Review*, 77(2), 106–117.

Hardy, C. (1996). Understanding power: Bringing about strategic change. *British Journal of Management*, Special Issue, 7(1), S3–S16.

Hardy, C. and Phillips, N. (1998). Strategies of engagement: Lessons from the critical examination of collaboration and conflict in an interorganizational domain. *Organization Science*, 9(2), 217–230.

Hardy, C., Phillips, N. and Lawrence, T. B. (2003). Resources, knowledge and influence: The organizational effects of interorganizational collaboration. *Journal of Management Studies*, 40(2), 321–347.

Harris, M. (2006). Technology, innovation and post-bureaucracy: The case of the British library. *Journal of Organizational Change Management*, 19(1), 80–92.

He, J., Butler, B. and King, W. R. (2007). Team cognition: Development and evolution in software project teams. *Journal of Management Information Systems*, 24(2), 261–292.

Hendriks, P. H. J. (2003). Managing innovation as knowledge work. In B. Dankbaar (Ed.) *Innovation Management in the Knowledge Economy*. London: Imperial College Press, pp. 321–342.

Hidalgo, A. and Albor, J. (2008). Innovation management techniques and tools: A review from theory and practice. *R&D Management*, 38(2), 113–127.

Hill, S. (1995). The social organization of boards of directors. *The British Journal of Sociology*, 46(2), 245–279.

Hislop, D., Newell, S., Scarbrough, H. and Swan, J. (2000). Networks, knowledge and power: Decision making, politics and the process of innovation. *Technology Analysis & Strategic Management*, 12(3), 399–411.

Hobday, M. (2000). The project-based organization: An ideal form for managing complex products and systems? *Research Policy*, 29, 871–893.

Horwitz, F., Heng, C. T. and Quazi, A. (2003). Finders keepers? Attracting, motivating and retaining knowledge workers. *Human Resource Management Journal*, 13(4), 23–44.

Hosking, D. M. and Morley, I. E. (1991). *A Social Psychology of Organizing: People, Processes and Contexts*. London: Harvester Wheatsheaf.

Huang, J., Newell, S., Poulson, B. and Galliers, R. (2007). Creating value from a commodity process: A case study of a call center. *Journal of Enterprise Information Management*, 20(4), 396–413.

Iansiti, M. (1993). Real-world R&D: Jumping the product generation gap. *Harvard Business Review*, 71(3), 138–147.

Janis, I. L. (1982). *Groupthink*. Boston, Mass.: Houghton Mifflin.

Jennex, M. and Olfman, L. (2003). Organizational memory. In C. Holsapple (Ed.) *Handbook of Knowledge Management*, 2nd edn. New York: Springer, pp. 207–234.

Jones, G. and George, J. (1998). The experience and evolution of trust: Implications for cooperation and teamwork. *Academy of Management Review*, 23(3), 531–546.

Jones, O., Conway, S. and Steward, F. (2001). *Social Interaction and Organisational Change*. London: Imperial College Press.

Kabanoff, B. and Holt, J. (1996). Changes in the espoused values of Australian organizations 1986–1990. *Journal of Organizational Behavior*, 17(3), 201–220.

Kanter, R. (1984). *The Change Masters*. London: Allen & Unwin.

Keegan, A. and Turner, R. (2001). Quantity versus quality in project-based learning practices. *Management Learning*, 32(1), 77–98.

Kelley, R. (1990). *The Gold Collar Worker – Harnessing the Brainpower of the New Workforce*. Reading, Mass.: Addison-Wesley.

Knights, D. and Wilmott, H. (1997). The hype and hope of interdisciplinary management studies. *British Journal of Management*, 8, 9–22.

Knorr-Cetina, K. (1999). *Epistemic Cultures: How the Sciences Make Knowledge*. Cambridge, MA: Harvard University Press.

Kofman, F. and Senge, P. (1993). Communities and commitment: The heart of learning organizations. *Organizational Dynamics*, 22(2), 5–22.

Korte, W. and Gareis, K. (2002). *E-work in Europe: Spread and Measurement – the SIBIS Survey*. Paris: Europe Conference.

Kotnour, T. (1999). A learning framework for project management. *Project Management Journal*, 30(2), 32–38.

Kreiner, K. and Schultz, M. (1993). Informal collaboration in R&D. The formation of networks across organizations. *Organization Studies*, 14(2), 189–209.

Kumar, K. and Hillegersberg, J. V. (2000). ERP experiences and evaluation. *Communications of the ACM*, 43(4), 23–26.

Kunda, G. (1992). *Engineering Culture: Control and Commitment in a High-Tech Corporation*. Philadelphia: Temple University Press.

Lampel, J. (2001). The core competencies of effective project execution: The challenge of diversity. *International Journal of Project Management*, 19(8), 471–783.

Latene, B., Williams, K. and Harkins, S. (1979). Many hands make light work: The causes and consequences of social loafing. *Journal of Personality and Social Psychology*, 37, 822–832.

Latour, B. (1988). The politics of explanation: An alternative. In Woolgar, S. (Ed.) *Knowledge and Reflexivity: New Frontiers in the Sociology of Knowledge*. London: Sage, pp. 155–176.

Lave, J. and Wenger, E. (1991). *Situated Learning: Legitimate Peripheral Participation*. Cambridge: Cambridge University Press.

Leonard-Barton, D. (1988). Implementation as mutual adapation of technology and organization. *Research Policy*, 17, 251–267.

Leonard-Barton, D. (1995). *Well-Springs of Knowledge: Building and Sustaining the Sources of Innovation*. Boston, Mass.: Harvard Business School Press.

Lewin, A. Y. and Peeters, C. (2006). Offshoring work: Business hype or the onset of fundamental transformation? *Long Range Planning*, 39, 221–239.

Lindkvist, L. (2005). Knowledge communities and knowledge collectivities: A typology of knowledge work in groups. *Journal of Management Studies*, 42(6), 1189–1210.

Locke, E. A. (1999). Some reservations about social capital. *Academy of Management Review*, 24(1), 8–9.

Lowendahl, B. (1997). *Strategic Management of Professional Service Firms.* Copenhagen: Copenhagen Business School Press.

Lowendahl, B. (2000). *Strategic Management of Professional Service Firms,* 2nd edn. Copenhagen: Copenhagen Business School Press.

Luhmann, N. (1988). Familiarity, confidence, trust: Problems and alternatives. In D. Gambetta (Ed.) *Trust: Making and Breaking Cooperative Relations.* New York: Basil Blackwell, pp. 94–107.

Luker, W. and Lyons, D. (1997). Employment shift in high-technology industries, 1988–96. *Monthly Labor Review,* June, 12–25.

Lukes, S. (1974). *Power: A Radical View.* London: Macmillan Press.

Lyotard, J. F. (1988). The Differend: Phrases in Dispute, trans. G. van den Abbeele. Minneapolis: Uni of Minnesota Press.

March, J. G. (1991). Exploration and exploitation in organizational learning. *Organization Science,* 2, 71–87.

March, J. G. and Olsen, J. P. (1995). *Democratic Governance.* New York: Free Press.

Martin, J. (1992). *Cultures in Organizations.* New York: Oxford University Press.

Mayer, R., Davis, J. and Schoorman, F. (1995). An integration model of organizational trust. *Academy of Management Review,* 20(3), 709–719.

McAfee, A. (2006). Enterprise 2.0: The dawn of emergent collaboration. *MIT Sloan Management Review,* 47(3), 21–28.

McDermott, R. (1999). Why information technology inspired but cannot deliver Knowledge Management. *California Management Review,* 41, 103–117.

McDermott, R. (2004). How to avoid a mid-life crisis in your cops. *Knowledge Management Review,* 7, 10–13.

McLoughlin, I. (1999). *Creative Technological Change.* London: Routledge.

McLoughlin, I., Badham, R. and Couchman, P. (2000). Rethinking political process in technological change: Socio-technical configurations and frames. *Technology Analysis & Strategic Management,* 12(1), 17.

Mclure, W. M. and Faraj, S. (2005). Why should I share? Examining social capital and knowledge contribution in electronic networks of practice. *MIS Quarterly,* 29, 35.

Meyerson, D., Weick, K. E. and Kramer, R. M. (1996). Swift trust and temporary groups. In R. M. Kramer and T. R. Tyler (Eds) *Trust in Organizations: Frontiers of Theory and Research.* New York: Sage.

Miles, I. (2003). Services innovation: Coming of age in the knowledge based economy. In B. Dankbarr (Ed.) *Innovation Management in the Knowledge Economy.* London: Imperial College Press, pp. 59–82.

Milgram, S. (1964). Behavioral study of obedience. *Journal of Abnormal and Social Psychology,* 67, 371–378.

Milgram, S. (1967). The small world problem. *Psychology Today,* 2, 60–67.

Mintzberg, H. (1979). *Structures in Fives, Designing Effective Organizations.* Englewood Cliffs, NJ: Prentice-Hall.

Moorhead, G., Ference, R. and Neck, C. (1991). Group decision fiascos continue: Space shuttle Challenger and a revised groupthink framework. *Human Relations,* 44(6), 539–551.

Muzio, D. and Ackroyd, S. (2005). On the consequences of defensive professionalism: Recent changes in the legal labour process. *Journal of Law and Society,* 32(4), 615–642.

Nadler, D., Hackman, J. and Lawler, E. (1979). *Managing Organizational Behaviour.* Boston, Mass.: Little, Brown.

Nahapiet, J. and Ghoshal, S. (1998). Social capital, intellectual capital and the organizational advantage. *Academy of Management Review,* 23(2), 242–266.

Nelson, R. (1992). *National Systems of Innovation.* Oxford: OUP.

Newell, S., Edelman, L., Scarbrough, H., Swan, J. and Bresnen, M. (2003). 'Best practice' development and transfer in the NHS: The importance of process as well as product knowledge. *Health Services Management Research*, 16, 1–12.

Newell, S., Swan, J. and Scarbrough, H. (2001). From global knowledge management to internal electronic fences: L Contradictory outcomes of intranet development. *British Journal of Management*, 12(2), 97–111.

Nicolini, D. (2008). Zooming in and zooming out: A package of method and theory to study work practices. In S. Ybema, D. Yanow, H. Wels, and F. Kamsteeg (Eds) *The Complexity of Everyday Organizational Life: An Ethnographic Approach*. London: Sage.

Nicolini, D., Gherardi, S. and Yanow, D. (Eds) (2003). *Knowing in Organizations: A Practice-Based Approach*. New York: M.E. Sharpe.

Nonaka, I. (1994). A dynamic theory of organizational knowledge creation. *Organization Science*, 5(1), 14–37.

Nonaka, I. and Konno, N. (1998). The concept of 'ba': Building a foundation for knowledge creation. *California Management Review*, 40(3), 40–54.

Nonaka I. and Takeuchi, H. (1995). *The Knowledge-Creating Company*. Oxford: Oxford University Press.

Nowotny, H., Scott, P. and Gibbons, M. (2001). *Rethinking Science: Knowledge and the Public in an Age of Uncertainty*. Cambridge: Polity Press.

Nowotny, H., Scott, P. and Gibbons, M. (2003). 'Mode 2' revisited: The new production of knowledge, *Minerva*, 41, 179–194.

O'Neill, B. and Adya, M. (2007). Knowledge sharing and the psychological contract. *Journal of Managerial Psychology*, 22(4), 411–436.

Okhuysen, G. and Eisenhardt, K. (2002). Integrating knowledge in groups: How formal interventions enable flexibility. *Organization Science*, 13, 370–386.

Oliver, A. L. and Liebeskind, J. P. (1998). Three levels of networking for sourcing intellectual capital in biotechnology. *International Studies of Management and Organization*, 27(4), 76–103.

Orlikowski, W. J. (2000). Using technology and constituting structures: A practice lens for studying technology in organizations. *Organization Science*, 11(4), 404–428.

Orlikowski, W. J. (2002). Knowing in practice: Enacting a collective capability in distributed organizing. *Organization Science*, 13(3), 249–273.

Orlikowski, W. J. (2006). Material knowing: The scaffolding of human knowledgeability. *European Journal of Information Systems*, 15(5), 460–466.

Orlikowski, W. J. (2007). Sociomaterial practices: Exploring technology at work. *Organization Studies*, 28(9), 1435.

Orlikowski, W. J. and Barley, S. (2001). Technology and institutions: What can research on information technology and research on organizations learn from each other? *MIS Quarterly*, 25(2), 145–165.

Orlikowski, W. J. and Yates, J. A. (2002). It's about time: Temporal structuring in organizations. *Organization Science*, 13(6), 684.

Orr, J. (1990). Sharing knowledge, Celebrating identity in War stories and Community memory in a service culture. In D. Middleton and D. Edwards (Eds) *Collective Remembering: Remembering in a Society*. Beverly Hills, Calif: Sage.

Owen-Smith, J. and Powell, W. W. (2004). Knowledge networks as channels and conduits: The effects of spillovers in the Boston biotechnology community. *Organization Science*, 15(1), 5–21.

Owen-Smith, J., Riccaboni, M., Pammolli, F. and Powell, W. (2002). A comparison of US and Eurepean university-industry relations in the Life Sciences. *Management Science*, 48(1), 24–43.

Ozcelik, Y. (2008). Globalization and the internet: The digitization of the nonprofit sector. *Journal of Global Business Issues*, 2(1), 149–153.

Perez Perez, M., Martinez-Sanchez, A., De Luis Carnicer, P. and Jose Vela Jimenez, M. (2007). Modelling the adoption of teleworking: An empirical study of resources and organizational factors. *International Journal of Services Technology and Management*, 8(2/3), 188.

Perrow, C. (1967). *Organizational Analysis: A Sociological View*. London: Tavistock.

Peters, T. and Waterman, R. (1982). *In Search of Excellence: Lessons from America's Best-Run Companies*. New York: Harper & Row.

Pettigrew, A. M. (1973). *The Politics of Organisational Decision Making*. London: Tavistock.

Pfeffer, J. and Salancik, G. (1978). *The External Control of Organizations: A Resource Dependence Perspective*. New York: Harper & Row.

Pfeffer, J. and Sutton, R. I. (2000). *The Knowing-Doing Gap: How Smart Companies Turn Knowledge into Action*. Cambridge, MA: Harvard Business School Press.

Pittaway, L., Robertson, M., Munir, K., Denyer, D. and Neely, A. (2004). Networking and innovation: A systematic review of the evidence. *International Journal of Management Reviews*, 5/6(3 and 4), 137–168.

Polanyi, M. (1962). *Personal Knowledge*. Chicago, Ill.: University of Chicago Press.

Powell, W., Koput, K. and Smith-Doerr, L. (1996). Interorganizational collaboration and the locus of innovation: Networks of learning in biotechnology. *Administrative Science Quarterly*, 41, 116–145.

Proehl, R. (1997). Enhancing the effectiveness of cross-functional teams. *Team Performance Management*, 3(3), 137–147.

Prusak, L. (1997). *Knowledge in Organizations*. Oxford: Butterworth-Heinemann.

Pyoria, P. (2007). Informal organizational culture: The foundation of knowledge workers' performance. *Journal of Knowledge Management*, 11(3), 16–27.

Raelin, J. A. (1991). *The Clash of Cultures: Managers Managing Professionals*. Boston, Mass.: Harvard Business School Press.

Raelin, J. A. (2001). Public reflection as the basis of learning. *Management Learning*, 32(1), 11–30.

Raisch, S. and Birkinshaw, J. (2008). Organizational ambidexterity: Antecedents, outcomes and moderators. *Journal of Management*, 34(3), 982–993.

Redpath, L., Hurst, D. and Devine, K. (2007). Contingent knowledge worker challenges. *Human Resource Planning*, 30, 33.

Ring, P. S. and Van de Ven, A. H. (1994). Developmental processes of cooperative interorganizational relationships. *Academy of Management Review*, 19(1), 90–118.

Ringlemann, M. (1913). Recherches sur moteurs animŽs: Travail de l'homme. *Annales de l'Institut National Agronomique*, 2e sŽrie, XII, 1–40.

Robertson, M. (2007). Translating breakthroughs in genetics into biomedical innovation: The case of UK genetic knowledge parks. *Technology Analysis & Strategic Management Journal*, 19(2), 189–204.

Robertson, M. and Swan, J. (2004). Going public: The emergence and effects of soft bureaucracy in a knowledge intensive firm. *Organization*, 11(1), 123–148.

Robertson, M., Scarbrough, H. and Swan, J. (2003). Knowledge creation in professional firms: Institutional effects. *Organization Studies*, 24(6), 831–857.

Robertson, M., Swan, J. and Newell, S. (1996). The role of networks in the diffusion of technological innovation. *Journal of Management Studies*, 33, 333–359.

Robey, D. and Boudreau, M.-C. (1999). Accounting for the contradictory consequences of information technology. *Information Systems Research*, 10(2), 167–186.

Rogers, E. (1995). *Diffusion of Innovations*, 3rd edn. New York: Free Press.

Rothwell, R., Freeman, C., Horsley, A., Jervis, V. T. P., Robertson, A. B. and Townsend, J. (1974). Sappho updated – Project Sappho phase II. *Research Policy*, 3, 258–291.

Ruggles, R. (1998). The state of the notion: Knowledge management in practice. *California Management Review*, 40(3), 80–89.

Sako, M. (1992). *Prices, Quality and Trust: How Japanese and British Companies Manage Buyer–Supplier Relations*. Cambridge: Cambridge University Press.

Scarbrough, H. (1995). Blackboxes, hostages and prisoners. *Organization Studies*, 16(6), 991–1019.

Scarbrough, H. (2003). Why your employees don't share what they know. *KM Review*, 6, 16–19.

Scarbrough, H. (Ed.) (2008a). *The Evolution of Business Knowledge*. Oxford: OUP.

Scarbrough, H. (2008b). 'Organizational knowledge' entry in S. Clegg and J. R. Bailey. *International Encyclopedia of Organization Studies*. Thousand Oaks, CA: Sage, pp. 1087–1092.

Scarbrough, H. and Elias, J. (2002). *Evaluating Human Capital*. London: CIPD Publishing.

Scarbrough, H. and Swan, J. (2001). Explaining the diffusion of knowledge management: The role of fashion. *British Journal of Management*, 12(1), 3–12.

Scarbrough, H., Swan, J., Laurent, S., Edelman, L. and Newell, S. (2004). Project-based learning: An exploratory study. *Management Learning*, 35(4), 491–506.

Schatzki, T. (2001). Practice theory. In T. Schatzki, K. Knorr-Cetina, and E. von Savigny (Eds) *The Practice Turn in Contemporary Theory*. London: Routledge, pp. 1–14.

Schatzki, T. R., Knorr-Cetina, K. and von Savigny, E. (2001). *The Practice Turn in Contemporary Theory*. London: Routledge.

Schein, E. (1983). The role of the founder in creating organizational culture. *Organizational Dynamics*, Summer; 12, 13–28.

Schein, E. (1992). *Organizational Culture and Leadership*, 2nd edn. San Francisco: Jossey-Bass.

Schultze, U. and Leidner, D. (2002). Studying knowledge management in information systems research: Discourses and theoretical assumptions. *MIS Quarterly*, 26(3), 213–242.

Schultze, U. and Orlikowski, W. J. (2004). A practice perspective on technology-mediated network relations: The use of Internet-based self-serve technologies. *Information Systems Research*, 15(1), 87–106.

Schultze, U. and Vandenbosch, B. (1998). Information overload in a GroupWare environment: Now you see it, now you don't. *Journal of Organizational Computing and Electronic Commerce*, 8(2), 127–148.

Schweitzer, L. and Duxbury, L. (2002). Benchmarking the use of teleworking arrangements in Canada. *Canadian Journal of Administrative Sciences*, 23(2), 105–117.

Scott, W. R. (1995). *Institutions and Organizations*. London: Sage.

Scott, W. R. and Meyer, J. W. (1994). *Developments in Institutional Theory, Institutional Environments and Organizations*. Thousand Oaks, CA: Sage, pp. 1–8.

Sewell, G. (1998). The discipline of teams: The control of team-based industrial work through electronic and peer surveillance. *Administrative Science Quarterly*, 43(2), 397–428.

Sewell, G. and Wilkinson, B. (1992). Someone to watch over me: Surveillance, discipline and the just-in-time labour process. *Sociology*, 26: 271–289.

Shapiro, D., Sheppard, B. and Cheraskin, L. (1992). Business on a handshake. *Negotiation Journal*, 8, 365–377.

Sharp, D. (2003). Knowledge management today: Challenges and opportunities. *Information Systems Management*, 20(2), 32–37.

Sinclair, A. (1992). The tyranny of a team ideology. *Organization Studies*, 13(14), 611–626.

Slappendel, C. (1996). Perspectives on innovation in organizations. *Organization Studies*, 17(1), 107–129.

Spender, J.-C. (1996). Organisational knowledge, learning and memory: Three concepts in search of a theory. *Journal of Organisational Change and Management*, 9(1), 63–78.

Spender, J.-C. (1998). Pluralist epistemology and the knowledge-based theory of the firm. *Organization*, 5(2), 233–256.

Standish Group (2007). *CHAOS Report: The laws of Chaos*. Standish Group International Inc.

Star, S. L. and Griesemer, J. (1989). Institutional ecology, translations and boundary objects: Amateurs and professionals in Berkley's Museum of Vetebrate Zoology 1907–1939. *Social Studies of Science*, 19(3), 387–420.

Starbuck, W. (1992). Learning by knowledge-intensive firms. *Journal of Management Studies*, 29(6), 713–740.

Stoner, J. (1968). Risky and cautious shifts in group decision: The influence of widely held values. *Journal of Experimental Social Psychology*, 4, 442–459.

Suchman, L. (1987). *Plans and Situated Actions: The Problem of Human/Machine Communication*. Cambridge, UK: Cambridge University Press.

Swan, J. (2007). 'Knowledge' entry in James R. Bailey and Stewart Clegg (Eds). *International Encyclopedia of Organization Studies*. London: Sage Publications, Vol. 2.

Swan, J. (2008). 'Knowledege' entry in S. Clegg and J. R. Bailey (Eds). *International Encyclopedia of organization Studies*. Thousand Oaks, CA: Sage, pp. 750–755.

Swan, J. and Clark, P. (1992). Organizational decision-making in the appropriation of technological innovation: Cognitive and political dimensions. *European Work and Organizational Psychologist*, 2, 103–127.

Swan, J. and Newell, S. (1995). The role of professional associations in technology diffusion. *Organization Studies*, 16(5), 847–874.

Swan, J. and Scarbrough, H. (2005). The politics of networked innovation. *Human Relations*. 58(7), 913–943.

Swan, J., Newell, S. and Robertson, M. (1999a). Central agencies in the diffusion and design of technology: A comparison of the UK and Sweden. *Organization Studies*, 20, 905–932.

Swan, J., Newell, S. and Robertson, M. (1999b). The illusion of best practice in information systems for operations management. *European Journal of Information Systems*, 8, 284–293.

Swan, J., Scarbrough, H. and Robertson, M. (2002). The construction of 'communities of practice' in the management of innovation. *Management Learning*, 33(4), 477–496.

Swan, J., Scarbrough, H. and Robertson, M. (2003). The construction of 'communities of practice' in the management of innovation. *Management Learning*, 33(4), 477–496.

Swan, J., Bresnen, M., Newell, S. and Robertson, M. (2007a). The object of knowledge: The role of objects in interactive innovation. *Human Relations*, 60(12), 1809–1837.

Swan, J., Goussevskaia, A., Newell, S., Robertson, M., Bresnen, M. and Obembe, A. (2007b) Modes of organizing biomedical innovation in the UK and US and the role of integrative and relational capabilities. *Research Policy*, 36(4), 529–547.

Taylor, F. W. (1911). *The Principles of Scientific Management*. New York: Harper.

Teece, D. J., Pisano, G. and Shuen, A. (1997). Dynamic capabilities and strategic management. *Strategic Management Journal*, 18(7), 509–533.

Thompson, J. (1967). *Organizations in Action*. New York: McGraw-Hill.

Thompson, M. (2005). Structural and epistemic parameters in Communities of Practice. *Organization Science*, 16(2), 151–164.

Thompson, M. and Heron, P. (2006). Relational quality and innovative performance in R&D based science and technology firms. *Human Resource Management Journal*, 16, 28.

Tidd, J., Bessant, J. and Pavitt, K. (1997). *Managing Innovation: Integrating Technological Market and Organizational Change*. Chichester: Wiley.

Tseng, S. (2007). The effects of information technology on knowledge management systems. *Expert Systems with Applications*, 35(1–2), 1–11.

Tsoukas, H. (1996). The firm as a distributed knowledge system: A social constructionist approach. *Strategic Management Journal*, 17 (Winter Special Issue), 11–25.

Tsoukas, H. (2003). Do we really understand tacit knowledge. In M. Easterby-Smith and M. A. Lyles (Eds) *The Blackwell Handbook of Organizational Learning and Knowledge Management*. Oxford: Blackwell, pp. 410–427.

Tsoukas, H. and Vladimirou, E. (2001). What is organizational knowledge? *Journal of Management Studies*, 38(7), 973–993.

Tushman, M. and Scanlon, T. (1981). Boundary spanning individuals: Their role in information transfer and their antecendents. *Academy of Management Journal*, 24, 289–305.

Ulrich, D. (1998). Intellectual Capital = Competence X commitment. *Sloan Management Review*, 39, 15–26.

Utterback, J. (1994). *Managing the Dynamics of Innovation*. Boston, Mass.: Harvard Business School Press.

Van de Ven, A. H. (1986). Central problems in the management of innovation. *Management Science*, 32, 590–607.

van der Panne, G., van Beers, C. and Kleinknecht, A. (2003). Success and failure of innovation: A literature review. *International Journal of Innovation Management*. London: Imperial College Press.

Vermeulen, P. (2003). Does it really matter that services differ? New product development in financial services. In B. Dankbarr (Ed.) *Innovation Management in the Knowledge Economy*. London: Imperial College Press, pp. 117–136.

Volberda, H. W. (1998). *Building the Flexible Firm: How to Remain Competitive*. New York: Oxford University Press.

von Hippel, E. (2005). Open Source Software Projects as 'User Innovation Networks'. In J. Feller, B. Fitzgerald, S. Hissam, and K. R. Lakhani (Eds) *Perspectives on Free and Open Source Software*. Cambridge, MA: The MIT Press, pp. 267–278.

von Hippel, E. and von Krogh, G. (2003). Open source software and the 'Private- Collective' innovation model: Issues for organization science. *Organization Science*, 14(2), 209–223.

von Hippel, E. and von Krogh, G. (2006). Free revealing and the private-collective model for innovation incentives. *R&D Management*, 36(3), 295–306.

Von Krogh, G., Ichijo, K. and Nonaka, I. (2000). *Enabling Knowledge Creation: How to Unlock the Mystery of Tacit Knowledge and Release the Power of Innovation*. Oxford: Oxford University Press.

Von Zedtwitz, M. (2002). Organizational learning through post-project reviews in R&D. *R&D Management*, 32(3), 255–268.

Wageman, R. (1995). Interdependence and group effectiveness. *Administrative Science Quarterly*, 145–180.

Wagner, E., Scott, S. and Galliers, R. (2006). The creation of 'best practice' software: Myth, reality and ethics. *Information and Organization*, 16, 251–275.

Wagner, E. and Newell, S. (2007). Exploring the importance of participation in the post-implementation period of an Enterprise System Project: A neglected area. *Journal of the Association of Information Systems, 8, 10, article 32*.

Wagner, E. and Newell, S. (2004). Best for whom: The tension between 'Best Practice' ERP packages and diverse epistemic cultures in a university context. *Journal of Strategic Information Systems*, 14(4), 305–328.

Wallace, T. and Kremzar, M. (2001). *Making It Happen: The Implementers' Guide to Success with ERP*. New York: John Wiley.

Walsham, G. (2002). What can knowledge management systems deliver? *Management Communication Quarterly*, 16(2), 267–273.

Walton, R. E. (1985). From control to commitment. *Harvard Business Review*, 63, 77–84.

Weick, K. E. (1990). Technology as equivoque. In P. S. Goodman and L. S. Sproull (Eds) *Technology and Organizations*. San Fransisco, CA: Jossey-Bass.

Weick, K. E. (1995). *Sensemaking in Organizations*. Thousand Oaks, Calif: Sage.

Weick, K. E. (1990). Technology as equivoque: Sensemaking in new technologies. In P. S. Goodman, L. S. Sproull, and Associates (Eds) *Technology and Organizations*. Oxford: Jossey-Bass.

Weick, K. E. (2001). *Making Sense of the Organization*. Oxford; Malden, Mass.: Blackwell Business.

Wenger, E. (1998). *Communities of Practice: Learning, Meaning, and Identity*. Cambridge, UK; New York, NY, Cambridge University Press.

Wenger, E. C. and Snyder, W. M. (2000). Communities of practice: The organizational frontier. *Harvard Business Review*, 78(1), 139.

Wenger, E., McDermott, R. A. and Snyder, W. (2002). *Cultivating Communities of Practice: A Guide to Managing Knowledge*. Cambridge, MA: Harvard Business School Press.

West, M., Borrill, C. and Unsworth, K. (1998). Team effectiveness in organizations. In C. Cooper and I. Robertson (Eds) *International Review of Industrial and Organizational Psychology*, Vol. 13. Chichester: Wiley, pp. 1–48.

Whyte, J., Ewenstein, B., Hales, M. and Tidd, J. (2008). Managing knowledge representation in design. In H. Scarbrough (Ed.) *The Evolution of Business Knowledge*. Oxford: OUP, pp. 189–214.

Willem, A. and Scarbrough, H. (2006). Social capital and political bias in knowledge sharing: An exploratory study. *Human Relations*, 59, 1343.

Willmott, H. (1993). Strength is ignorance; slavery is freedom: Managing culture in modern organisations. *Journal of Management Studies*, 30, 515–552.

Wittgenstein, L. (1958). *Philosophical Investigations,* trans. G. E. M. Anscombe, 3rd Edn. Oxford: Blackwell. New York: Harper.

Witzeman, S., Slowinski, G., Dirkx, R., Gollob, L., Tao, J., Ward, S. and Miraglia, S. (2006). Harnessing external technology for innovation. *Research-Technology Management*, 49(3), 19–27.

Wolfe, R. A. (1994). Organizational innovation: Review, critique and suggested research directions. *Journal of Management Studies*, 31, 405–431.

Wood, S. (1995). The four pillars of HRM: Are they connected? *Human Resource Management Journal*, 5(5), 48–58.

Woodward, J. (1965). *Industrial Organizations: Theory and Practice*. Oxford: Oxford University Press.

Xu, J. and Quaddus, M. (2005). Adoption and diffusion of knowledge management systems: An Australian survey. *Journal of Management Development*, 24(4), 335–361.

Zollo, M. and Winter, S. G. (2002). Deliberate learning and the evolution of dynamic capabilities. *Organization Science*, 13(3), 339.

Zucker, L. G. (1986). Production of trust: Institutional sources of economic structure, 1840–1920. In B. M. Staw and L. L. Cummings (Eds) *Research in Organisational Behaviour*, Vol. 8. Greenwich, Cann.: JAI, pp. 53–111.

Index

CPI Antony Rowe
Chippenham, UK
2017-12-22 11:43